AF621978

Charlotte Brontë's

Jane Eyre

MODERN CRITICAL INTERPRETATIONS

Charlotte Brontë's

Jane Eyre

Edited and with an Introduction by

Harold Bloom

Viva Books

New Delhi | Mumbai | Chennai | Kolkata | Bengaluru | Hyderabad | Kochi | Guwahati

Copyright © Chelsea House Publishers, a subsidiary of Haights Cross Communications
Introduction © Harold Bloom

First Indian Edition 2007
Reprinted 2011

VIVA BOOKS PRIVATE LIMITED

- 4737/23 Ansari Road, Daryaganj, New Delhi 110 002
  E-mail: vivadelhi@vivagroupindia.net, Tel. 42242200
- 76, Service Industries, Shirvane, Sector 1, Nerul, Navi Mumbai 400 706
  E-mail: vivamumbai@vivagroupindia.net, Tel. 27721273, 27721274
- Jamals Fazal Chambers, 26 Greams Road, Chennai 600 006
  E-mail: vivachennai@vivagroupindia.net, Tel. 28290304, 28294241
- B-103, Jindal Towers, 21/1A/3 Darga Road, Kolkata 700 017
  E-mail: vivakolkata@vivagroupindia.net, Tel. 22836381, 22816713
- 7, Sovereign Park Apartments, 56-58, K. R. Road, Basavanagudi, Bengaluru 560 004
  E-mail: vivabangalore@vivagroupindia.net, Tel. 26607409, 26607410
- 101-102 Mughal Marc Aptt., 3-4-637 to 641, Narayanguda, Hyderabad 500 029
  E-mail: vivahyderabad@vivagroupindia.net, Tel. 27564481, 27564482
- First Floor, Beevi Towers, SRM Road, Kaloor, Kochi 682 018, Kerala
  E-mail: vivakochi@vivagroupindia.net, Tel: 0484-2403055, 2403056
- 232, GNB Road, Beside UCO Bank, Silpukhuri, Guwahati 781 003
  E-mail: vivaguwahati@vivagroupindia.net, Tel: 0361-2666386

Published by arrangement with:

Facts on File, Inc.
132 West 31st Street
New York NY 10001
USA

All rights reserved. No part of this book may be reproduced or transmitted in any form or by any means now known or to be invented, electronic or mechanical, including photocopying, recording or by any information storage or retrieval system without written permission from the publisher.

This edition is for sale in the Indian subcontinent only. Not for export elsewhere.

ISBN : 978-81-309-1886-0

Published by Vinod Vasishtha for Viva Books Private Limited, 4737/23, Ansari Road, Daryaganj New Delhi - 110 002. Printed and bound by Anand Sons, Delhi - 110 092.

Contents

Editor's Note

My Introduction considers the vitalizing Byronism of *Jane Eyre*, which is clearly sadistic, particularly evident in Jane's dominance over the partly maimed and partly blinded Rochester.

Sally Shuttleworth begins this volume with the argument that even the "most private realms are constructed socially."

Colonialism, another current mode of critical cant, is invoked by Susan Meyer, while Susan Ostrov Weisser refreshingly acknowledges that *Jane Eyre* attempts to achieve a private morality.

Sandra M. Gilbert, the major feminist literary critic, even more refreshingly emphasizes Jane's fierce sexuality, after which Marianne Thormählen centers upon St. John Rivers, Jane's more spiritual "double," whose character is allowed by Charlotte Brontë to remain rather ambiguous, an enigma partly resolved by Jerome Beaty's Bakhtinian reading.

In Heather Glen's interpretation, the novel's religious conclusion points toward Charlotte Brontë's own public era, while Warren Edminster finds in Chaucer's Wife of Bath a feminist precursor to the sexually vibrant Jane Eyre.

James Buzard concludes this volume by describing Jane Eyre as a wild being self-tamed, as Wordsworth and Coleridge had been, before her.

HAROLD BLOOM

Introduction

The three Brontë sisters—Charlotte, Emily Jane, and Anne—are unique literary artists whose works resemble one another's far more than they do the works of writers before or since. Charlotte's compelling novel *Jane Eyre* and her three lesser yet strong narratives—*The Professor*, *Shirley*, *Villette*—form the most extensive achievement of the sisters, but critics and common readers alike set even higher the one novel of Emily Jane's, *Wuthering Heights*, and a handful of her lyrical poems. Anne's two novels—*Agnes Grey* and *The Tenant of Wildfell Hall*—remain highly readable, although dwarfed by *Jane Eyre* and the authentically sublime *Wuthering Heights*.

Between them, the Brontës can be said to have invented a relatively new genre, a kind of northern romance, deeply influenced both by Byron's poetry and by his myth and personality, but going back also, more remotely yet as definitely, to the Gothic novel and to the Elizabethan drama. In a definite, if difficult to establish sense, the heirs of the Brontës include Thomas Hardy and D.H. Lawrence. There is a harsh vitalism in the Brontës that finds its match in the Lawrence of *The Rainbow* and *Women in Love*, though the comparison is rendered problematic by Lawrence's moral zeal, enchantingly absent from the Brontës' literary cosmos.

The aesthetic puzzle of the Brontës has less to do with the mature transformations of their vision of Byron into Rochester and Heathcliff, than with their earlier fantasy-life and its literature, and the relation of that life and literature to its hero and precursor, George Gordon, Lord Byron. At his rare worst and silliest, Byron has nothing like this scene from Charlotte Brontë's "Caroline Vernon," where Caroline confronts the Byronic Duke of Zamorna:

> The Duke spoke again in a single blunt and almost coarse sentence, compressing what remained to be said, "If I were a bearded Turk, Caroline, I would take you to my harem." His deep voice as he uttered this, his high featured face, and dark, large eye burning bright with a spark from the depths of Gehenna, struck Caroline Vernon with a thrill of nameless dread. Here he was, the man Montmorency had described to her. All at once she knew him. Her guardian was gone, something terrible sat in his place.

Byron died his more-or-less heroic death at Missolonghi in Greece on April 19, 1824, aged thirty-six years and three months, after having set an impossible paradigm for authors that has become what the late Nelson Algren called "Hemingway all the way," in a mode still being exploited by Norman Mailer, Gore Vidal, and some of their younger peers. Charlotte was eight, Emily Jane six, and Anne four when the Noble Lord died and when his cult gorgeously flowered, dominating their girlhood and their young womanhood. Byron's passive-aggressive sexuality—at once sadomasochistic, homoerotic, incestuous, and ambivalently narcissistic—clearly sets the pattern for the ambiguously erotic universes of *Jane Eyre* and *Wuthering Heights*. What Schopenhauer named (and deplored) as the Will to Live, and Freud subsequently posited as the domain of the drives, is the cosmos of the Brontës, as it would come to be of Hardy and Lawrence. Byron rather than Schopenhauer is the source of the Brontës' vision of the Will to Live, but the Brontës add to Byron what his inverted Calvinism only partly accepted, the Protestant will proper, a heroic zest to assert one's own election, one's place in the hierarchy of souls.

Jane Eyre and Catherine Earnshaw do not fit into the grand array of heroines of the Protestant will that commences with Richardson's Clarissa Harlowe and goes through Austen's Emma Woodhouse and Fanny Price to triumph in George Eliot's Dorothea Brooke and Henry James's Isabel Archer. They are simply too wild and Byronic, too High Romantic, to keep such company. But we can see them with Hardy's Tess and, even more, his Eustacia Vye, and with Lawrence's Gudrun and Ursula. Their version of the Protestant will stems from the Romantic reading of Milton, but largely in its Byronic dramatization, rather than its more dialectical and subtle analyses in

Blake and Shelley, and its more normative condemnation in Coleridge and in the Wordsworth of *The Borderers*.

II

The Byronism of Rochester in *Jane Eyre* is enhanced because the narrative is related in the first person by Jane Eyre herself, who is very much an overt surrogate for Charlotte Brontë. As Rochester remarks, Jane is indomitable; as Jane says, she is altogether "a free human being with an independent will." That will is fiercest in its passion for Rochester, undoubtedly because the passion for her crucial precursor is doubly ambivalent; Byron is both the literary father to a strong daughter, and the idealized object of her erotic drive. To Jane, Rochester's first appearance is associated not only with the animal intensities of his horse and dog, but with the first of his maimings. When Jane reclaims him at the novel's conclusion, he is left partly blinded and partly crippled. I do not think that we are to apply the Freudian reduction that Rochester has been somehow castrated, even symbolically, nor need we think of him as a sacrificed Samson figure, despite the author's allusions to Milton's *Samson Agonistes*. But certainly he has been rendered dependent upon Jane, and he has been tamed into domestic virtue and pious sentiment, in what I am afraid must be regarded as Charlotte Brontë's vengeance upon Byron. Even as Jane Eyre cannot countenance a sense of being in any way inferior to anyone whatsoever, Charlotte Brontë could not allow Byron to be forever beyond her. She could acknowledge, with fine generosity, "that I regard Mr. Thackeray as the first of modern masters, and as the legitimate high priest of Truth; I study him accordingly with reverence." But *Vanity Fair* is hardly the seedbed of *Jane Eyre*, and the amiable and urbane Thackeray was not exactly a prototype for Rochester.

Charlotte Brontë, having properly disciplined Rochester, forgave him his Byronic past, as in some comments upon him in one of her letters (to W.S. Williams, August 14, 1848):

> Mr. Rochester has a thoughtful nature and a very feeling heart; he is neither selfish nor self-indulgent; he is ill-educated, misguided; errs, when he does err, through rashness and inexperience: he lives for a time as too many other men live, but being radically better than most men, he does not like that degraded life, and is never happy in it. He is taught the severe lessons of experience and has sense to learn wisdom from them. Years improve him; the effervescence of youth foamed away, what

> is really good in him still remains. His nature is like wine of a good vintage, time cannot sour, but only mellows him. Such at least was the character I meant to portray.

Poor Rochester! If that constituted an accurate critical summary, then who would want to read the novel? It will hardly endear me to feminist critics if I observe that much of the literary power of *Jane Eyre* results from its authentic sadism in representing the very masculine Rochester as a victim of Charlotte Brontë's will-to-power over the beautiful Lord Byron. I partly dissent, with respect, from the judgment in this regard of our best feminist critics, Sandra M. Gilbert and Susan Gubar:

> It seems not to have been primarily the coarseness and sexuality of *Jane Eyre* which shocked Victorian reviewers ... but ... its "anti-Christian" refusal to accept the forms, customs, and standards of society—in short, its rebellious feminism. They were disturbed not so much by the proud Byronic sexual energy of Rochester as by the Byronic pride and passion of Jane herself.

Byronic passion, being an ambiguous entity, is legitimately present in Jane herself as a psychosexual aggressivity turned both against the self and against others. Charlotte Brontë, in a mode between those of Schopenhauer and Freud, knows implicitly that Jane Eyre's drive to acknowledge no superior to herself is precisely on the frontier between the psychical and the physical. Rochester is the outward realm that must be internalized, and Jane's introjection of him does not leave him wholly intact. Gilbert and Gubar shrewdly observe that Rochester's extensive sexual experience is almost the final respect in which Jane is not his equal, but they doubtless would agree that Jane's sexual imagination overmatches his, at least implicitly. After all, she has every advantage, because she tells the story, and very aggressively indeed. Few novels match this one in the author's will-to-power over her reader. "Reader!" Jane keeps crying out, and then she exuberantly cudgels that reader into the way things are, as far as she is concerned. Is that battered reader a man or a woman?

I tend to agree with Sylvère Monod's judgment that "Charlotte Brontë is thus led to bully her reader because she distrusts him ... he is a vapid, conventional creature, clearly deserving no more than he is given." Certainly he is less deserving than the charmingly wicked and Byronic Rochester, who is given a lot more punishment than he deserves. I verge upon saying that Charlotte Brontë exploits the masochism of her male readers, and I may as well say it, because much of *Jane Eyre*'s rather nasty power as a novel depends upon its author's attitude towards men, which is nobly sadistic as befits a disciple of Byron.

"But what about female readers?" someone might object, and they might add: "What about Rochester's own rather nasty power? Surely he could not have gotten away with his behavior had he not been a man and well-financed to boot?" But is Rochester a man? Does he not share in the full ambiguity of Byron's multivalent sexual identities? And is Jane Eyre a woman? Is Byron's Don Juan a man? The nuances of gender, *within literary representation*, are more bewildering even than they are in the bedroom. If Freud was right when he reminded us that there are never two in a bed, but a motley crowd of forebears as well, how much truer this becomes in literary romance than in family romance.

Jane Eyre, like *Wuthering Heights*, is after all a romance, however northern, and not a novel, properly speaking. Its standards of representation have more to do with Jacobean melodrama and Gothic fiction than with George Eliot and Thackeray, and more even with Byron's *Lara* and *Manfred* than with any other works. Rochester is no Heathcliff; he lives in a social reality in which Heathcliff would be an intruder even if Heathcliff cared for social realities except as fields in which to take revenge. Yet there is a daemon in Rochester. Heathcliff is almost nothing but daemonic, and Rochester has enough of the daemonic to call into question any current feminist reading of *Jane Eyre*. Consider the pragmatic close of the book, which is Jane's extraordinary account of her wedded bliss:

> I have now been married ten years. I know what it is to live entirely for and with what I love best on earth. I hold myself supremely blest—blest beyond what language can express; because I am my husband's life as fully as he is mine. No woman was ever nearer to her mate than I am; ever more absolutely bone of his bone and flesh of his flesh.
>
> I know no weariness of my Edward's society: he knows none of mine, any more than we each do of the pulsation of the heart that beats in our separate bosoms; consequently, we are ever together. To be together is for us to be at once as free as in solitude, as gay as in company. We talk, I believe, all day long: to talk to each other is but a more animated and an audible thinking. All my confidence is bestowed on him, all his confidence is devoted to me; we are precisely suited in character—perfect concord is the result.
>
> Mr. Rochester continued blind the first two years of our union: perhaps it was that circumstance that drew us so very near—that

> knit us so very close! for I was then his vision, as I am still his right hand. Literally, I was (what he often called me) the apple of his eye. He saw nature—he saw books through me; and never did I weary of gazing for his behalf, and of putting into words the effect of field, tree, town, river, cloud, sunbeam—of the landscape before us; of the weather round us—and impressing by sound on his ear what light could no longer stamp on his eye. Never did I weary of reading to him: never did I weary of conducting him where he wished to go: of doing for him what he wished to be done. And there was a pleasure in my services, most full, most exquisite, even though sad—because he claimed these services without painful shame or damping humiliation. He loved me so truly that he knew no reluctance in profiting by my attendance: he felt I loved him so fondly that to yield that attendance was to indulge my sweetest wishes.

What are we to make of Charlotte Brontë's strenuous literalization of Gen. 2:23, her astonishing "ever more absolutely bone of his bone and flesh of his flesh"? Is *that* feminism? And what precisely is that "pleasure in my services, most full, most exquisite, even though sad"? In her "Farewell to Angria" (the world of her early fantasies), Charlotte Brontë asserted that "the mind would cease from excitement and turn now to a cooler region." Perhaps that cooler region was found in *Shirley* or in *Villette*, but fortunately it was not discovered in *Jane Eyre*. In the romance of Jane and Rochester, or of Charlotte Brontë and George Gordon, Lord Byron, we are still in Angria, "that burning clime where we have sojourned too long—its skies flame—the glow of sunset is always upon it—."

SALLY SHUTTLEWORTH

Jane Eyre: *Lurid Hieroglyphics*

In *Jane Eyre* Brontë extends her analysis of the ways in which ideological pressures of class, gender and economics are played out in the domain of subjectivity. Traditional readings of the novel which regard it primarily as a drama of the psyche, where society is consigned to the role of backdrop, fail to register the ways in which the language of psychology in the novel is itself politically defined and charged. Similarly, feminist celebrations of Brontë's depictions of sexual rebellion fail to take into account the ways in which the novel is framed by the discourses of Victorian psychology.[1] Medical texts of the era foregrounded the same three concerns which dominate Brontë's novel: the mechanics of self-control, the female body and sexuality, and the insurgence of insanity.

Psychology however, has never been an innocent discipline: in the Victorian period, as today, the writing of the self is a political act. In this conflict-ridden tale of upward female mobility, and flagrant female rebellion, Brontë's own political ambivalences are recorded in the ways in which she mobilizes contemporary psychological discourse. Cutting across the overarching narrative of self-improvement through self-control, one finds depictions of internal struggle cast in terms of both racial and class conflict. Although Brontë does not, as in *Shirley*, foreground the political dimensions of class and gender polarities in this novel, the realm of psychic struggle is

---

From *Charlotte Brontë and Victorian Psychology*. © 1996 by Cambridge University Press.

clearly associated in her mind with the dynamics of social struggle and insurrection. The drama of social interaction is played out, however, on the terrain of the female body, which is treated, by Jane's antagonists and lovers alike, as an object to be regulated, controlled and decoded.

Jane Eyre follows a similar social trajectory to *The Professor*. Each text records the transition of an outcast figure from a position of social marginality to confirmed membership of the gentry. Both Jane and Crimsworth make their way by hard work, thus avoiding the taint of upper-class idleness, and the overt money-grubbing of trade. The relationship between this plot and the analysis of surges of energy within Jane's inner emotional life, and the depiction of Bertha's madness is not tangential, I will argue, but fundamental. The issue of 'madness' or female sexuality cannot be isolated out from this wider social and economic context which actively defines them.[2]

The drama of social ascent and erotic exchange is once more focused on the activities of reading and surveillance. Jane's courtships with both Rochester and St. John, for example, are competitive exercises in interpretative penetration. A preoccupation with unveiling is not restricted to the thematics of the text, however. In the preface to the second edition of *Jane Eyre*, Brontë, responding to those who had criticized the religious tendency of the book, significantly aligns her own authorial stance with the act of unmasking: 'To pluck the mask from the face of the Pharisee, is not to lift an impious hand to the Crown of Thorns'.[3] Invoking the authority of the Bible for her own stance, Brontë warns that her work will constitute a radical, political act of unveiling. The world, 'may hate him who dares to scrutinize and expose—to rase the gilding, and show base metal under it—to penetrate the sepulchre, and reveal charnel relics: but, hate as it will, it is indebted to him' (p. xxxi).[4] The connections of this sexualized rhetoric of unveiling to the overt political sphere are made explicit in Brontë's own comments on the preface, which she had concluded with a eulogy of Thackeray as the 'first social regenerator of the day'. In a letter to W. S. Williams, Brontë makes clear that she had associated Thackeray's role as regenerator, mastering and rectifying a warped social body, with the contemporary revolution in France. The letter passes from praise of Thackeray as the high priest of the goddess of truth to the observation that 'I read my preface over with some pain—I did not like it. I wrote it when I was a little enthusiastic, like you, about the French Revolution.'[5]

For Brontë, the connection between the rhetoric of unveiling the truth and an overt political movement of insurrection is painfully evident. Writing again two weeks later, Brontë returns once more to the topic of the French Revolution, contrasting her scepticism about the end results with her faith in the Germans' 'rational and justifiable efforts for liberty'. Using the language of earthquakes and tremors, which occurs throughout *Jane Eyre* to describe upheavals in the psychological domain, she makes clear that she perceives England to lie under similar threat of social insurrection:

> It seems, as you say, as if change drew near England too. She is divided by the sea from the lands where it is making thrones rock, but earthquakes roll lower than the ocean, and we know neither the day nor the hour when the tremor and heat, passing beneath our island, may unsettle and dissolve its foundations.

Like the forces of female violence and insanity in *Jane Eyre*, that 'crime ... that lived incarnate in this sequestered mansion, and could neither be expelled nor subdued by the owner ... [but] broke out, now in fire and now in blood, at the deadest hours of night' (p. 264) the forces of political rebellion are figured as latent, secretive, and beyond control. England might be 'sequestered' by the sea, but is nonetheless liable to find her foundations shaken and her mansion rased by fire to the ground. The implicit associative connections in this letter between the psychological and political domains are confirmed in the ensuing praise of Thackeray whose power stems from his calm 'self-control': '*he* borrows nothing from fever; his is never the energy of delirium—his energy is sane energy, deliberate energy, thoughtful energy ... Thackeray is never borne away by his own ardour—he has it under control.'[6] Thackeray's activities as social unveiler are thus aligned not with the delirium of revolution but with the Germans' 'rational and justifiable efforts for liberty', not with female excess but masculine control. The text of *Jane Eyre* itself, however, is by no means so clear-cut with reference either to social and gender politics, or authorial stance, as these subsequent reflections might imply. The firm distinctions Brontë is proposing here are themselves the subject of interrogation in the novel.

Brontë's observations on the different forms of energy reveal the ideological hegemony established in nineteenth-century discourse by ideas of the controlled circulation of energy: the same model could be applied to the economy, the social body and the psyche, or the production of writing; to working-class riots in England, political revolutions in France, or slave rebellions in the colonies; to the processes of the female body and the eruptions of insanity, or the novels of Thackeray. The dividing line between the forceful, useful channelling of energy, the full utilization of all resources, and the overspill into revolution or insanity was a thin one. The problem was particularly acute because the nineteenth century had witnessed the dissolution of binary divisions between health and sickness, both social and physiological. The new paradigm emerging in physiological and social discourse was one in which the old 'Manichean' divide between health and sickness, good and ill, had been supplanted by a sliding scale of the normal and pathological.[7] The differentiation between activities which would lead to health or disease was now only one of degree; depending on the state of the organism, the same activity could lead to perfect health or dangerous excess. Central to this new discursive regime was the elusive concept of the 'normal': the power to determine and define the normative state hence became crucial.

In the discourses of both political economy and psychiatry one can see the same preoccupation with the normal, the same attempt to define when control modulates into hysteria. Political economy concerned itself with that indefinable line which marked the transition from a healthy, expanding economy producing useful goods, to a sick system characterized by gluts, overstocked markets and financial panic. Psychiatry employed a similar economic model of the psyche, exploring the ways in which healthy attempts to develop all the faculties to the full could quickly shade over into monomania, delirium, insanity; the only demarcating factors would be those of balance, and control. Insanity and ill-health were not absolutes, but rather states of health pushed to extremes. The discourses of political economy, medicine and psychology all converged in their preoccupation with the balanced channelling of energy within the individual body.

Brontë's depiction of Thackeray's 'sane', 'deliberate energy' contrasts the useless waste of energy in the delirious movements of insanity, with the social power and productivity deriving from self-control. In *Jane Eyre* she brings a similar model of interpretation to bear. The incipient parallel which runs throughout the novel between Jane and the 'mad' Bertha turns on the issue of the flow of energy: at what point does productive forcefulness turn into self-destructive anarchy? For a Victorian woman the question was peculiarly fraught since women were biologically defined as creatures of excess, throbbing with reproductive energy which had to be sluiced away each month, and yet could not be dammed up or controlled without real threat to the balance of the psyche. In constructing the parallel histories of Jane and Bertha, Brontë constantly negotiates between these different models of womanhood, trying to find an image of female empowerment and control which would not also be a negation of femininity.

Although the question of energy control is played out primarily on the terrain of the female body, its ramifications in the text concern all social groups who seek to overturn the established lines of demarcation between 'normal' and 'pathological' behaviour; between praiseworthy exertion and self-help, and destabilizing 'revolutionary' activity. The famous passage in *Jane Eyre* where Jane compares the plight of women, condemned to lives of inactivity, to that of workers who are forced by the social paralysis imposed on their faculties into revolutionary action, is not merely an isolated allusion, but rather raises to the level of explicit statement the implied parallels which run through the text.

At a linguistic level, the narrative of *Jane Eyre* enacts the novel's central thematic: order and structure are imposed on disruptive, inchoate material. Jane's claims to have achieved social success, to have moved out of her initial state of social and psychological marginality, are vindicated by her ability to tell a 'credible' tale and thus win from readers a conviction of her probity and sanity. The measure of her success is the degree to which we as readers believe we are listening to the workings of 'sane energy', rather than the ravings of delirium. Syntactically, Jane's prose gives the impression of surges of energy which are yet restrained within legitimate social bounds. As Margot Peters has pointed out, Brontë's style is characterized by a practice of syntactic inversion, which creates a sense of pervasive tension.[8] The novel replicates linguistically Jane's attempts to transgress social boundaries whilst remaining within an accepted social framework; to maintain energy at the highest level of excitation without bursting through into pathology.

Like its predecessor, the history of 'Jane Eyre' describes an arc through a whole series of problematic social boundaries. As a child Jane occupies the difficult terrain between servant and kin: kept at a distance from the family she is also 'less than a servant, for you do nothing for your keep' (p. 9). Her life as an adult repeats this pattern: as a governess, she is again neither servant nor kin. Fulfilling the role of wife or mother for monetary gain, she is aligned with the members of that other 'anathematized race', prostitutes, who similarly substitute an economic relation for a familial one, and who together with that other marginal female figure, the madwoman, haunted the Victorian imagination.[9] With her flight from Thornfield, Jane transgresses the social demarcations of class, occupying simultaneously the positions of lady and beggar; the Rivers' servant, Hannah, immediately places her once more in recognized categories of social liminality, prostitution and criminality: 'You are not what you ought to be' (p. 423).

In traversing the domains of social and psychological marginality, *Jane Eyre* explores the intersection of models of the psyche and of social order. Jane's problematic status in the social and economic sphere is replicated in the psychological domain where she is aligned with the two figures from the discourse of Victorian psychiatry who demarcated the sphere of excess: the passionate child and madwoman. Following her eruption of childhood temper she comes to reside, in the household's eyes, within the borderland of insanity, and on the cusp between humanity and animality, thus preparing for her later association with Bertha. In both the social and psychological domains, wasteful, polluting excess is set against productive, healthy regulation. Jane depicts her history as a battle on two fronts: the internal struggle to regulate her own flow of energy, and the external, social fight to wrest control of the power of social definition. Her battle with the Reeds concerns the issue of denomination: where the boundary demarcating the normal and 'natural' should be drawn. As in *The Professor*, the site of struggle rests in the dual sphere of control and penetration: regulating the self and unveiling the other.

From the opening paragraphs of the novel, where a defiant note of self-assertion is quickly introduced, it becomes clear that the narrator of *Jane Eyre* is a figure involved in the processes of self-legitimation. Jane's reference to her sense of being 'humbled by the consciousness of my physical inferiority' to her cousins actually suggests an opposing sense of *mental* superiority. Her account of her alienation from the family circle reveals a curious blend of envy and disdain. Jane is writing as an outsider who longs to be included, but yet whose self-definition and sense of self-worth stems precisely from her position of exclusion and sense of difference. Like the upwardly-mobile middle classes, Jane is fighting a battle for definitional control. Her relatives, the Reeds, have usurped the categories of both society and nature: Jane is to be excluded, Mrs Reed declares, until she learns, paradoxically, to acquire a more 'natural' disposition. At issue is the clash between two models of mind and the 'natural'. Against Mrs Reed's identification of the 'natural' with her own social expectations, Jane, by contrast, identifies herself with an independent realm of physiological energy and innate capacity: a 'natural' endowment which cannot, without violence, be constrained within the gentry's normative rules for social behaviour. Her physiological model of the self thus aligns her with the phrenologists, and the social economists who sought to analyse social dynamics entirely in terms of energy circulation.

Brontë's representation of Jane's adolescence draws on two fundamental strands in nineteenth-century psychology: the phrenological depiction of the mind as the site of warring faculties, conceived not as abstract intellectual powers but as distinct sources of physiological energy; and a separate tradition which focused on the female reproductive system as the source of destabilizing energies. Whereas the phrenologists emphasized the goals of self-control, and the hierarchical ordering and directing of mental energies, medical theories of the uterine economy suggested that female mental energy would always be overwhelmed by the forces of the reproductive system. Although in practice the two strands often overlapped, it is important, for analytic purposes, to maintain a distinction in order to explain why, in *Jane Eyre*, the rhetoric of liberating energy is also allied to the language of self-defeat and disgust. In dramatizing the ebbs and flows of Jane's internal conflicts, Brontë explores in depth the complex forms of female subjectivity engendered by contradictory formulations within Victorian discourse.

Jane's strategy of response to oppression is concealment, a retreat to a physiologically suggestive interiority, 'enshrined' behind the red curtain. In dragging her out of her shrine and exposing her to public view, John Reed enacts a gross physical parody of the more subtle forms of female unveiling in psychiatric discourse. His literal unveiling is matched, however, by Jane's own figurative unveiling in her sudden eruption into passion, thus confirming Victorian fears of the latent fires within the female body. In the class and gender war in which she is engaged Jane is bound to lose. Her attempts to pit her ideational wealth against his material power prove futile. To John Reed she becomes a 'rat', a term which demotes her from humanity to the animality reserved in contemporary rhetoric for the violence of the lower classes. As a dweller in the sewers, she is, furthermore, associated with both class and sexual contamination.[10]

The red room in which Jane is subsequently imprisoned functions, like the third story of Thornfield, as a spatialized configuration of Victorian notions of female interiority.[11] The flow of blood which had marked Jane's entrance, associates her confinement both with the onset of puberty, and the polluting effects of suppression within the female frame. Jane's responses capture the bewildering, contradictory formulations of femininity in Victorian discourse. Catching sight of herself in the mirror, she is not reassured by a comforting specular identification with the physical coherence of her image, but rather precipitated into spirals of increasing terror.[12] That 'visionary hollow' confirms only her own insubstantiality, an endlessly retreating centre of self (p. 12). The fears of spirits and phantoms it engenders set in motion the extended network of imagery which draws Jane and Bertha together within an associative nexus of the 'non-human'.

Jane's own language for herself in childhood repeatedly stresses her lack of a sense of coherence. She is a 'heterogeneous thing', an 'uncongenial alien' distinguished from her cousins by her innate endowment of 'propensities' (pp. 13–14). Her oscillation between defiant self-assertion and a sense of internal fragmentation can be traced not simply to contradictory constructions of femininity but also to contradictions within the dominant Victorian theories of self-control. According to Combe, 'Man is confessedly an assemblage of contradictions', a conflict-ridden association of 'heterogeneous elements'.[13] His fierce advocacy of the doctrines of self-improvement and advancement is based, paradoxically, on a physiological model of the psyche which undercuts earlier theories of a unified psychological principal. Combe's domain of selfhood is not the originating source of emotion, thought or action, but rather the shifting balance or product of internal conflicts: a battleground of warring, autonomous energies, where conflict is inscribed not as an occasional lapse, but as a necessary principle of existence. As a model of mind it takes to an extreme the principles of laissez-faire economics.

Whereas in *The Professor* Brontë had been content to chart the difficulties attending Crimsworth's ascent to an achieved state of repressive self-control, in *Jane Eyre* she explores the contradictions at the heart of theories of unified selfhood. Jane dwells repeatedly on her internal divisions, her lack of a unifying, controlling centre of self: In her conversations with Mrs Reed, 'something spoke out of me over which I had no control' (p. 28). Although constrained grammatically to the use of 'I', Brontë draws attention to the illusory fiction of unified control connoted by that term. The language of Jane's self-representation at this time emphasizes the implied political parallel between the upsurge of psychic energies, and the swell of revolutionary fervour both in England and Europe, and in the slave revolts in the West Indies. Jane's mood is that of a 'revolted slave', her brain is in 'tumult' and 'my heart in insurrection' (pp. 12–13). Taking the contemporary Tory rhetoric of social revolt as the eruption of animal energies, the convulsive thrashings of insanity, Brontë reverses its import to suggest a necessary, though equally unstoppable, outflow of constrained psychological force, whose release is essential for the health of the organism.

Brontë's analysis of the shifts and turns in Jane's emotions traces the material, physiological flow of her energies. The figure 'Jane' exists not as controlling agent but rather as the site of violent, contradictory charges of material energy. Following the 'gathering' and 'launching' of her energies in a verbal assault on Mrs Reed, Jane depicts her sensation of expansion and exultation: 'It seemed as if an invisible bond had burst, and that I had struggled out into unhoped-for liberty' (p. 39). This notion of an emergence into selfhood occurring with an unleashing of physiological powers is reiterated later by St John Rivers in describing the impact of his decision to become a missionary: 'my cramped existence all at once spread out to a plain without bounds ... the fetters dissolved and dropped from every faculty' (p. 462). In each case, responsibility for social rebellion is displaced onto a material sphere; it is not the individual, but rather the physiological faculties which act to overthrow the fetters of social constraint.

The phrenological theory of innate, unrealized capacity lies behind this dual image of justified revolt and of the psychological exhilaration to be obtained from faculty exertion. Each faculty, Combe argued, 'has a legitimate sphere of action, and, when properly gratified, is a fountain of pleasure'.[14] Moving beyond the instrumentalist basis of Bentham's 'felicific calculus' with its integrated, associationist model of selfhood, Combe offers the alluring notion of buried treasure within the self, multiple sources of gratification, only waiting to be released. Brontë's novel reveals the seductive attractions of this philosophy which simultaneously privileged ideas of a private, interiorized domain of authenticity, and authorized movements of social revolt—the challenging of entrenched systems of social interest and power. Yet Combe's theories were no more divorced from the sphere of economic interest than those of Bentham. Behind the rhetoric of pleasure and social liberation lies the dominant economic principle of Victorian industrial expansionism: full maximization, utilization and free circulation of all resources.

At the end of *The Professor* Brontë had offered a tantalizing portrait of female self-development in the image of Lucia. *Jane Eyre* looks more chillingly at the difficulties faced by a Victorian woman in fulfilling this goal. In Jane's case the rhetoric of liberation conflicts with her internalized fears of the disruptive forces of female energy. Searching for a fit 'emblem' to depict the processes of her mind she turns to the image of fire, which recurs so frequently in mid-Victorian medical representations of the dangerous, destabilizing energies of the uterine economy: 'A ridge of lighted heath, alive, glancing, devouring, would have been a meet emblem of my mind when I accused and menaced Mrs Reed: the same ridge, black and blasted after the flames are dead, would have represented as meetly my subsequent condition' (pp. 40–1). In Brontë's hands, the common rhetorical image of female sexuality is transformed into an analytic tool to suggest the ways in which the internalization of conflicting models of the psyche creates a sensation of self-defeat, of self-consuming energy. Jane is left once more in fear of herself, and of the seemingly unrestrainable force of her own faculties. She dreads offering an apology to Mrs Reed lest she re-excite, 'every turbulent impulse of my nature. I would fain exercise some better faculty than that of fierce speaking; fain find nourishment for some less fiendish feeling than that of sombre indignation' (p. 41). The language of the passage encapsulates Victorian social hopes and fears: doctrines of self-improvement through the 'nourishment' and 'exercise' of the faculties, are set against more deep-rooted fears of social turbulence, and 'fiendish' female behaviour.

Images of turbulence and fire permeate Victorian discussions of working-class life and political organisation.[15] Sir James Kay Shuttleworth's work, *The Moral and Physical Condition of the Working Classes*, warns of the dangers of 'the turbulent riots of the people—of machine breaking—of the secret and sullen organization which has suddenly lit the torch of incendiarism'.[16] Similar rhetoric occurred in psychiatric texts. The physician

Georget gave a more sympathetic warning of the consequences of women's social situation; prohibited from outward expression of their sexual feelings, they are forced 'to feign a calmness and indifference when an inward fire devours them and their whole organization is in tumult'.[17] The association between fire and femininity is not solely metaphorical, however. There were also abundant medical accounts of the 'insane cunning' of women which could be seen in 'the perpetration of *secret* murders by wholesale poisoning, or in secret incendiarism'.[18] The working classes and women alike are accused of secrecy, of suddenly erupting after years of quiescence into turbulence and both literal and figural incendiarism.

Jane's primary crime, in her aunt's eyes, is her sudden flaring into violence which suggests a history of secrecy and concealment. On her deathbed, Mrs Reed recurs once more to her bewilderment as to 'how for nine years you could be patient and quiescent under any treatment, and in the tenth break out all fire and violence' (p. 300). At the time of Jane's outbreak the servants had scrutinized her face 'as credulous of my sanity', wondering how a girl of her age could have 'so much cover' (p. 10). Mrs Reed similarly gazed at her 'as if she really did not know whether I were child or fiend' (p. 28). Jane defies her oppressors' theories of physiognomical correspondence, secretly nursing within her, in a hideous parody of motherhood, the hidden germs or 'minute embryos' of insanity and social disruption.[19] As passionate child, Jane Eyre is one of the first literary embodiments of that new object of fear in Victorian social and medical discourse. Together with the hysterical woman, the passionate child was perceived as a being dominated by the processes of the body, outside rational control; both were therefore viewed as disruptive, marginal groups, on the borders of 'real' humanity.[20] This simultaneously lowly, yet threatening, status was further reinforced by writings within political economy and anthropology which linked women and children together with savages and operatives as figures on the bottom rungs of civilization.[21]

In its focus on passion, *Jane Eyre* has been seen as a very un-Victorian text; its organising psychological assumptions, as I have suggested however, are drawn directly from the energy dynamics of nineteenth-century economic and psychological discourse. The problems of an industrial culture, of simultaneously maximizing and restraining energy resources, are replicated in the psychological sphere. According to Combe's Malthusian economy of the psyche, 'All the faculties, when in excess, are insatiable, and, from the constitution of the world, never can be satisfied.'[22] In the mind, as in society, the economics of scarcity and competition are in operation. Development must work hand in hand with control: Jane desires to starve her 'fiendish' feelings and to find 'nourishment' for her more socially acceptable faculties. Her mingled exultation in, and fear of, her new-found powers is mirrored in the social realm where pride in the seemingly endless potentiality of the industrial economy, with its liberation of previously unutilized and imprisoned energies, was indissolubly linked with fear of the monster they had created, whose powers might turn out to be unstoppable.

The psychological correlative of this position is complex. Passion could not, in itself, be dismissed as fiendish. Indeed in Combe's work this preoccupation with energy flow gives rise, significantly, to a validation of passion. 'PASSION', he observes, 'is the highest degree of activity of any faculty ... Hence there can be no such thing as *factitious* passion.'[23] His model of the mind is of a constant, competitive struggle between different forms of passion. Against the rationalist philosophers who had insisted on the illusory nature of strong emotions, Combe proclaims the psychological and material validity of all passionate sensations. His stance also has significant ramifications with regard to childhood. Whereas Locke had argued that passion could only be the outcome of extensive experience, and thus was an attribute solely of adult life, Combe suggests that it could be experienced with equal force by children.[24] The Victorians' fears of the passionate child, and the enthusiasm with which they policed the borders of childhood, establishing it as an explicit social and psychological category, can be linked to this shattering of the developmental continuum.[25] The sacred ideas of hierarchy and linear progression were under threat: children had now been granted the same unruly energies as undisciplined adults.

The narrative structure of *Jane Eyre* mirrors this challenge to developmental hierarchy. Like that other mid-Victorian portrait of a passionate child, *The Mill on the Floss*, it seems to follow the developmental pattern of a *Bildungsroman*, whilst in actuality offering the very reverse of a progressive, linear history.[26] Jane, as child, presents the same psychological formation as Jane in adulthood. The history she offers is that of a series of moments of conflict, a series, moreover, which does not display the characteristics of progression, but rather the endless reiteration of the same. This non-progressive format is demonstrated most clearly in her comments on her response to the loss of Miss Temple. On the day of Miss Temple's marriage, Jane recounts, 'I altered': 'I tired of the routine of eight years in one afternoon' (pp. 99–101). Jane represents her mind as a microcosm of the asylum in which she had been placed; while it had seemed that 'better regulated feelings had become the inmates of my mind' her mind now 'put[s] off all it had borrowed of Miss Temple ... I was left in my natural element; and beginning to feel the stirring of old emotions' (pp. 99–100). Jane's life is a history of eternal recurrence, offering a challenge to the forces of institutional order; no matter how firmly the 'inmates' might be subject to external direction and regulation, they remain essentially unchanged, ready at any moment to 'break bounds'. The Freudian model of the mind, and the 'scandalous' notion of infant sexuality, find their roots in mid-Victorian economies of the psyche.

The Victorian preoccupation with simultaneously maximizing and restraining energy, which underlies the repetitive cycle of Jane's history, reverberates throughout contemporary discourse: in debates on the 'machinery question', and the problems of labour or in medical and social discussions of the female role.[27] As with the productive working-class body, the reproductive energies of the female body had to be fully utilized, without transgressing the fine line of regulatory social control. The problem was particularly fraught with regard to women since the very energies which fuelled their essential role of reproduction were also deemed to be dangerously at odds with their required domestic role. Brontë explores in *Jane Eyre* two alternate institutional models for the disciplining and controlling of female energy, two forms of 'asylum': Lowood and the third floor of Thornfield.

The system at Thornfield represents the vestiges of a prior era, when the 'animal' insane were kept hidden and mechanically restrained (as Bertha is after each outbreak) and no attempt was made at cure or recuperation. 'Nature' was given free rein, but the inmates were in consequence cast out from the ranks of humanity. Lowood, by contrast, conforms more to the system of moral management (with a leaven of physical violence); individuals are to be 'saved' for society by the careful regulation of their inner impulses. As Brocklehurst declares, 'we are not to conform to nature' (p. 73). Discipline is achieved both by mortification of the flesh, and constant inspection and surveillance. Jane's punishment for being a liar is to stand on a stool and be displayed to the public gaze.

In depicting events at Lowood, Brontë explores the consequences of restraining female energy. Two models are offered, both associated with death. Whereas the other girls die of the contagious disease of typhus, Helen is granted a more dignified death from consumption, which as I noted earlier, was consistently linked in Victorian medical texts with a repression of sexuality. In physiological terms, her internal productive forces, turned inward upon themselves, become self-consuming. Helen achieves her wish to become a 'disembodied soul', burning in purifying fire the forces of sexual desire (p. 298). The other girls, however, are brought to a death which reeks of putrid animality. Whereas Helen is permitted a form of transcendence, the other girls in the asylum are driven inwards into their own materiality which, once restrained, obstructed in its flow, becomes a source of pollution. The two forms of death prefigure that of Bertha who is not allowed to be consumed, like Helen, by purifying fire, but smashes down to her native earth in an apotheosis of her intrinsic animality: 'dead as the stones on which. her brains and blood were scattered' (p. 548).

Surviving the fires of self-consumption, and the diseases of obstruction, Jane depicts her escape from Lowood in terms of the upsurge of clamorous, independent energies. Her initial responses to Thornfield are framed outside any personal sense of agency: 'My faculties ... seemed all astir. I cannot precisely define what they expected, but it was something pleasant' (p. 118). The 'I' who speaks is differentiated both from the source and experience of emotion. This famous novel of defiant self-assertion persistently undercuts notions of an originating, unified self. Jane's restlessness, which translates into social discontent, is defended on the grounds of physiology: 'Who blames me? Many no doubt; and I shall be called discontented. I could not help it. The restlessness was in my nature; it agitated me to pain sometimes' (p. 132). Seemingly aware of the accusations which might be levelled at her text, Brontë permits her heroine to draw on the discourse of internal, competing energies in order to absolve herself of responsibility for her rebellious thoughts. It was precisely such passages, however, which caused Elizabeth Rigby to attack the novel as a 'proud and perpetual assertion of the rights of man': 'We do not hesitate to say that the tone of the mind and thought which has overthrown authority and violated every code human and divine abroad, and fostered Chartism and rebellion at home, is the same which has also written *Jane Eyre*.'[28]

Rigby's indignant review picks up on the implied parallels between female and working-class revolt which run through the narrative, and are later to be foregrounded in *Shirley*. Jane's famous assertion of female rights makes these parallels quite explicit:

> It is in vain to say human beings ought to be satisfied with tranquillity: they must have action; and they *will* make it if they cannot find it. Millions are condemned to a stiller doom than mine, and millions are in silent revolt against their lot. Nobody knows how many rebellions besides political rebellions ferment in the masses of life which people earth. Women are supposed to be very calm generally: but women feel just as men feel; they need exercise for their faculties, and a field for their efforts as much as their brothers do; they suffer from too rigid a restraint, too absolute a stagnation, precisely as men would suffer; and it is narrow-minded in their more privileged fellow-creatures to say that they ought to confine themselves to making pudding and

> knitting stockings, to playing on the piano and embroidering bags. (p. 133)

Ostensibly the passage articulates support for the reformist position adopted by Combe, that women, as well as men, should be allowed to exercise their faculties to the full. The demand is not for radical change, but rather that women should be allowed to participate in the given social order in more decisive fashion. But against this reformist reading we must place the explosive energy of the passage, and the explicit linking of the position of women and workers. The vision is that of a silent but seething revolt, merely waiting to erupt.

Writing in the era of Chartism, and at a time when political revolution was about to explode throughout Europe, Brontë was not employing her terms loosely. Her letters of 1847 and 1848 show a recurrent preoccupation with the phenomenon of political rebellion, though her shifting responses reveal a significant ambivalence. In April 1848 she speaks of Chartism as an 'ill-advised movement ... judiciously repressed': collective political action should be replaced by 'mutual kindliness' and the 'just estimate of individual character'.[29] Two months later, when the focus of her letter is the more personally implicative issue of the plight of governesses, this individualist perspective and emphasis on restraint is ultimately overthrown. After insisting initially that what governesses most require is 'self'-control' and 'the art of self-possession' Brontë reverses her position in the postscript:

> I conceive that when patience has done its utmost and industry its best, whether in the case of women or operatives, and when both are baffled, and pain and want triumph, the sufferer is free, is entitled, at last to send up to Heaven any piercing cry for relief, if by that cry he can hope to obtain succour.[30]

This same ambivalent shifting between the politics of control, and the inescapability of rebellion, underlies the passage in *Jane Eyre*.

The ideological power of Combe's phrenological social platform and the whole self-help movement lay in its ability to defuse the political challenge of working-class insurgency: in its individualist focus on self-improvement, it directed attention away from class-based action, and facilitated the internalization of social controls. Yet the reformist implications of this position are only operative if emphasis is placed firmly on the processes of regulation and control. Jane's strident utterance, by contrast, seems to focus rather on the impossibility of restraint and the inevitability of rebellion. Combining ruling-class fears of the animal masses, with the reformist platform of self-development, Brontë articulates a political position which extends beyond, and undercuts, the bourgeois ideology of the dominant narrative. Rebellion is figured as an irresistible physiological process which 'ferments' not in the masses (understood as human subjects) but in 'the masses of life which people earth'. Social and political rebellion is conceived as an inevitable upswelling of a homogeneous animal life-force.

Brontë is drawing here jointly on the rhetoric of the medical obsession with the disruptive potentiality of female reproductive energies, and on depictions of working-class animality. Sir James Kay Shuttleworth, for example, traced many of the problems of society to the working-class body. There was, he maintained, 'a licentiousness capable of corrupting the whole body of society, like an insidious disease, which eludes observation, yet is equally fatal in its effects'. Unlike criminal acts, this disease was so insidious and secretive as to escape even the controlling, classificatory powers of statistics: 'Sensuality has no record, and the relaxation of social obligations may coexist with a half dormant, half restless impulse to rebel against all the preservative principles of society; yet these chaotic elements may long smoulder, accompanied only by partial eruptions of turbulence or crime.'[31] Working-class sensuality stands as a figure of political rebellion; like the workings of latent insanity, and the hidden processes of the female body, it smoulders in secret, gathering its forces of disruption beyond the control of social regulation.

In Brontë's text, the associative connections lying behind Jane's vehement defence of female faculty development are made clear in the continuation of the passage where Jane suggests that it is thoughtless of men to laugh at women,

> if they seek to do more or learn more than custom has pronounced necessary for their sex.
>
> When thus alone, I not unfrequently heard Grace Poole's laugh: the same peal, the same low, slow ha! ha! which, when first heard, had thrilled me: I heard, too, her eccentric murmurs; stranger than her laugh. (p. 133)

From men's laughter at women, Jane moves to the uncanny laughter of female response, which she initially locates in a member of the servant class. Her own bodily 'thrill' of response directly implicates her within this disruptive domain.[32] Brontë's attitudes to the sexual and social challenge offered by the figure of Bertha/Grace are, however, far more ambivalent than Rigby's review might lead one to believe.

The 'Mad Wife'

Recent feminist criticism has tended to adopt a celebratory response towards Brontë's 'mad-wife', suggesting that the representation offers a clear critique of the Victorian repression of the 'innate' forces of female sexuality.[33] To figure woman as a sexualized creature, liable to outbreaks of insanity, is not to move beyond the parameters of Victorian thought, however, but rather to give them explicit inscription. Setting aside the romanticized view which depicts female madness as the natural rebellion of the oppressed, we should consider rather the ways in which Victorian discourse had pre-defined the forms both of rebellion and conformity. Brontë's originality lies less in her focus on the issue of sexuality, than in her resolute juxtaposition of conflicting formulations within Victorian psychological thought, and her tracing through of the implications of these contradictions for the formation of female subjectivity. The measured rhetoric of self-development and control is placed alongside its feared inverse image, the eruption of uncontrollable energies; in the careful structuring of her narrative, Brontë breaks through the binary divide which policed the borders of category ascription, suggesting that the forces of conformity and rebellion are one and the same. Bertha's laughter and 'eccentric murmurs' constitute another narrative within the text, running in counterpoint to Jane's rational discourse. Yet her voice is not that of the semiotic (as defined by Kristeva), the upswell of madness outside the dominant patriarchal sphere of the symbolic.[34] Rather, as incarnation of an alternate male model of the female psyche, a gendered inflection of the doctrine of control, the figure of Bertha functions to call attention to the tenuous, fragile foundations of Jane's imperialist claims to self-dominion.

The issue of imperial control is one which has both psychological and political dimensions. Bertha is not only mad but is also, a Creole; placed on the border between European and non-European blood and culture, she is a literal realization of Jane's self-depiction as an 'heterogeneous thing', 'an uncongenial alien' within that first upper-class household.[35] Bertha functions less as a 'self-consolidating Other' for Jane than as a destabilizing agent, undermining her attempts to construct a fiction of integrated selfhood.[36] The explicit textual parallels drawn between Jane and Bertha have been well documented in feminist criticism: the red room and the attic, the imagery of blood and fire, the references to Jane as 'mad' and a 'fiend' and her famous question to Mrs Fairfax, 'am I a monster?' (p. 334).[37] To Rochester the division is absolute: Jane is 'my good angel' and Bertha is a 'hideous demon' (p. 402). Yet the very scene in which he hopes to offer a visible demonstration of this polarity to an assembled public audience is ambiguous.[38] Rochester asks the 'spectators' of his physical struggle with Bertha to 'Compare these clear eyes with the red balls yonder—this face with that mask—this form with that bulk' (p. 371). His ostensible meaning is clear: defined form is set against the shapelessness of sheer excess; open transparency against the practices of concealment. Yet if we recall the nineteenth-century rhetoric of insanity, and the rise of interest in the physiognomy of the insane, concealment and deception were the very attributes that the insane were assumed to lack. According to Esquirol, the capacity for concealment was a fundamental pre-condition for a state of sanity, and civilized humanity. It is Jane, the child who possessed 'so much cover' and defied her critics' physiognomical powers, who possesses the ability to 'mask' herself. Bertha's insanity is in fact visible proof of her inability to mask her feelings or actions.

Madness, John Reid argued, stemmed from a 'deficiency in the faculty of self-control', an inability to command the thoughts and passions: 'The veil is rent which concealed, the resistance is overcome which controlled them.'[39] Lacking any form of veil herself, Bertha literally rends Jane's bridal veil in a symbolic gesture which focuses narrative attention on the associated network of interconnections between the exposure of female sexuality and insanity. Jane is saved from casting her hymenal veil aside, and only returns to Rochester once she is veiled from his sight. With Bertha, by contrast, we are presented with the 'lurid hieroglyphics' of a sexuality too evidently displayed. Rochester recounts his meeting with his destiny, a hag, as in Macbeth, who writes in 'lurid hieroglyphics all along the house-front' his memento: 'Like it if you can! Like it if you dare!' (p. 175). The challenge is that of the demon who has usurped the domestic space of the household angel; the threatening 'other' who, refusing to recognize the barriers of race or geographical space, has staked her own territorial claim in the heart of English patriarchal and upper-class culture.

In depicting Bertha, Brontë draws on the animal imagery which pervaded contemporary representations of the 'savage', the working classes and the insane. With the rise of theories of moral management, the insane were no longer automatically assimilated to the category of animal; yet this rhetoric was retained, only in a more subtle register, particularly with reference to female forms. Our first sight of Bertha is not, significantly, as the beast grovelling on all fours, but rather as a woman gazing into Jane's mirror. Her 'savage face' with its 'red eyes and the fearful blackened inflation of the lineaments' (p. 358), her black hair, sanguine colouring, and tremendous strength, all conform to contemporary images of the most violent form of maniac.[40] Her laughter, and propensity to destruction, and attacks on her closest relatives also form part of the contemporary repertoire of images.[41]

On our second sighting of Bertha she has crossed the border from human to animal: 'it grovelled, seemingly, on all fours; it snatched and growled like some strange wild animal: but it was covered with clothing; and a quantity of dark, grizzled hair, wild as a mane, hid its head and face' (p. 370). When the 'clothed hyena' stands on its 'hind feet' it becomes, significantly, a masculinized figure which shows 'virile force' in its contest with Rochester. Following this 'spectacle'. Bertha seems irrecuperable for femininity or humanity. Yet Rochester's ensuing reveries on what Jane would be like if she were mad, and Jane's mirroring of Bertha's animal posture, 'crawling forwards on my hands and knees' (p. 410) as she pursues her flight from Thornfield, reduced to a social status lower than that of a lost dog, all suggest a more searching, interrogative attitude towards the social demarcations which separate the animal from the human, and the insane from the sane, underscoring once more the parallels between Jane and Bertha.

The reasons given for Bertha's insanity are all drawn, as Showalter has pointed out, from the discourse of Victorian psychiatry.[42] Rochester's accounts combine two forms of explanation which yoke together the idea of inherited taint with the notion of personal responsibility. Bertha inherits her insanity from her mother, 'the Creole', who was 'both a mad woman and a drunkard' but it was her 'excesses' which had 'prematurely developed the germs of insanity' (p. 391). In addition to her specific legacy from her mother, Bertha is also plagued by the generic functions of her female body, the sexual heat associated with menstrual flow. Her attacks occur, significantly, on occasions when there is a blood red moon,[43] in line with medical belief that, in some women, insanity 'bursts forth at each menstrual period'.[44] Court reports in newspapers and medical texts popularized ideas of the 'insane cunning' of women, when under the influence of their reproductive organs. Laycock's graphic accounts of the 'grotesque forms' this cunning assumed in the 'hysterical female' cover all the ground detailed by Rochester in his complaints of his wife who 'is prompted by her familiar to burn people in their beds at night, to stab them, to bite their flesh from their bones, and so on' (p. 384).[45] Incendiarism, and the 'ovarian perversions of appetite' which prompted the desire to eat human flesh (usually of the husband) were a common theme.[46] The eruption of Bertha Rochester into the text does not signify the intrusion of an outmoded Gothic form into a realist novel; she stands, rather, as the crystallization of the negative images of womanhood available in contemporary social and scientific discourse.[47] Given Rochester's eagerness to tell Jane all the details of his affairs with his previous mistresses, he is curiously inexplicit in his account of Bertha's early crimes. Her first failings, significantly, are those of household management: she cannot keep servants, and fails to give the correct angelic responses to his expansive conversation. To this image of domestic inadequacy, which already inspires Rochester's 'disgust', is added that of the sexually depraved female: Bertha is 'at once intemperate and unchaste'. The forms of Bertha's unchastity are unclear; evidently she displayed too avid a sexual appetite towards Rochester himself, but it is also possible, as no other partners are specified, that he is here referring also to the 'vice' of masturbation which was widely treated as a major cause of insanity, in women as well as men. Laycock, for example, warns that allowing girls to associate together at school when they are 'influenced by the same novel feelings towards the opposite sex' will lead them to 'indulge in practices injurious to both body and soul'. The 'young female' will return home, 'a hysterical, wayward, capricious girl; imbecile in mind, habits, and pursuits'.[48] At a more popular level, a best-selling tract on female complaints describes 'self-pollution' as 'the *fashionable* vice of young women' which causes the 'moral economy of the mind [to be] completely overthrown'.[49] Significantly, the writer, like Freud in his later theories of child seduction, does not situate the originating cause of masturbation in the upper-class body, but rather traces it to the seductive practices of 'depraved servant women'.[50] Bertha, as an upper-class, but exotic, racial 'other' represents a threatening conjunction between high breeding, and the sexual depravity attributed to the lower classes and alien races.[51]

It is significant that Jane explicitly demurs from Rochester's condemnation of Bertha: she remains for her 'an unfortunate lady' who 'cannot help being mad' (p. 384). Nowhere does she endorse Rochester's statements of disgust. Her own revulsion is reserved, rather, for the idea of a sexual connection between Rochester and the lower-class Grace:

> I hastened to drive from my mind the hateful notion I had been conceiving respecting Grace Poole: it disgusted me. I compared myself with her, and found we were different. Bessie Leaven had said I was quite a lady; and she spoke truth: I was a lady. (p. 196)

The child who had not been 'heroic enough to purchase liberty at the price of caste' (p. 24) has not changed. Even in her raging madness Bertha remains to her a 'lady': caste overrides the boundaries of race, and of animal/human, insane/sane behaviour. Despite the mobilization or images of the animal grotesque, Jane places herself; Bertha and Blanche on the same side of the class divide, in opposition to the servant Grace.[52]

It is important to the structure of Jane's narrative of self-improvement that her two rivals, Bertha and Blanche, should both belong to the same social strata, and thus represent alternate models of upper-class womanhood.

The parallels between Blanche and Bertha are insistent. Blanche is 'dark as a Spaniard' (p. 216), and serves as a model in Rochester's description of the former appearance of his wife (p. 389). More subtly, Rochester, in the proposal scene, draws attention to the surprising intrusion of a West Indian-looking insect, a 'large and gay ... nightrover', and accuses Jane of questing after the moth as he speaks of his marriage to 'my beautiful Blanche' (pp. 313–14). Such parallels function to suggest that what we see in Bertha is merely the full flowering of the flagrant, 'depraved' sexuality which the upper-class male fears exists not only in the females of exotic races but also amongst the ranks of 'respectable' English ladies.

The fate meted out to Bertha, locked away in an attic as soon as she ceased to please her husband sexually, is a precise enactment of Jane's own fears. In defending her sexually elusive conduct during courtship, Jane refers to the 'books written by men' which assign the period of six months as 'the farthest to which a husband's ardour extends' (p. 327).[53] Jane assumes that she will retain Rochester's liking, but not his 'love'—a distinction which, cutting across Victorian literary niceties, clearly aligns the latter term with sexual interest. Brontë's novel offers a devastating dissection of Victorian constructions of male sexual desire, exposing the ideological double bind which underpins cultural dominance (whether of race, sex or class). Marriage for Rochester, the explicit ownership of an ideologically-constituted inferior, necessarily brings with it a sense of self-loathing and pollution: 'a nature the most gross, impure, depraved I ever saw, was associated with mine, and called by law and by society a part of me' (p. 391). Legal dominance is purchased at the cost of self-hatred which carries over into his subsequent sexual activity: 'I tried dissipation—never debauchery: that I hated, and hate. That was my Indian Messalina's attribute: rooted disgust at it and her restrained me much, even in pleasure' (p. 397). The distinction between dissipation and debauchery might seem to twentieth-century eyes a rather subtle one: for Rochester the crucial differentiation rests in the notion of enjoyment. In this brilliant anatomy of Victorian attitudes to male sexuality, Brontë suggests that pleasure could be legitimately experienced only if wedded to a just sense of degradation. The despised debauchery assumes a frank enjoyment of sex, whilst dissipation is always constrained by a feeling of disgust.

Once Rochester has had connection with Bertha, she becomes 'my secret' which he is afraid will be revealed to the world, and Thornfield, with its 'lurid hieroglyphics' becomes 'this accursed place—this tent of Achan—... this narrow stone hell, with its one real fiend, worse than a legion of such as we imagine' (p. 383). Brontë turns this Biblical tale against the teller to suggest that his 'narrow stone hell' is of his own making: it is Rochester who has, like Achan, stolen the 'accursed thing' and thus he who is the 'real fiend' who will cause his own house and innocent wife to be destroyed by fire.[54] In defining Bertha as 'accursed' he has prepared for his own (partial) immolation.

Brontë's text offers a fierce critique of the perverted, self-destructive forces of Rochester's sexual tyranny, but also implicates Jane in the act of collusion. In another telling Biblical reference, Rochester locates Jane as Esther, in relation to his own role as King Ahasuerus, an association which then aligns Bertha, the scorned wife, with the defiant figure of Vashti (p. 329). The story could operate as a parable of *Jane Eyre*: Vashti's open rebellion is countered by Esther's strategic pliancy, as she undergoes extensive purification rituals in order to gain control of the king. Esther, in her single-minded defence of her people, has long been a heroine in Jewish and Christian religion, just as Jane, in her quest for self-fulfillment has become the heroine of recent feminist criticism. Jane, like Esther, quietly achieves her aims (with slightly less bloody results), but only at the expense of her rival who represents an alternate model of female power. Bertha, that complex symbol of abused innocence, female rebellion and sexual depravity, must be sacrificed in order for Jane to achieve her ambitions. Brontë, however, does not offer an unambiguous endorsement of Jane's progress. Her fears at the costs exacted, subtly registered through this text, are flamboyantly displayed in *Villette* where Bertha is revived as Vashti, a figure whose 'unholy power' acts even more forcibly than that of her predecessor to destabilize the realist narrative of self-improvement.

Courtship Rituals

The courtship of Jane and Rochester, over which Bertha presides, is framed in very different terms to that of Rochester's account of his relations with Bertha. The dominant discourse here is not that of sexuality and the body, but rather that of phrenology and the economic and psychological principles of Victorian individualism. Sexuality is displaced into erotic power play. While Jane might not openly defy Rochester, she is not meekly submissive. Both figures treat their association as a fierce battle for the preservation of autonomy. As Rochester says to Jane, shortly alter his proposal, 'Encroach, presume, and the game is up' (p. 330). The rules of their 'game' are defined, as in all Brontë's novels, by an attempt to read the inner territory of the other while preserving the self unread. On their first evening together Rochester reads Jane's character from her sketches, and on the second she is invited to read his skull. Her unquestioning assertion that Rochester is not handsome confirms that we are in the domain of phrenology, not physiognomy. Neither Rochester nor Jane, who constantly stresses her own lack of physical beauty, conform to the rules of physiognomy which suggest, as Spurzheim observes, that 'an unsightly person ought to be the concomitant of an unenviable soul'.[55] The external signs of the head and countenance do not directly express inner qualities, but rather offer a language that has to be decoded. Rochester offers his skull for Jane's perusal:

> 'Criticize me: does my forehead not please you?'
>
> He lifted up the sable waves of hair which lay horizontally over his brow, and showed a solid enough mass of intellectual organs; but an abrupt deficiency where the suave sign of benevolence should have risen.
>
> 'Now, ma'am, am I a fool?'
>
> 'Far from it, sir. You would perhaps think me rude if I inquired in return whether you are a philanthropist?' (p. 161)

In this phrenological exchange the barriers of class and status are overthrown; all that matters is innate endowment and interpretative proficiency. As an equally skilled reader, Jane is momentarily placed on equal terms with Rochester.

Surveillance and interpretative penetration form the groundworks of Jane and Rochester's erotic struggles. He attempts constantly to baffle her powers of deciphering external signs: he withholds information, offers misleading explanations, and even engages in masquerade, as in his courtship of Blanche, and his impersonation of a gypsy. Jane is never allowed to rest secure in her own interpretative powers. Following Rochester's stories concerning Grace Poole, she is 'amazed—confounded' by the discrepancies between her attributed character of would-be murderer and that suggested by her features and 'hard-forehead' (p. 192). Bodies cease to be legible. Rochester's explanations, indeed, trespass on the tremulous borders of Jane's own sanity. He denies, initially, the physical existence of the woman who tore her veil, thrusting on Jane, rather, the label of hysteric with his suggestion that it was 'the creature of an overstimulated brain' (p. 360). Not content with defining one wife as 'maniac', he places his future bride in that other category of female weakness: the nervous, hysterical woman. Their attempted marriage, in which he attempts to impose a false name and role on Jane, represents the culmination of his bid for control of interpretative and definitional power.

Like Jane, Rochester aims to read the other, while keeping the self firmly veiled. Although critics have celebrated the novel's depiction of a romantic union of souls, close reading suggests that even their moments of greatest apparent union are in fact based on power struggles centered on the withholding of self.[56] In the gypsy scene, which directly parallels Jane's earlier phrenological reading of Rochester, he offers to analyse her destiny from her face and forehead. Disguised as a woman, Rochester enjoys free access to Jane's unprotected interiority. There follows an extraordinary passage, in which the gypsy's ventriloquizing of the 'speech' of Jane's forehead is set in dialogue with her inner self. The divisions of self and other seem to break down, and inner and outer to meld into one. In that external voice Jane believes she hears the 'speech of my own tongue' (p. 253), but as soon as Rochester unveils himself the preceding events take on a different complexion. By exposing herself, unguarded, to his gaze, Jane has betrayed herself, temporarily, into his power, allowed him both to penetrate and control the articulation of her psyche.

Yet the struggle is not all one-sided: the retaining and withholding of self also constitutes part of Jane's 'system' for handling Rochester. Her depiction of this 'system' (as she designates it), represents a decisive innovation in the genre of the novel. Whereas Pamela and Clarissa mobilized their resources of defence to protect their 'hidden treasure' of virginity against a very real physical threat, Jane's system of withholding operates within the domain of knowledge. A physical threat to virginity is no longer even the ostensible issue. The erotic charge created in readers of the eighteenth-century novel, hovering always on the brink of violation, is here openly defined and analysed, and explicitly appropriated by the protagonist as a mode of regulating social and sexual interaction. Jane delights in 'vexing and soothing' Rochester 'by turns'; though 'beyond the verge of provocation I never ventured; on the extreme brink I liked well to try my skill' (p. 197). Such tactical play now figures not only as a goal in itself (to be continued, Jane asserts, even into marriage) but also as a source of pleasure.

Jane Eyre offers an anatomy of the 'perpetual spirals of power and pleasure' which were incited by the nineteenth-century regulation of sexuality.[57] Erotic excitement is produced by evading interpretative penetration, while a sense of selfhood is actively created by the demand for disclosure. Under this regime romantic union is impossible. Rochester's demonstrations of tenderness constitute a threat, rather than desired end: 'Soft scene, daring demonstration, I would not have: and I stood in peril of both: a weapon of defence must be prepared' (p. 343). Jane's 'weapon' is that of language: throughout their courtship she aims constantly to gain control by contradicting his expectations, and challenging his interpretative skills. Only by maintaining herself unread can she maintain the balance of power. Her system is therefore to 'thwart' and 'afflict' him since she realizes that this keeps him 'excellently entertained' (p. 345).

What we are offered in these descriptions is not an invariant, ahistoric model of sexual dynamics, but rather an analysis of the specific forms of erotic enjoyment engendered by nineteenth-century models of economic, psychological and sexual regulation.[58] Although erotic surveillance is clearly to be found in Restoration comedy, for example, it is not tied in with the same economic theory of regulated selfhood. With its dual emphasis on external surveillance and the internal channelling and restraining of competing energies, phrenology may be taken, as I suggested earlier, as the paradigmatic model of the psyche during the rise of the industrial economy. The courtship of Jane and Rochester, which revolves around the activities of surveillance, and the maintenance of the energies of both self and other in a state of productive, dynamic tension, inscribes these economic principles in the domain of romance. As in the economy, energies were to be both fully maximized, and firmly restrained. Jane's most intense experience of erotic excitement arises not from sexual contact but from involvement in a triadic structure of surveillance. Carefully positioning herself so that she can watch Blanche without being observed, she notes that her scrutiny is being duplicated by 'other eyes besides mine ... the future bridegroom, Mr. Rochester himself, exercised over his intended a ceaseless surveillance' (p. 232). In feeling united to Rochester by their shared readerly skills, and mutual conviction of Blanche's gross textual incompetence, Jane feels herself to be 'at once under ceaseless excitation and ruthless restraint' (p. 233). Stimulated, but controlled, Jane enacts in her love life the ideologically-prescribed role of the industrial worker. Energy is to be maintained at its highest level without 'breaking bounds'.

To romantic souls, *Jane Eyre* must seem to offer a very perverted model of interaction. Jane revels in the pleasures of dominance even in the agonised moments after her aborted marriage. Looking at Rochester's incipient frenzy, she realizes that 'the passing second of time—was all I had in which to control and restrain him ... I felt an inward power; a sense of influence, which supported me. The crisis was perilous; but not without its charm' (p. 386). Brontë cuts through the niceties of romance tradition, daring to give her heroine (and not, as in earlier fiction, just her readers) a sense of enjoyment at the conventional moment of supposed greatest suffering. Control and regulation have moved from being mere agents in the service of wider social concerns to being ends in themselves, and ones which are, on the psychological level, decidedly pleasurable.

The Pleasures of Control

In order to understand the centrality of ideas of regulation and control in *Jane Eyre* it is necessary to place the novel within a wider frame of cultural reference. Throughout nineteenth-century psychological theory one can see the emergence of a new emphasis on the centrality of opposition as the defining category of selfhood: in Esquirol's insistence that selfhood only emerges with the ability to conceal, and in the phrenologists' grounding of self in the experience of conflict, both internal, between the faculties themselves, and external, between the self and the world, a theory which, in turn, bears a strong relation to aspects of German Romantic psychology.[59] Nowhere are these principles of opposition given more prominence than in a series of articles by James Ferrier entitled 'An Introduction to the Philosophy of Consciousness', published in Brontë's favourite periodical, *Blackwood's*, 1838–9. While Brontë would probably have read these articles, I am less concerned with questions of influence, than with Ferrier's role in articulating and isolating one of the emerging principles of nineteenth-century psychological thought which frames Brontë's writing. In Ferrier's work, the German Romantic ideal of striving and becoming is assimilated to the antagonistic, individualistic principles of Victorian economic culture. The self, he insists, only comes into being by an act of opposition or negation.[60] Consciousness is not the 'harmonious accompaniment' but rather 'the antagonist and the violator of sensation'.[61] The violent, implicitly sexual, imagery, which parallels that of Brontë, is indicative: his work is suffused with a sense of perpetual embattlement. In a passage of importance for *Jane Eyre*, Ferrier maintains that one cannot 'lay hold of the good' by remaining unconscious of evil,

> for the passions are real madmen, and consciousness is their only keeper; but man's born amiabilities are but painted masks, which, (if consciousness has never occupied its post) are liable to be torn away from the face of his natural corruption, in any dark hour in which the passions may choose to break up from the dungeons of the heart.[62]

Like Esquirol, Ferrier situates selfhood and sanity in the act of masking. He emphasizes the absolute primacy of control; surrender to any passion, whether judged morally 'good' or 'bad' leads to the total erasure of selfhood.[63] In the light of this philosophy, Jane's fears of Rochester's tenderness become clear: to surrender to passion is to surrender the very basis of selfhood. The 'real madwoman' of Thornfield breaks out on each occasion when Jane allows herself to be almost submerged within Rochester. On the night when she follows him 'in thought through the new regions he disclosed', and slips free from her usual 'painful restraint' his bed is set on fire (p. 180). Her sense of union with Rochester in his gypsy guise is similarly followed by the attack on Mason, and the final eruption occurs before the wedding when Jane has been absorbed, imaginatively, in Rochester's world, thinking 'of the life that lay before me—*your* life, sir' (p. 354). Her nightmares culminate in the tearing of the bridal veil. Jane's amiability is a 'cover' or 'mask' which is liable to be torn away each time she surrenders to passion and loses sense of herself as individualized being, a being defined by the active process of opposition.

The significance of Ferrier's text lies in its separation of the doctrine of self-control from any vestiges of a moral framework. The only category of evil he seems to acknowledge is that of passivity of response, an inertness of control; thus to bask in the warmth of another's love is to become little better than an 'automaton'.[64] Opposition has become an end in itself, to be activated whatever the content or the character of the desires or individual being opposed might be. Jane flees Rochester not because of moral scruples, but so that she can retain her own oppositional sense of self. With Rochester she had felt called to an Edenic 'paradise of union' (p. 321). She had wished to deny separation, the founding condition of selfhood, and to return once more to the harmonious, passive, pre-conscious state of paradisiacal existence which for Ferrier (anticipating contemporary psychoanalysis) defined our original state of union before the emergence of the 'rebellious I' which marked our Fall.[65] Jane has been guilty of trying to create a false Eden; in ceasing to oppose the promptings of her passions she is in danger of becoming, 'an automaton'. She is saved from such a lapse by her pursuit of individualism on the economic front: her letter to her uncle functions as the primary agency in averting the impending wedding.

Her response to this situation is clearly in line with Ferrier's theories of self-suppression; she becomes her own violator: 'you shall, yourself, pluck out your right eye; yourself cut off your right hand: your heart shall be the victim; and you, the priest, to transfix it' (p. 379). Such self-mutilation constitutes for Ferrier the ultimate act of liberty, the only possible way of attaining inviolate selfhood. Its foundation in an ever-vigilant state of opposition and warfare, whether towards inner emotion or external forces, suggests, however, the very essence of slavery. In shifting the definition of freedom from a social and political register to that of a qualitative measure of psychological experience, he, like the phrenologists, has inscribed the social battleground within the self.

Brontë explores the impact of these oppositional principles of selfhood on the genre of romance. If the self is only an unstable point, which exists only to the degree that a sense of conscious opposition between both self and other, and emotional prompting and repressive control, can be instituted, then the romantic ideal of harmonious union between two integral units is firmly undercut. Yet Jane Eyre should not therefore be considered as a heroine of feminist self-fulfillment, overthrowing the tyrannous demands of a patriarchal society for female submission. In subscribing to the oppositional principles of selfhood, seeking power through concealment and self-control, she is adhering to the competitive, individualist principles which underpinned Victorian social and economic theory.

Jane Eyre is a heroine of individualism who exposes the contradictions of individualist ideology. She attempts to found a sense of personal agency and power on a concept of selfhood which, lacking all unity, is merely the shifting relation of internal conflicts. At the very time when individualist theories of social and economic interaction held ideological sway, and contemporary rhetoric was filled with references to individual rights, psychological theories of individuality, applying the competitive principles of the market place to the psychological economy, started to stress internal divisions, and the lack of a unified centre of self. This principle holds true across the wide spectrum of psychological theories, whether in the aggressively individualistic premises of phrenology, which nonetheless rested on a theory of internal contradiction, in the fierce assertiveness of Ferrier's theories which reduced selfhood to a state of negativity, an ever-shifting point of opposition, or in the more popular interest in the unconscious processes of the mind which developed, in the hands of physiological psychology, into an energy-dynamics of the psyche which grounded selfhood in the conflicting flows of physiological force. Selfhood thus becomes, not an invincible bastion of sovereignty, the unshakeable bedrock of the imperialist project, but rather the interiorized site of social conflict.

Jane's narrative plots a series of defiant assertions of a self which threatens, imminently, to fragment and rupture. After her flight from Thornfield, and her experience of being reduced to the level of animal existence on the moors, her re-entry into selfhood is marked not by her articulation of the self, but rather by her experience of the power to withhold. After refusing to offer an account of herself to the Rivers family she remarks, 'I began once more to know myself' (p. 431). The self is only conjured into existence by an act of refusal.

With St John Rivers, Jane enters into a new cycle of her battles for self-definition. As before, the struggles are played out on the field of knowledge, both parties withholding the self while trying to read the other. St John's initial diagnosis of her physical condition is followed by a reading of her character: 'I trace lines of force in her face which make me sceptical of her tractability' (p. 433). Their relationship is founded on the power of the gaze; each treats the other as a text to be decoded. St John seemed 'to read my face, as if its features and lines were characters on a page' (p. 452). Jane refers repeatedly to the qualities of his gaze; to his piercing eyes, and 'coruscating radiance of glance' (p. 452); she finds herself falling 'under the influence of the ever-watchful blue eye' (p. 507). Like Lucy before Dr John, Jane feels reduced to the status of an object, examined and controlled by the scientific gaze. St John waits, 'looking like a physician watching with the eye of science an expected and fully-understood crisis in a patient's malady' (p. 511). Jane becomes the figure of a disease whose external symptoms are monitored, anticipated and controlled by medical expertise.

St John acquires dominion through his own indecipherability. Extending the medical analogy, Jane observes that he uses his eyes, 'rather as instruments to search other people's thoughts, than as agents to reveal his own' (p. 441). Nonetheless, St John is not impervious to interpretation. To Jane's eyes the physiognomical harmony of his Greek features is suggestive not of perfection, but rather of elements 'restless, or hard, or eager' (p. 440). Both characters use the vocabulary of phrenology to diagnose in the other 'insatiate' faculties which need to be 'pruned', 'trained' and 'eradicated'. The force of St John's sermon, 'compressed, condensed, controlled', seems to Jane to spring from 'a depth where lay turbid dregs of disappointment—where moved troubling impulses of insatiate yearnings and disquieting aspirations' (p. 449). The language recalls her own emotional outbreak as a child when angry thoughts 'were turned up in my disturbed mind like a dark deposit in a turbid well' (p. 12). In addition, it associates both figures with the upswell of working-class discontent, the social 'turbulence' of contemporary rhetoric, where the 'dregs' of society seek to further their destructive ambitions (the officers in the nearby town; we learn, are there to control the riots). The minds of both Jane and St John are represented as microcosms of the social whole: an assemblage of conflicting elements, where the higher faculties seek to impose control on the turbulent lower orders.

St John, with his resolute, mechanized timing of a permitted period of submission to the 'nectarous flood' of sensual desire, stands as paradigm of a ruthless, repressive organization of energies, whether in the social or psychological system. In the debates between Jane and St John, the potential subjects of his imperialist mission in India are almost entirely omitted: the social is shifted, metonymically, into the psychological. Discussion focuses on the interaction of the faculties, conceived as an independent sphere of competing energies, distanced both from the control of the speaking subject, and the people who are to be subject to this dominion. Jane colludes with St John in this writing out of the native subjects, shifting the politics of imperialism into an issue of internal psychology and geographical space. She agrees that St John's faculties are 'paralysed' (p. 454) and 'stagnate' in

England, and that the 'Himalayan ridge, or Caffre bush' would enable him to develop them to advantage (p. 502). But she refuses, however, to accompany him on the grounds that, 'I want to enjoy my own faculties as well as to cultivate those of other people' (p. 198). Such a 'selfish' demand for enjoyment and pleasure is deemed impermissible by St John who fiercely rebuts Jane's claims to be able to impose harmonious control on her energies: the inner scene of the psyche, and the outer terrain of social action, must always be characterized by conflict and a relentless struggle to control.

Whilst Rochester literally imprisoned his Creole wife, St John fixes Jane with his 'freezing spell', exerting on her the imperial authority he hopes to unleash overseas. Like members of other oppressed groups, Jane nurses sentiments which belie her apparent quiescence: 'I did not love my servitude' (p. 508). The cycle of their mutual struggles for dominance is disrupted by St John's proposal of marriage which shifts the question of control onto an explicit material ground, forcing Jane to confront, finally, the question of the relationship between sexuality and selfhood. The problem of marriage to St John would not lie, as critics sometimes assume, in its asexuality, but rather in his physical obedience to the letter but not the spirit of the marriage contract. In terms remarkably explicit for the Victorian age, Jane wonders whether she could endure for St John to 'scrupulously observe ... all the forms of love' whilst knowing that his 'spirit was quite absent'. Unlike the later Dorothea Brooke, she decides that 'such a martyrdom would be monstrous' (p. 517).[66] She fears that, as St John's wife, she would be 'forced to keep the fire of my nature continually low, to compel it to burn inwardly and never utter a cry, though the imprisoned flame consumed vital after vital—*this* would be unendurable' (pp. 520–1). Jane's image of the agony of self-consuming energy recalls her early responses when she first discovered her love for Rochester: 'it is madness in all women to let a secret love kindle within there, which, if unreturned and unknown, must devour the life that feeds it' (p. 201).[67] Jane believes that, if forced to marry St John, she could 'imagine the possibility of conceiving an inevitable, strange, torturing kind of love for him' while he would find her exhibition of desire, 'a superfluity, unrequired by him, unbecoming in me' (p. 531). A cultural system which defines women as aggressively sexual beings, but maintains that *both* repression and expression of sexuality will lead to madness, establishes the perfect model for self-mutilation. As the image of 'torturing love' suggests, women are rendered doubly abject, their own persecutors and destroyers.

By forcing Jane to overcome her dualistic model of selfhood and actively confront the question of the relationship between sexuality and self definition, St John offers her a model of empowerment. Much has been made of the 'Gothic' voice which rescues Jane from self-destructive commitment, but of equal importance here is the way in which Brontë self-confidently intercuts different genres: the supernatural and the theological are directly tied to overtly materialist depictions of energy flow. The supernatural is invoked only to be negated: the voice was, Jane firmly decides, no miracle but 'the work of nature' (p. 536). In one of her most daring Biblical rewritings, Brontë recasts St John the Divine's cry, 'Even so, come Lord Jesus', (which is also to conclude her novel) into overtly secular and sexual terms: 'I am coming! ... Oh, I will come!' (p. 536). The onrush of sexual energy rouses Jane's senses from their 'torpor' and brings about a total reversal of the power dynamics in her relations with St John. Whereas before she had been tempted to 'rush down the torrent of his will into the gulf of his existence, and there lose my own', she feels it was now 'my turn to assume ascendancy. My powers were in play, and in force' (pp. 534, 536). We have moved swiftly from the Gothic to the social drama of aggressive, competing energies.

Jane's final ascendancy is set against the destruction of 'Bertha', that feared embodiment of female bodily excess, and the mutilation of Rochester whose physical injuries embody the acts of self-violation Jane had previously wished to impose on herself when her 'tyrant' conscience had decreed 'you shall, yourself, pluck out your right eye; yourself cut off your right hand' (p. 379). The depiction of Rochester as 'some wronged and fettered wild-beast or bird, dangerous to approach in his sullen woe' (p. 552) clearly recalls, however, descriptions of the imprisoned Bertha, and of Jane's earlier desires to cast off the fetters from her faculties, setting an ominous note for this final stage in their mutual struggles.

On returning to Rochester, Jane enters directly into a replay of the power games which had marked their earlier relations, only this time it is she who is in command, withholding herself and information, and deliberately allowing him to misconstrue her relations with St John. Her assumption of social dominance is figured in her assertion that 'I was then his vision, as I am still his right hand' (pp. 576–7). She becomes, in terms which confirm Brontë's explicit secular rewriting of the conclusion of Revelations, literally, Rochester's 'alpha and omega' (p. 572).[68] Not only is Jane hidden, through Rochester's blindness, from the controlling power of his gaze; she holds interpretative authority over his entire world: 'He saw nature—he saw books through me; and never did I weary of gazing for his behalf, and of putting into words the effect of field, tree, town, river, cloud, sunbeam' (p. 577). The description recalls Rochester's statement of how he would behave to Jane if she were mad. As her sole 'watcher and nurse' he would 'never weary of gazing into your eyes, though they had no longer a ray of recognition for me' (p. 384). Jane inverts this image of male delight in female powerlessness; where Rochester had committed himself to an inward-looking gaze, striving to find himself in the non-reflecting eyes of female madness, Jane takes more active command, seeking not to find herself directly, but rather through the exercise of interpretative control.[69] Jane begins her autobiographical narrative with her struggle against the Reeds for the power of social definition, and concludes with her attainment of this power. Throughout she has been forced to listen to others' narratives of herself that of Mrs Reed's which 'obliterates hope' from her future existence, Mr Brocklehurst's account of her to Lowood, Rochester's gypsy reading, and St John's story of one, 'Jane Eyre'. In each case the accounts represent an overt bid for control, offering a narrative which takes over the role of self-definition. The conclusion reverses this situation: Jane literally articulates Rochester's world.

Despite the foregrounding of romance, *Jane Eyre* does not end, as one might expect, with a celebration of Jane's romantic or maternal role. Final place is actually given to St John Rivers, raving in perpetual restlessness, transplanting the bourgeois ideology of self-improvement into an imperial exercise in control: 'full of energy, and zeal, and truth, he labours for his race: he clears their painful way to improvement; he hews down like a giant the prejudices of creed and caste that encumber it' (p. 578). Just as the eruptions of Bertha had earlier disrupted the surface meaning of Jane's text, so this final vision of St John, internally torn and violently hewing down external opposition, undercuts Jane's claims to have achieved harmonious union.

Jane's history, like that of Crimsworth, seems to endorse popular ideologies of self-improvement: by acquiring self-control she is able to move into a position of social power. Her will to control has not been allayed, however, but rather projected outwards more forcibly onto her relations with Rochester. While Jane's calm assertions of domestic serenity endorse the overt moral message of Combe's philosophy, the underlying implications of his worldview are more accurately conveyed in the final picture of St John's savage discontent. If, following the conflictual theories of selfhood which emerged in the nineteenth century, the self is not a unified entity, but rather a site of internal struggle between competing energies; and self-consciousness arises only through the experience of oppositional control, then a sense of unified harmony can never be attained. Competition and opposition, as in the economy, are the defining elements of selfhood. Total fulfillment could come, indeed, only with total vanquishment. The novel ends fittingly, therefore, with St John, like his name-sake, calling on God for death. If, in the figure of Rochester, chained and fettered, we have an image of sullen energy, poised to re-enact Jane and Bertha's rebellion against constraint, in Brontë's final return to the words of St John the Divine, we have the startling suggestion that the sexual awakening to which Jane 'comes' is a form of living death.

The brooding, dank atmosphere of Ferndean, with air so 'insalubrious' that Rochester had declined to place Bertha there, forms a setting which ill accords with Jane's attempts to claim happiness for all. Just as the violence of Crimsworth's murder of his son's dog in *The Professor* revealed Brontë's clear awareness of the costs exacted by a culture of control, so the final foregrounding of the figure of St John signals a similar unease. Where Crimsworth sends Victor away to Eton, to subdue his 'electrical ardour', Rochester's ward, Adèle, in parallel with the young Jane, is sent away from the family home until she too learns to acquire a more 'natural' disposition. Jane's celebration of the fact that Adèle learns to become 'docile, good-tempered and well-principled' places her unnervingly close to the position of the detested Mrs Reed, whose social status she has now assumed. Such statements of happy conformity sit awkwardly in a text whose power and motivating force lies in its clamour against injustice, its desire to 'break bounds' whether of social prescriptions for femininity or the generic conventions of the realist text. The spirit of Bertha is not quite so easily subdued.

The difficulties of interpreting *Jane Eyre* lie in its internal contradictions, which in turn mirror those of the social, psychological and economic discourse of the age. The text yearns towards the powerful ideal of romantic union, whilst simultaneously exposing it as a further expression of the competitive dynamics which govern the marketplace. It seems to take us inward into the most private recesses of selfhood, but then shatters illusions of individual autonomy by showing how even these most private realms are constructed socially, in a silent drama of conflict and withdrawal. It espouses ideologies of self-development and improvement, and economic ideas of energy flow, only to reveal their intrinsic opposition; the self is figured both as a striving, integrated unit, and as the divided, unstable product of conflicting energies. The ideals of self-control are set, furthermore, against alternate models of female subordination to the forces of the body, and their social and psychological implications are explored and interrogated. Jane's defiant assertions of selfhood in the text are cut across by fears of imminent dissolution, and the upsurge of energies which cannot be controlled.

In many ways *Jane Eyre* can be read as a quintessential expression of Victorian individualism. Whilst George Eliot's heroines ask where social duty can lie, Charlotte Brontë's ask only how individual desires and ambitions can be achieved. In the mouth of an industrialist, such sentiments would express the spirit of the age. Coming from a socially-marginal female their import is radical, if not revolutionary. The spirit of defiance can find no social locus, however; the red room and the attic cannot be socially contained. Brontë's novels move reluctantly, defiantly, towards a conventional ending in marriage whose harmony and stasis suggest, to an individual defined by conflict, a form of self-annihilation.

NOTES

1. See Sandra Gilbert and Susan Gubar, *The Madwoman in the Attic: The Woman Writer and the Nineteenth-Century Literary Imagination* (New Haven: Yale University Press, 1979), and Barbara Hill Rigney, *Madness and Sexual Politics in the Feminist Novel* (Madison: University of Wisconsin Press, 1978).

2. It is on this point that I would like to differentiate my work from Elaine Showalter's excellent study, *The Female Malady: Women, Mildness, and English Culture, 1830–1980* (New York: Pantheon, 1985), which considers the notion of female madness within a narrower framework of social explanation.

3. Charlotte Brontë, *Jane Eyre*, eds. Jane Jack and Margaret Smith (Oxford: Clarendon Press, 1969), p. xxxi. All references to this edition will be given in future in the text.

4. See Matthew 23: 27.

5. T. J. Wise and J. A. Symington, *The Brontës: their Lives, Friendships and Correspondence*, 4. vols. (Oxford: Basil Blackwell, 1933), II, p. 198. Hereafter cited as *Letters*. To W. S. Williams, 11 March 1848.

6. *Letters*, II, p. 201. To W. S. Williams, 29 March 1848.

7. See Georges Canguilhem, *Essai sur quelques problèmes concernant le normal et le pathologique* (Publications de la Faculté des Lettres de l'Université de Strasbourg) (Paris: 1950), p. 18

8. Margot Peters, *Charlotte Brontë: Style in the Novel* (Madison: University of Wisconsin Press, 1973), p. 57.

9. See Mary Poovey, *Uneven Developments: The Ideological Work of Gender in Mid-Victorian England* (London: Virago, 1989), ch. 5, and M. Jeanne Peterson, 'The Victorian Governess: Status Incongruence in Family and Society' in Martha Vicinus, ed., *Suffer and Be Still: Women in the Victorian Age* (Bloomington: Indiana University Press, 1972), pp. 3–19.

10. See Peter Stallybrass and Allon White, *The Politics and Poetics of Transgression* (Ithaca, NY: Cornell University Press, 1986), ch. 3.

11. For a further reading of this interiority see Elaine Showalter, *A Literature of their Own: British Women Novelists from Brontë to Lessing* (Princeton: Princeton University Press, 1977) and Karen Chase, *Eros and Psyche: The Representation of Personality in Charlotte Brontë, Charles Dickens, and George Eliot* (London: Methuen, 1984), chs. 3 and 4.

12. Brontë's text points to the inadequacies of forms of Lacanian analysis which do not take full account of the contradictory subject positions offered within a given culture.

13. George Combe, *Elements of Phrenology*, 3rd edn (Edinburgh: John Anderson, 1828), p. 60.

14. George Combe, *The Constitution of Man Considered in Relation to External Objects*, 7th edn (Boston: Marsh, Capen and Lyon, 1836), p. 104.

15. As Susan Meyer has pointed out in her excellent article, 'Colonialism and the Figurative Strategy of *Jane Eyre*', *Victorian Studies*, 33 (1990), the language of fire was also employed in representations of the revolt of that other oppressed group whose presence informs the text of *Jane Eyre*, the West Indian Slaves (p. 254).

16. James Kay Shuttleworth, *The Moral and Physical Condition of the Working Classes*

employed in the Cotton Manufacture in Manchester (London, 1832; repr. Shannon: Irish University Press, 1971), p. 47.

17. Quoted by John Conolly in 'Hysteria', in J. Forbes, A. Tweedie and J. Conolly (eds.), *The Cyclopaedia of Practical Medicine*, 4 vols. (London: Sherwood et al., 1833), II, p. 572.

18. 'Woman in her Psychological Relations', *Journal of Psychological Medicine and Mental Pathology*, 4 (1851), p. 33. The writer here is echoing the work of Thomas Laycock. See for example, the section on 'Insane Cunning' in *A Treatise on the Nervous Diseases of Women; Comprising an Inquiry into the Nature, Causes, and Treatment of Spinal and Hysterical Disorders* (London: Longman, 1840), p. 353.

19. John Reid, *Essays on Hypochondriasis and other Nervous Afflictions*, 2nd edn (London: Longman, 1821). p. 314

20. See Laycock, *An Essay on Hysteria* (Philadelphia: Haswell, Barrington and Haswell, 1840), p. 107.

21. See Nancy Stepan, 'Race and Gender: the Role of Analogy in Science', *Isis*, 77 (1986), p. 264.

22. Combe, *Constitution of Man*, p. 72.

23. Combe, *A System of Phrenology*, 3rd edn (Edinburgh: John Anderson, 1830), p. 540.

24. *Ibid.*

25. For an examination of the fears aroused by the passionate child, see Michel Foucault, *The History of Sexuality*, vol 1, trans. R. Hurley (Harmondsworth: Penguin, 1981).

26. See Penny Boumelha, 'George Eliot and the End of Realism', in Sue Roe, ed., *Women Reading Women's Writing* (Brighton: Harvester Press, 1987), pp. 15–35; George Eliot, *The Mill on the Floss*, ed. S. Shuttleworth (London: Routledge, 1991), p. 495; and Susan Fraiman, *Unbecoming Women: British Women Writers and the Novel of Development* (New York: Columbia University Press, 1993), chs. 4 and 5.

27. For a discussion of the economic side of this debate see Maxine Berg, *The Machinery Question and the Making of Political Economy, 1815–48* (Cambridge: Cambridge University Press, 1980).

28. Elizabeth Rigby, Review of *Jane Eyre*, *Quarterly Review*, 15 (April 1848); repr. in Miriam Allott, *The Brontës: The Critical Heritage* (London: Routledge and Kegan Paul, 1974), pp. 109–10.

29. *Letters*, II, 203. To W. S. Williams, 20 April 1848.

30. *Letters*, II, 216. To W. S. Williams, 12 May 1848.

31. Kay Shuttleworth, *The Moral and Physical Condition*, p. 38.

32. Susan Fraiman in chapter 4 of *Unbecoming Women* offers a very insightful reading of the centrality of Grace, the servant figure, in the text, highlighting the importance of Jane's concern with her relations to the working class.

33. See, for example, Rigney, *Madness*, ch. 1, and Gilbert and Gubar, *Madwoman*.

34. Julia Kristeva, *Revolution in Poetic Language* (New York: Columbia University Press, 1984).

35. Bertha's racial designation has been the subject of debate in recent criticism. In 'Three Women's Texts and a Critique of Imperialism', *Critical Inquiry*, 12 (1985) Gayatri Spivak identified Bertha as a 'native female' (p. 245). Susan Meyer, however, in 'Colonialism and the Figurative Strategy of *Jane Eyre*' has highlighted the complex associations surrounding the term Creole, and the slippages in Spivak's own designations. Meyer argues very convincingly for the centrality of race in Brontë's works, showing clearly how awareness of shared oppression does not preclude racism.

36. Spivak, 'Three Women's Texts', p. 255. My reading of *Jane Eyre* differs from that of Spivak in that the challenge to imperialism which she locates solely in Jean Rhys' rewriting of the novel in *Wide Sargasso Sea* I find also, to a lesser degree, in the original. Philip Martin in *Mad Women in Romantic Writing* (Brighton: Harvester Press, 1987) offers an interesting reading of the text in the light of the development of the figure of the madwoman in Romantic psychiatry and literature. Like Spivak, however, he emphasises the divide between Jane and Bertha, and sees in *Wide Sargasso Sea* a novel which splits apart the double standards of *Jane Eyre* (ch. 5).

37. See, for example, Showalter, *A Literature of their Own* and *The Female Malady*; Rigney, *Madness*, and Gilbert and Gubar, *Madwoman.*

38. Hermione Lee has pointed out in 'Emblems and Enigmas in *Jane Eyre*', *English*, 29–30 (1981), pp. 235–55, the ways in which Brontë is drawing on a theological, pre-novelistic tradition of emblematic display which is in conflict with her sense of the enigmas of psychological states.

39. John Reid, *Essays on Hypochondriasis and other Nervous Afflictions*, 2nd edn (London: Longman, 1821). This passage was added in the second edition, in line with the emergence of a new emphasis on self-control as the defining characteristic of sanity.

40. J. E. D. Esquirol, *Mental Maladies: A Treatise on Insanity*, trans. E. K. Hunt (1845: repr., New York: Hafner, 1964). 'In general those who have black hair, who are strong, robust, and of a sanguine temperament, are maniacs, and furious. The course of their insanity is more acute, its crises more marked, than among those composing the other classes' (p. 38).

41. Prichard outlines the stages of an often cited case of raving madness, starting with the 'impetuous, audacious, shameless habits, a bold menacing aspect' which are soon followed by 'shrieking, roaring, raging, abusive expressions and conduct towards the dearest friends and relatives who are now looked upon as the bitterest enemies. The patient tears his clothes to tatters, destroys, breaks in pieces whatever comes in his way.' As the violence increases, so does the physical strength of the patient, and in the final stage when the paroxysms subside, that patient 'sings or laughs in a strange manner, or chatters with incessant volubility'. James Cowle Prichard, *A Treatise on Insanity and other Disorders Affecting the Mind* (London: Sherwood, Gilbert and Piper, 1835), pp. 64–5

42. Showalter, *The Female Malady*, pp. 66–9.

43. *Ibid.*, p. 67.

44. Esquirol, *Mental Maladies*, p. 392.

45. Laycock, *Nervous Diseases*, p. 353

46. 'Woman in her Psychological Relations', p. 31.

47. My reading clearly differs from that of Nancy Armstrong in *Desire and Domestic Fiction: A Political History of the Novel* (New York and Oxford: Oxford University Press, 1987), who sees Bertha as part of the ahistorical 'Gothic claptrap' of the Brontës' fictions (p. 197).

48. Laycock, *Nervous Diseases*, p. 141.

49 Goss and Company, *Hygeniana; a Non-Medical analysis of the Complaints Incidental to Females*, 20th edn (London: Sherwood, 1829), p. 66. See also 'Woman in her Psychological Relations', on the 'vicious habit' of lesbian pleasures (p. 38).

50. See Sander L. Gilman, *Difference and Pathology: Stereotypes of Sexuality, Race, and Madness* (Ithaca: Cornell University Press, 1985), p. 58.

51. *Ibid.*, p. 213.

52. My argument here diverges from that of Fraiman in *Unbecoming Women* who, in highlighting the associations between Jane and Grace, tends to overplay Jane's sense of community with the working class.

53. A similar opinion had earlier been voiced by Brontë in a letter to Ellen Nussey in 1840. See *Letters*, I, p. 206.

54. See Joshua, 7: 11.

55. J. G. Spurzheim, *Phrenology in Connexion with the Study of Physiognomy* (Boston: Marsh, Capen and Lyon, 1836), p. 182.

56. Kucich has also drawn attention to this oppositional structure in Brontë's fiction: 'Reciprocal combat defines passion as an aggressive opposition to others, rather than as an unguarded relaxing of personal boundaries.' *Repression in Victorian Fiction* (Berkeley: University of California Press, 1987), p. 47.

57. Foucault, *History of Sexuality*, p. 45.

58. Although Foucault's *History of Sexuality* illuminates the sexual dynamics in play, he does not explore the complex inter-relationship with the economic sphere.

59. Jason Y. Hall in 'Gall's Phrenology: A Romantic Psychology', *Studies in Romanticism*, 16 (1977), draws attention to the emphasis on internal and external conflict in the writings of Gall, and to Gall's links, in this respect, with German Romantic psychology, p. 316.

60. J. F. Ferrier, 'An Introduction to the Philosophy of Consciousness'. Part VII, *Blackwood's Edinburgh Magazine*, 4.8 (1839), p. 429.

61. *Ibid.*, part V, 44 (1838), p. 550.

62. *Ibid.*, part VII, 48 (1839), p. 423.

63. *Ibid.*, part V, 44 (1838), p. 547.

64. *Ibid.*, part VI, 48 (1839), p. 207 and part VII, 48 (1839), p. 419.

65. *Ibid.*, part VII, 48 (1839), pp. 420–4.

66. See George Eliot, *Middlemarch*, Cabinet edition, 3 vols. (Edinburgh: William Blackwood, 1878–80), I, p. 337.

67. For similar sentiments expressed in the medical literature of the day, see Conolly's article on 'Hysteria' in J. Forbes, A. Tweedie and J. Conolly, *The Cyclopaedia of Practical Medicine*, 4 vols., (London: Sherwood et al., 1833), II, p. 572.

68. Jane has thus reversed her position in relationship to Rochester. In a cancelled passage in II, ch. 9 she had observed, 'The name Edward Fairfax Rochester was then my Alpha and Omega of existence' (p. 346).

69. For a discussion of the male need to identify selfhood through the reflecting female gaze see Shoshana Felman, 'Women and Madness: the Critical Phallacy', *Diacritics*, 5 (1975), p. 8.

SUSAN MEYER

"Indian Ink": Colonialism and the Figurative Strategy of *Jane Eyre*

The colonies play an important metaphorical role in each of Charlotte Brontë's major novels. The heroines of *Shirley* (1849) and *Villette* (1853) are both compared to people of nonwhite races experiencing the force of European imperialism. Louis Moore and M. Paul, the men whom the heroines love, either leave or threaten to leave Europe for the colonies, and in each case the man's dominating relationship with a colonial people is represented as a substitute for his relationship with the rebellious heroine. In order to determine if Shirley loves him, Louis Moore tells her that he intends to go to North America and live with the Indians, where, he immediately suggests, he will take one of the "sordid savages" as his wife.[1] Similarly, at the end of *Villette*, M. Paul departs for the French West Indian colony of Guadeloupe to look after an estate there instead of marrying Lucy. Such an estate would indeed have needed supervision in the early 1850s, as the French slaves had just been emancipated in 1848. Brontë suggests the tumultuous state of the colony by the ending she gives the novel: M. Paul may be killed off by one of the tropical storms that Brontë, like writers as diverse as Monk Lewis and Harriet Martineau, associates with the rage and the revenge of the black West Indians.[2] If M. Paul is a white colonist, Lucy is like a native resisting control: Brontë has Lucy think of her own creative impulse as a storm god, "a dark Baal." These metaphors make the novel's

---

From *Imperialism at Home*. © 1996 by Cornell University.

potentially tragic ending more ambiguous: it may not be entirely a tragedy if M. Paul is indeed killed by a storm and does not return from dominating West Indian blacks to marry the Lucy he calls "sauvage."[3]

The metaphorical use of race relations to represent conflictual gender relations is even more overt in Brontë's *The Professor* (1846). The novel begins as an unreceived letter, whose intended recipient has disappeared into "a government appointment in one of the colonies."[4] William Crimsworth's own subsequent experiences among the young women of a Belgian boarding school are represented as a parallel act of colonization. Crimsworth discreetly compares his Belgian-Catholic girl students to blacks whom he must forcibly keep under control. He likens one Caroline, for example, to a runaway West Indian slave when he describes her curling, "somewhat coarse hair," "rolling black eyes," and lips "as full as those of a hot-blooded Maroon" (86).[5] Even the atypical half-Swiss, half-English Frances Henri whom Crimsworth marries shows a potential rebelliousness against male domination that the novel figures using the imagery of race. Frances tells Crimsworth, with "a strange kind of spirit," that if her husband were a drunkard or a tyrant, marriage would be slavery, and that "against slavery all right thinkers revolt" (255). The metaphor is even more explicit when Frances tells Hunsden, who is matching wits with her in an argument about Switzerland, that if he marries a Swiss wife and then maligns her native country, his wife will arise one night and smother him "even as your own Shakespeare's Othello smothered Desdemona" (242). This imaginary wife's rebellion against women's subordination and against her gender role—she behaves like an angry man—precipitates her figurative blackness.

Even in the two existing chapters of Brontë's final and unfinished novel *Emma* (1853), race seems to be about to play an important figurative role: the heroine's suddenly apparent blackness suggests her social disenfranchisement due to gender, age, and social class. The two chapters are set in a boarding school and focus on a little girl, known as Matilda Fitzgibbon, who appears at first to be an heiress, but whose father disappears after leaving her at the school and cannot be located to pay her fees at the end of the first term. Matilda Fitzgibbon is revealed, at the end of the second chapter, to be of a race, or at least a physical appearance, that renders her susceptible to the following insult: "'If we were only in the good old times' said Mr Ellin 'where we ought to be—you might just send Miss Matilda out to the Plantations in Virginia—sell her for what she's worth and pay yourself—'"[6] This revelation has been prepared for by several previous passages. Matilda, the narrator has informed us, has a physical appearance that makes her inadequate as a wealthy "shew-pupil," a physiognomy that repels the headmistress and causes her a "gradually increasing peculiarity of feeling"

(309, 312), and "such a face as fortunately had not its parallel on the premises" (313). Brontë has also given Matilda the name "Fitz/gibbon," one that suggests racist epithets when it is read in the context of the nineteenth-century scientific commonplace that blacks were low on the scale of being, closer to apes than to white Europeans: Matilda's last name is a patronymic that brands her the offspring of a monkey. Yet in a sense Matilda becomes black only at the moment in the novel in which she loses her social standing. Only then do any of those around her make any explicit references to her race or skin coloring, and only then does the reader become aware of what it is that is "repulsive" in her "physiognomy." When Matilda becomes isolated, orphaned, unrooted, and poor—and more vulnerable and sympathetic—she is transformed by the narrative into a black child.

Brontë uses these references to relations between Europeans and races subjected to the might of European imperialism—in these instances, primarily native Americans and African slaves in the West Indies and the United States, although elsewhere in her fiction other peoples serve a similar metaphorical function—to represent various configurations of power in British society: female subordination in sexual relationships, female insurrection and rage against male domination, and the oppressive class position of the female without family ties and a middle-class income. She does so with a mixture of both sympathy for the oppressed and a conventional assertion of white racial supremacy: Matilda's apparently dark face is represented as repulsive, yet the situation that provokes Mr. Ellin's harsh racism also evokes the reader's sympathy for Matilda. Lucy Snowe's strength of character is one of her most admirable traits—and yet to represent it Brontë invokes the Eurocentric idea of colonized savages. The figurative use of race relations in Brontë's major fiction reveals a conflict between sympathy for the oppressed and a hostile sense of racial supremacy, one that becomes most apparent in *Jane Eyre* (1847).

I

In the opening chapters of *Jane Eyre*, race is a controlling metaphor—the young Jane is compared to a slave both at Gateshead, as she resists John Reed's tyranny, and at Lowood where she argues the need to resist unjust domination and angrily states that she would refuse to be publicly "flogged," only later to find herself subjected to another form of public humiliation like "a slave or victim."[7] Although in a few of these references Brontë represses the recent and immediate history of British slaveholding by alluding in the same passages to a safely remote history of Roman acts of enslavement ("You are like a murderer—you are like a slave-driver—you are like the Roman emperors!" Jane cries out to John Reed in the opening chapter [8]) the history of Britain's slaveholding, only nine years past at the time the novel was published, is inescapably evoked by such references. Indeed the novel will later hint at unflattering links between the British and the Roman empire. As the novel continues, the metaphor of slavery takes on such a central status that, although the novel remains situated in the domestic space, Brontë imports a character from the territory of the colonies (that territory also of her childhood writings) to give the metaphor a vivid presence. This realization of the metaphor through the creation of a character brings Brontë into a more direct confrontation with the history of British race relations. And Brontë's metaphorical use of race has a certain fidelity to the history of British imperialism. Brontë alludes to nonwhite races in the novel—primarily African slaves and Indians, though also Persians, Turks, and native Americans—in passages where she is evoking the idea of unjust oppression. But Brontë makes class and gender oppression the overt significance of these other races, displacing the historical reasons why nonwhite people might suggest the idea of oppression, at some level of consciousness, to nineteenth-century British readers. What begins then as an implicit critique of British domination and an identification with the oppressed collapses into merely an appropriation of the imagery of slavery, as the West Indian slave becomes the novel's archetypal image of the oppressed "dark races." Nonetheless, the novel's closure fails, in interesting ways, to screen out entirely the history of British imperialist oppression.

This complex metaphorical use of race explains much of the difficulty of understanding the politics of *Jane Eyre*. In an important reading of the significance of colonialism in this novel, Gayatri Spivak argues that "the unquestioned ideology of imperialist axiomatics" informs Brontë's narrative and enables the individualistic social progress of the character Jane that has been celebrated by "U.S. mainstream feminists." For her, Bertha, a "white Jamaican Creole," is a "native 'subject,'" indeterminately placed between human and animal and consequently excluded from the individualistic humanity that the novel's feminism claims for Jane.[8] While I agree with Spivak's broad critique of an individualistic strain of feminism, I find problematic her analysis of the workings of imperialist ideology and its relation to feminism, both in general and in *Jane Eyre*.

Spivak describes Bertha as at once a white woman and (as a native-born Jamaican white) a native, that is, as what she terms with little definition a "native 'subject.'"[9] She is thus able to designate Bertha as either native or white in order to criticize both Brontë's *Jane Eyre* and Jean Rhys's *Wide Sargasso Sea* as manifestations of exclusive feminist individualism. *Jane Eyre*, she argues, gives the white Jane individuality at the expense of the "native"

Bertha; *Wide Sargasso Sea*, on the other hand, retells the story of *Jane Eyre* from Bertha's perspective and thus merely "rewrites a canonical English text within the European novelistic tradition in the interest of the white Creole rather than the native" (253). Bertha is either native or not native to suit Spivak's critique. Thus it is by sleight of hand that Spivak shows feminism to be inevitably complicitous with imperialism.

My own proposition is that the interconnection between the ideology of male domination and the ideology of racial domination, manifested in the comparisons between white women and people of nonwhite races in many texts in this period of European imperialist expansion, in fact resulted in a very different relation between imperialist ideology and the developing resistance of nineteenth-century British women to the gender hierarchy. *Jane Eyre* was written in an ideological context in which white women were frequently compared to people of nonwhite races, especially blacks, in order to emphasize the inferiority of both to white men. But as Brontë constructs the trope in *Jane Eyre*, the yoking between the two terms of the metaphor turns not on shared inferiority but on shared oppression. Although this figurative strategy does not preclude racism, it inevitably produces the suggestion that people of these "other" races are also oppressed. While for the most part the novel suppresses the damning history of racial oppression and slavery, its ending betrays an anxiety that imperialism and oppression of other races constitute a stain upon English history and that the novel's own appropriation of nonwhite races for figurative ends bears a disturbing resemblance to that history. Thus although the ending of the novel does essentially permit the racial hierarchies of European imperialism to fall back into place, *Jane Eyre* is characterized not by Spivak "unquestioned ideology" of imperialism but by an ideology of imperialism that is questioned—and then reaffirmed—in interesting and illuminating ways.

An interpretation of the significance of the British empire in *Jane Eyre* must begin by making sense of Bertha Mason Rochester, the mad, drunken West Indian wife whom Rochester keeps locked up on the third floor of his ancestral mansion. Bertha functions in the novel as the central locus of Brontë's anxieties about the presence of oppression in England, anxieties that motivate the plot and drive it to its conclusion. The conclusion of the novel then settles these anxieties, partly by eliminating the character who seems to embody them. Yet Bertha only comes into the novel after about a third of its action has already taken place. As she emerges in the novel, anxieties that have been located elsewhere, notably in the character of Jane herself, become absorbed and centralized in the figure of Bertha, thus preparing the way for her final annihilation.

I read Bertha's odd ambiguity of race—an ambiguity that is constructed by the text itself, rather than one that needs to be mapped onto it—as directly related to her function as a representative of dangers that threaten the world of the novel. She is the heiress to a West Indian fortune, the daughter of a father who is a West Indian planter and merchant, and the sister of the yellow-skinned yet socially white Mr. Mason. She is also a woman whom the younger son of an aristocratic British family would consider marrying, and so she is clearly imagined as white—or as passing for white—in the novel's retrospective narrative. Critics of the novel, including Spivak, who describes her as a white Creole, have consistently assumed that Bertha is a white woman, basing the assumption on this part of the narrative, although Bertha has often been described as a "swarthy" or "dark" white woman.[10] But when she actually emerges as a character in the action of the novel, the narrative associates Bertha with blacks, particularly with the black Jamaican antislavery rebels, the maroons. In the form in which she becomes visible in the novel, Bertha has become black as she is constructed by the narrative, much as Matilda Fitzgibbon becomes black in *Emma*.

Even in Rochester's account of the time before their marriage, when Bertha Mason was "a fine woman, ... tall, dark, and majestic," there are hints, as there are in the early descriptions of Matilda Fitzgibbon, of the ambiguity of her race. Immediately after Rochester describes Bertha as "tall, dark, and majestic," he continues, "Her family wished to secure me, because I was of a good race" (389). In the context of a colony where blacks outnumbered whites by twelve to one, where it was a routine and accepted island practice for white planters to force female slaves to become their mistresses, and where whites on the island were uneasily aware of the growing population of people of mixed race, Rochester's phrase accrues a significance beyond its immediate reference to lineage, to his old family name.[11] Spoken in the context of a colony in which race relations were growing increasingly explosive and were becoming a constant preoccupation, Rochester's phrase cannot avoid evoking other meanings of the word "race," and thus suggesting that Bertha herself may not be of as "good" a race as he. Bertha is the daughter, as Richard Mason oddly and, it would seem, unnecessarily declares in his official attestation to her marriage with Rochester, "of Jonas Mason, merchant, and of Antoinetta his wife, a Creole" (366).

The ambiguity of Bertha's race is marked by this designation of her mother as a creole. The word "creole" was used in the nineteenth century to refer to both blacks and whites born in the West Indies, a usage that caused some confusion: as the India-born British barrister and historian John Malcolm Forbes Ludlow put it in 1862, "There are creole whites, creole negroes, creole horses, &c.; and creole whites are, of all persons, the most anxious to be deemed of pure white blood."[12] When Rochester exclaims of

Bertha, "She came of a mad family:—idiots and maniacs through three generations! Her mother, the Creole, was both a mad woman and a drunkard!" he locates both madness and drunkenness in his wife's maternal line, which is again emphatically and ambiguously labeled "Creole" (369). By doing so, he associates that line with two of the most common stereotypes associated with blacks in the nineteenth century.[13]

As Bertha emerges as a character in the novel, her blackness is made more explicit, despite Rochester's wish to convince Jane, and perhaps temporarily himself, that "the swelled black face" and "exaggerated stature" of the woman she has seen are "figments of imagination, results of nightmare" (360). But when Jane sees Bertha's face reflected in her mirror, and describes that face to Rochester, the *topoi* of racial "otherness" are very evident. Jane tells Rochester that the face was

> "Fearful and ghastly to me—oh, sir, I never saw a face like it! It was a discoloured face—it was a savage face. I wish I could forget the roll of the red eyes and the fearful blackened inflation of the lineaments!"
>
> "Ghosts are usually pale, Jane."
>
> "This, sir, was purple: the lips were swelled and dark; the brows furrowed; the black eye-brows wildly raised over the bloodshot eyes." (358)

The emphasis on Bertha's coloring in this passage—she is emphatically not "pale" but "discoloured," "purple," "blackened"—along with the references to rolling eyes and to full "swelled," "dark" lips, all insistently and conventionally mark Bertha as black. Jane's use of the word "savage" underlines the implication of her description of Bertha's features, and the redness that she sees in Bertha's rolling eyes suggests the drunkenness that, following the nineteenth-century convention, Brontë has associated with Africans since her childhood. When Bertha's "lurid visage flame[s] over" Jane (359) as she lies in bed, causing her to lose consciousness, the ambiguously dark blood Bertha has inherited from her maternal line becomes fully evident. The scene recalls the passage from Brontë's Roe Head journal in which the revolutionary African leader Quashia, victorious in an uprising against the white British colonists and triumphantly occupying the palace built by the colonists, revels drunkenly, in symbolic violation, on the "silken couch" of the white queen. Like the rebellious Quashia, leading an uprising against the white colonists, the Jamaican Bertha-become-black is the fiction's incarnation of the desire for revenge on the part of colonized peoples, and Brontë's language suggests that such a desire for revenge is not unwarranted.

The association of Bertha with fire recalls Jane's earlier question (264) to herself: "What crime was this, that lived incarnate in this sequestered mansion, and could neither be expelled nor subdued by the owner?—What mystery, that broke out, now in fire and now in blood, at the deadest hours of night?" The language of this passage strongly evokes descriptions of slave uprisings in the British West Indies, where slaves used fires both to destroy property and to signal to each other that an uprising was taking place. White colonists of course responded to slave insurrections with great anxiety, like that expressed by one writer for *Blackwood's* in October 1823, in response to the news of the Demerara slave uprising: "Give them [the abolitionists] an opportunity of making a few grand flowery speeches about liberty, and they will read, without one shudder, the narrative of a whole colony bathed in blood and fire, over their chocolate the next morning."[14]

Brontë began writing *Jane Eyre* in 1846, eight years after the full emancipation of the British West Indian slaves in 1838. At the time Brontë was writing the novel, emancipation and the recent British participation in human slavery were certainly in the national consciousness: having set their own slaves free, the British immediately began to put pressure on other countries, their economic competitors, to do likewise. The main events of the novel definitely occur prior to emancipation. Q. D. Leavis has shown that it may not be possible to pinpoint the closing moment of the novel further than within a range of twenty-seven years, between 1819 and 1846.[15] If we assume, when Jane says at the end of her autobiography, "I have now been married ten years" (576), that the date is at the latest 1846, when Brontë began the novel, then Jane's marriage with Rochester takes place no later than 1836. In the year before that marriage, Rochester tells Jane that he has kept Bertha locked for ten years in his third-story room: "She has now for ten years made [it] a wild beast's den—a goblin's cell" (394). At the latest, then, Rochester first locked Bertha in that room in 1825, and since he lived with her first for four years, again, at the latest, they would have been married in 1821. Brontë doubtless meant to leave the precise date of the novel ambiguous—she marks the year of Rochester and Bertha's wedding with a dash in Richard Mason's attestation to their marriage—but it is clear that even at the latest possible dates for the events of the novel, they occur well before emancipation, which was declared in 1834 but only complete in 1838. As I have suggested above, Brontë may have meant for the events of the novel to occur in the 1820s and 1830s. During these years, because of the economic decline of the British sugar colonies in the West Indies, planters imposed increasing hardship on the slaves and increasingly feared their revolt. When Bertha escapes from her ten years' imprisonment to attempt periodically to stab and burn her oppressors alive, and, as Rochester says, to hang her "black and scarlet visage over the nest of my dove" (395), she is symbolically enacting precisely the sort of revolt feared by the British colonists in Jamaica.

But why would Brontë write a novel permeated with the imagery of slavery, and suggesting the possibility of a slave uprising, in 1846, after the emancipation of the British slaves had already taken place? Indeed in 1846 it was evident that the British West Indian colonies were failing rapidly, and the focus of British colonial attention was shifting to India. Perhaps the eight years since emancipation provided enough historical distance for Brontë to make a serious and public, although implicit, critique of British slavery and British imperialism in the West Indies. Although that critique is suppressed, in some passages in the novel, by more overt references to other historical instances of slavery, and although the novel uses slavery for figurative purposes, nonetheless it in places does engage with the history of British slavery in the West Indies as a reality independent of its figurative uses. The story of Bertha, however finally unsympathetic to her as a human being, nonetheless does make an indictment of British imperialism in the West Indies and the stained wealth that came from its oppressive rule. When Jane wonders "what crime ... live[s] incarnate" in Rochester's luxurious mansion that can "neither be expelled nor subdued by the owner" (264) the novel suggests that the black-visaged Bertha, imprisoned out of sight in a luxurious British mansion, does indeed incarnate a historical crime. Rochester himself describes Thornfield as a "tent of Achan" (383), alluding to Joshua 7, in which Achan takes spoils wrongfully from another people and buries it under his tent, thus bringing down a curse upon all the children of Israel. The third floor of the mansion, where Bertha is imprisoned, Jane thinks, is "a shrine of memory" to which "furniture once appropriated to the lower apartments had from time to time been removed ... as fashions changed" (127). The symbolically resonant language Brontë uses as Jane tours the house suggests that Thornfield, and particularly its third floor, to which Bertha has been removed, stands as a material embodiment of the history of the English ruling class as represented by the Rochesters, whom Mrs. Fairfax, acting simultaneously as family historian and guide to the house—that is, guide to the house of Rochester in both senses—acknowledges to have been "rather a violent than a quiet race in their time" (128). The atmosphere of the third floor of this house is heavy in the novel with the repressed history of crimes committed by a violent race, crimes that have been removed from sight as fashions changed. Jane's response to this place dense with history—she is intrigued but "by no means covet[s] a night's repose on one of those wide and heavy beds" (128)—suggests her awareness of the oppressive atmosphere of imperialist history, and her uneasiness lest she, by lying in the bed of the Rochesters, should get caught up in it.

II

Brontë's description of the room where Bertha has been locked up for ten years—without a window, with only one lamp hung from a symbolic chain—also reveals her awareness that the black-visaged Bertha, like Quashia Quamina, has ample reason to be taking revenge on a "violent race." In *Jane Eyre* Brontë subtly suggests that the history locked up in the English "shrine of memory" is one of "crime incarnate" in Bertha. But the slavery evoked by Bertha's coloring and imprisonment, and the slave uprisings suggested by her nocturnal violence, have a more deliberate figurative function in the novel. Bertha represents the "dark races" in the empire, particularly African slaves, and gives them a human presence that lends a vividness to Brontë's metaphorical use of race.

As in her juvenilia and less prominently in her other major novels, Brontë uses black slavery in *Jane Eyre* as a metaphor for economic oppression. Several critics who analyze the novel's class politics determine that the novel is ultimately conservative in this respect. Terry Eagleton reads Brontë's novels as "myths" that work toward balancing individualistic bourgeois values and conservative aristocratic values. He argues that her novels, including *Jane Eyre*, do this in part through conservative endings in which the protagonists "negotiate passionate self-fulfillment on terms which preserve the social and moral conventions intact" by taking positions within the social system that has oppressed them earlier in the novel.[16] Some subsequent critics, notably Jina Politi and Kathryn Sutherland, concur with Eagleton's assessment of the novel's class politics, while expanding the critique to include the trajectory of the novel's gender politics. As Politi puts it, while Brontë "set[s] out to vindicate the socially underprivileged woman," the novel, through its anxiety about revolution, which is coded as French and immoral, "comes to celebrate the very ethos upon which bourgeois capitalism and its patriarchal ideology rest."[17]

Both Carol Ohmann and Igor Webb see a more radical thrust in the gender and class politics of *Jane Eyre*.[18] Ohmann argues that Brontë is concerned with gender and class "deprivation," and that, caught between her conservatism and her radicalism, she only offers a solution on an individual level. But, Ohmann argues, "in the very rendering of Jane Eyre's longing for fulfillment, Brontë conveys a moral imperative with broadly social implications" although the novel does not follow these out.[19] Webb sees Jane as the carrier of a "revolutionary individualism" through whom the novel struggles against inequality of gender and class. He too sees the novel as able to achieve revolutionary equality only on an individual level: "The full transformation of society seems daunting, and the novel retreats into its overgrown paradise. This paradise serves at once as a criticism of that other, public world and as an announcement of the deep, dispiriting gulf between active self-fulfillment and social possibility."[20]

With Ohmann and Webb, I see a more revolutionary impulse in *Jane Eyre* than do Eagleton, Politi, and Sutherland. Yet I find Brontë's struggle in *Jane Eyre* against inequality of class both broader and more limited than Ohmann and Webb do. Indeed, the critique of a realist novel for offering only an individual solution to an oppressive social system (a critique also made by Spivak) is itself problematic. Without slipping into the genre of utopian narrative, a realist novel, focusing, in the nature of the genre, on a limited number of characters, could hardly enact a social solution on a broader level than the individual. Yet such generic constraints do not necessarily render the critique of the novel as a perniciously individualistic genre an apt one. The relatively individual solutions to social problems necessarily enacted by a novel can have the larger suggestiveness of those evoked by a parable, or by that most populist of prose genres, the folk tale. The generalizable nature of Jane's problems, the language in which Jane Eyre's solution to social problems is worked out, and particularly the allusions to the French Revolution, suggest that Jane's individual story is that of a representative lower-middle-class woman, and that the story of her success emblematizes a solution to larger social problems. That individual story does argue the need for a broader redistribution of wealth, just as it argues the need for greater gender equality. At the same time, however, the novel specifically limits the recipients of this newly equalized wealth to one group, the lower middle class. The novel's position on economic redistribution and on gender politics is worked out through its central racial metaphor.

Throughout the novel, the marginality and disempowerment Jane experiences due to her class and gender are represented through a metaphorical linking between Jane and several of the nineteenth century's "dark races." In the novel's opening scene, she sits in her window seat, exiled from the drawing room, "cross-legged, like a Turk" (4). She cries out in rage against Mrs. Reed "in a savage, high voice" (40), and when she tells Helen that she believes in striking back against injustice, she is told that "heathens and savage tribes hold that doctrine, but Christians and civilised nations disown it" (65). That Helen's principle of civilized passivity in the face of oppression is an echo of the self-serving rhetoric of the powerful and is not at a deep level endorsed by the novel is evident in the repetition of her language a few pages later, when the sanctimonious Mr. Brocklehurst compares Jane to a Hindu, proclaiming that "this girl, this child, the native of a Christian land" is "worse than many a little heathen who says its prayers to Brahma and kneels before Juggernaut" (76–77). In Jane's adulthood, Rochester sees in her passions that "may rage furiously, like true heathens, as they are" (252), although held in check by her reason, and he finds in her resolute, wild spirit a "savage, beautiful creature" (405). When Jane confronts the angry, passionate Rochester, after the revelation of his previous marriage, she feels, in her attempt to assert control, "as the Indian, perhaps, feels when he slips over the rapid in his canoe" (386).

The novel compares the rebellious Jane, without much differentiation between them, to an entire array of "dark races" experiencing the force of European imperialism in the nineteenth century—Turks, Hindus, native Americans, and the generic "heathen" and "savage." Although Brontë's ambivalence is certainly evident in the recurring use of the words "heathen" and "savage," the novel nonetheless repeatedly affirms Jane's passionate rebellion against her social marginality. The most frequent recurrence of the racial metaphor in the novel is the sometimes covert, sometimes overt comparison of Jane to an African slave. The novel uses the idea of the enslaved Africans (eventually made spectacularly present through Bertha) as its most dramatic rendition of the concept of racial domination, and thus most frequently uses the slave to represent class and gender inequality in England.

As in the Roe Head journal entry, "Well, here I am at Roe Head," Brontë does not use slavery as a metaphor for the lot of the working class but for that of the lower middle class. Both Jane and the narrator invoke the metaphor not in response to the work Jane has to perform but in response to the attitude she has to endure from her class superiors. When as a child Jane first bursts out at John Reed, she cries, "You are like a murderer—you are like a slave-driver" and the adult Jane explains to the reader, "I had drawn parallels in silence, which I never thought thus to have declared aloud" (8). The adult narrator accepts the parallel, and in fact makes the child's simile into a more emphatic metaphor when she continues, "I was conscious that a moment's mutiny had already rendered me liable to strange penalties, and like any other rebel slave, I felt resolved, in my desperation, to go all lengths" (9). Although the use of the word "like" in this sentence almost disguises the trope as a simile, in fact the formulation "*like any other*" definitively designates Jane a slave and then describes her as behaving like others in the same position. Later, when Jane has been placed by Brocklehurst on the stool, she thinks of herself as "a slave or victim." The novel itself draws a parallel between slavery and Jane's social position as a child through Bertha.

Jane's sudden explosion of fury against her treatment at Gateshead occurs in her tenth year there. Mrs. Reed complains to the adult Jane, "To this day I feel it impossible to understand: how for nine years you could be patient and quiescent under any treatment, and in the tenth break out all fire and violence" (300). Jane brings herself to "mutiny" and becomes a "rebel slave" in her tenth year, like Bertha who after ten years in her third floor room "br[eaks] out, now in fire and now in blood" (264).

The imagery of social class as slavery recurs in Jane's adulthood. Rochester refers to her labor as "governessing slavery" (340), but Jane's work at Thornfield becomes like slavery to her only when Rochester arrives with his ruling-class friends and she comes into contact with the dehumanizing regard of her class superiors. Before this, those around Jane treat her as a social equal. Mrs. Fairfax helps Jane remove her bonnet and shawl when she first arrives, and Adèle is too young and also of too dubious an origin to treat her governess with superiority. Brontë explicitly constructs the atmosphere between the three of them—though significantly not between the three of them and the servants—as a utopian retreat from a world where inequalities of class are constantly present. Mrs. Fairfax distinctly marks the exclusion of the working class from this classless utopia when she tells Jane, just after expressing her delight that Jane has come to be her companion: "You know in winter time, one feels dreary quite alone, in the best quarters. I say alone—Leah is a nice girl to be sure, and John and his wife are very decent people; but then you see they are only servants, and one can't converse with them on terms of equality: one must keep them at a due distance, for fear of losing one's authority" (116). Some awareness of the costs even of having a class lower than one's own, a problem with which the novel is in general very little concerned, comes through in this passage. For the most part, however, Jane Eyre pays scant attention to the working class. Instead it draws parallels between slavery and Jane's social position as one of the disempowered lower middle class.

For Jane, the feeling of class slavery occurs most poignantly in the context of her awareness of the economic inequality between her and Rochester. She comments after their engagement that receiving his valuable gifts makes her feel like a degraded slave. Indeed, it is at this point that Jane writes to her uncle in Madeira, thus setting off the chain of events that will prevent her subjection to such financial slavery, first by impeding her wedding to Rochester, and then, when she finally does marry him, by bringing her the inherited wealth that enables her to meet him on more equal financial terms.

The crucial passage in which Jane sees Bertha's black face behind a wedding veil, in her own mirror, and then watches Bertha tear the veil in half, epitomizes the other form of slavery that Bertha both incarnates for Jane and then enables her to avoid. Feminist critics have frequently commented on this passage, interpreting Bertha as either the surrogate or the double who expresses Jane's rage against the restraints of gender. Gilbert and Gubar particularly elaborate on this pattern in the novel, describing Bertha as Jane's "dark double," the untamed, animal-like embodiment of Jane's flaming rage.[21] It is important to see this darkness in the context of the racial dynamics of nineteenth-century Britain: by invoking racially loaded terms—"blackened," "purple," "savage"—to describe the Jamaican Bertha, Brontë is using the emotional force of the idea of slavery and explosive race relations in the wake of British emancipation to represent the tensions of the gender hierarchy in England.

The imagery of slavery is both pervasive in the context of gender inequality in the novel and closely tied to the recent history of the British empire. When Rochester tells Jane, as he narrates the story of his life, "hiring a mistress is the next worst thing to buying a slave: both are often by nature, and always by position, inferior; and to live familiarly with inferiors is degrading" (397–98), his words take on a startling resonance in the context of the story he has just told. Rochester acquired a West Indian fortune by marrying a Jamaican wife and subsequently lived in Jamaica for four years. A wealthy white man living in Jamaica before emancipation would undoubtedly have had slaves to wait upon him, and his Jamaican fortune would have been the product of slave labor, so when Rochester discusses what it is like to buy and live with slaves he knows what he is talking about. When he compares his relationships with women to keeping slaves, then, the parallel is given a shocking vividness by his own history as a slave master. But it is in the character of Rochester's wife, somewhat surprisingly, not one of his mistresses, that the metaphor of slavery is most vividly realized. Rochester draws this parallel just after the reader, with Jane, has seen his wife's "black and scarlet" face emerging from her prison, an event that makes clear that a wife of Rochester, perhaps even more than a mistress, is in the position of being his "slave." When Jane, who has just been pondering over assuming the name "Mrs. Rochester," looks in the mirror and sees a black face behind a wedding veil, we realize that becoming even a wife to a man like Rochester, with his history in the colonies and his dominating character, is dangerous.

III

Jane Eyre associates nonwhite races with the idea of oppression by drawing parallels between people of the "dark races," black slaves in particular, and those oppressed by the hierarchies of social class and gender in Britain. So far the narrative function of the dark-featured Bertha and of the novel's allusions to the British empire has a certain fidelity to history. The novel's various allusions to people of nonwhite races, however, are not free from racism. The use of the slave as a figure focuses attention not so much on the oppression of blacks as on the domestic situation within England. By using the slave as the ultimate point on the scale of racial oppression, the novel also to some extent collapses all the other "dark races" to which it alludes into the figure of the slave, in a way not unlike the anatomist Robert Knox's conflation of all the "dark races" into the figure of the Negro: "Mr. Gibbon speaks of the obvious physical inferiority of the Negro; he means, no doubt, the dark races generally, for the remark applies to all."[22] Nonetheless, Brontë's metaphor at least implicitly acknowledges the oppressive situation of the peoples experiencing the force of the British empire. Oddly, however, the allusions to dark skin and to empire also arise in precisely the opposite context in the novel, one most strikingly represented in the descriptions of Blanche Ingram.

The haughty Blanche, with her "dark and imperious" eye, who treats Jane as hardly human, appears in the novel in part to illustrate the painful injustice of class inequality (231). Yet when Mrs. Fairfax describes Blanche to Jane, she emphasizes her darkness. "She was dressed in pure white," Mrs. Fairfax relates, and she had an "olive complexion, dark and clear," hair "raven-black ... and in front the longest, the glossiest curls I ever saw" (199). When Jane first sees Blanche, she too emphasizes her darkness—"Miss Ingram was dark as a Spaniard" Jane notes—adding that Blanche has a "low brow," a skull conformation that, like dark skin, was a mark of racial inferiority according to the nineteenth-century science of race differences (216). Rochester later describes Bertha as a woman "in the style of Blanche Ingram" (389), and he also directly compares Blanche to African women: he might be speaking of Bertha when he describes Blanche to Jane as "a real strapper ... big, brown, and buxom; with hair just such as the ladies of Carthage must have had" (275).

These references to Blanche's darkness, and to her similarities to non-British people with dark skin, only make sense in the context of the odd phrase, "dark and imperious." The use of the word "imperious" to describe Blanche's ruling-class sense of superiority recalls the contact between the British and the "dark races" of the British empire. In that contact, it was not the dark people who were imperious, or in the position of imperialist power, but the British themselves. By associating the qualities of darkness and imperiousness, Brontë suggests that imperialism brings out both these undesirable qualities in the imperialist, that the British aristocracy in particular has been sullied, darkened, and made imperious or oppressive by the workings of empire. The arrogance arising from the wielding of despotic force, as well as a contaminating contact with the "dark races," has sullied the British and in particular made the aristocracy unpleasantly imperious, the novel suggests.[23] Blanche Ingram dresses in white, is given by her mother the pet name "my lily-flower" (223), and her given name itself denotes her whiteness. But by mockingly juxtaposing this aristocratic Englishwoman's dark coloring, and her dark imperiousness, with her sense of herself as the lily-white flower of English womanhood, Brontë suggests that the class structure at home has been contaminated by imperialism abroad.

More mocking hints about the similarity between the British ruling class and nonwhite races occur in the descriptions of the Reeds. John Reed reviles his mother for "her dark skin, similar to his own" (13), and later grows into a young man whom some call handsome, the former nursemaid Bessie says uneasily, dissenting and pointing out that he has "such thick lips" (122).[24] Mrs. Reed's already dark face in her last illness becomes "disfigured and discoloured" (304)—and thus like Bertha's "discoloured face" (358). Mrs. Reed also has the "prognathous" skull, that is, one with a low measurement on the graduated scale of facial angles, typified by a protruding jaw and a low forehead, deemed characteristic of the lower races. This upper-class Englishwoman has "a somewhat large face, the under-jaw being much developed and very solid; her brow was low, her chin large and prominent" (38).[25]

Brontë also criticizes the aristocratic Lady Ingram by subtly comparing her both to Bertha and to the nonwhite races. Lady Ingram, who derides governesses in front of Jane, and who within her hearing pronounces that she sees in Jane's physiognomy "all the faults of her class" (221) has features "inflated and darkened" with pride (215), just as Bertha has a "blackened inflation of the lineaments" (358). Lady Ingram has "Roman features," and a haughty sense of superiority derived from her position in the British empire. She wears, Jane says, "a shawl turban of some gold-wrought Indian fabric [which] invested her (I suppose she thought) with a truly imperial dignity" (215). The novel draws unflattering parallels between the British empire, evoked by Lady Ingram's Indian shawl, and the Roman empire, whose emperors, the young Jane has implied, in comparing John Reed to them, are murderers and slave drivers. By associating the British empire with the Roman empire Brontë hints uneasily at a possibly parallel future: with these tainted, aristocratic representatives and with slaves of its own, the British empire may be headed for its own decline and fall. The despotism of the British upper classes, Brontë's mocking hints about their similarity to the nonwhite races imply, is one effect of the British involvement in empire.

By making these sly, intermittent allusions to nonwhite races when describing the British aristocracy, Brontë gives the "dark races" the metaphorical role of representing the presence of oppression in the novel. This elaboration of the metaphor relies on a sense of history considerably more Anglocentric than that which underlies the metaphorical yoking of white women and people of nonwhite races as mutually disempowered. Because it assigns these two contradictory associations to the nonwhite races, using them to represent both the oppressed and the oppressor, the novel follows this logic: oppression in any of its manifestations is foreign to the English, thus the nonwhite races signify oppression within England, either subjection to or participation in the unjust distribution of power.

This is the most equivocal move in the novel's figurative strategy. It can be seen, for instance, in the use of the word "caste" in the novel. When Jane, as a governess, reprimands herself sternly, as she feels herself falling in love with Rochester, "He is not of your order: keep to your caste" (203), and when she says that, as a child, she feared to leave the Reeds to go to the Eyre relatives she has heard termed a "beggarly set," noting that she "was not heroic enough to purchase liberty at the price of caste" (24), Brontë names what is unjust and humanly divisive in the English class system in such a way as to suggest that such injustices are not intrinsically English at all, that they belong by their nature instead to other races.[26] The novel's anti-imperialist politics, such examples suggest, are more self-interested than benevolent. The opposition to imperialism arises not primarily out of concern for the well-being of the people directly damaged by British imperialism—the African slaves in the West Indian colonies, the Indians whose economy was being destroyed under British rule—but out of concern for the British who were, as the novel's figurative structure represents it, being contaminated by their contact with the unjust social systems indigenous to the people with dark skin.

The novel also associates the oppression of women with the social practices of peoples other than the English. The allusions that do so arise primarily during the part of the novel describing Rochester and Jane's betrothal, as it is at this point that Rochester most directly asserts, and threatens in the future to assert, the power of his position in the gender hierarchy. In these passages, Brontë suggests that it is a characteristic of men of dark-skinned races to dominate women, as she repeatedly evokes imagery of Indian wives forced to die in "suttee," and of women imprisoned in Turkish harems. The word "slave" occurs in these passages, but Brontë here veers away from making a direct parallel with the British enslavement of Africans by associating Rochester's dominating masculine power over Jane with that not of a British but of an Eastern slave master. This part of the novel is rich in images of Turkish and Persian despots, sultans who reward their favorite slaves with jewels. The history of British participation in slavery arises at one point in this part of the novel—Rochester echoes the abolitionists' slogan when he tells Jane that she is too restrained with "a man and a brother" (170)—but the novel persistently displaces the blame for slavery onto the "dark races" themselves, only alluding directly to slavery as practiced by dark-skinned people. At one point, for example, the novel uses strong and shocking imagery of slavery to describe the position of wives, but despite references to such aspects of British slavery as slave markets, fetters, and mutiny, the scenario Brontë invokes is not of British imperialist domination but of the despotic, oppressive customs of nonwhites. Perhaps because he is guiltily conscious of his promiscuous past, or of his plans to commit bigamy, Rochester has just compared himself to "the Grand Turk," declaring that he prefers his "one little English girl" to the Turk's "whole seraglio" (339). Jane immediately picks up on this "eastern allusion" because she has been thinking that his treatment of her, now that she is to be his wife, has become like a sultan's treatment of a favorite slave. She responds:

> "I'll not stand you an inch in the stead of a seraglio.... [I]f you have a fancy for anything in that line, away with you, sir, to the bazars of Stamboul without delay; and lay out in extensive slave-purchases some of that spare cash you seem so at a loss to spend satisfactorily here."
>
> "And what will you do, Janet, while I am bargaining for so many tons of flesh and such an assortment of black eyes?"
>
> "I'll be preparing myself to go out as a missionary to preach liberty to them that are enslaved—your Harem inmates amongst the rest. I'll get admitted there, and I'll stir up mutiny; and you, three-tailed bashaw as you are, sir, shall in a trice find yourself fettered amongst our hands: nor will I, for one, consent to cut your bonds till you have signed a charter, the most liberal that despot ever yet conferred." (339)

Jane evidently has a sense of greater similitude with "enslaved" Turkish women than Rochester has anticipated. After all, she sits "cross-legged, like a Turk" in the novel's opening chapter, and has compared herself to a "revolted slave." As the passage begins she at first seems to be distancing herself from "them that are enslaved": she proclaims that she will not stand Rochester in "the stead of a seraglio," and she initially positions herself as a missionary to the enslaved women. But the continuity between the imagery in this passage and that elsewhere in the novel suggests that Jane knows how to help other women out of slavery because she has been a slave herself and because she now fears becoming one again. As the passage continues, it increasingly positions Jane *with* the owned, commodified Turkish women. She tells Rochester that he will find himself fettered "amongst *our* hands" and says that she "for one" will not free him until he has signed a charter, presumably freeing *all* women from his despotic superiority.

But if Jane is likened to enslaved Turkish women in this passage, Rochester, in his gender-authorized despotism, is also like a person of the "dark races," here the Turkish "three-tailed bashaw." By associating inequalities of gender with the "dark races" and with their practice of what it denominates "slavery," the novel marks all aspects of oppression as "other"—non-British, nonwhite, and the result of a besmirching contact with other peoples. In so doing it represses the history of British imperialist domination, and, in particular, British enslavement of Africans. Even when Rochester directly asserts his power over Jane, speaking of "attach[ing her] to a chain" (341), the novel compares him to a sultan, rather than to a white-skinned British slave master. All aspects of oppression, through this twist in the novel's figurative strategy, become something the British are in danger of being sullied by, something foreign and "other" to them.

IV

In opposition to this danger—the danger of the contagious inequality characteristic of other races—Brontë poses an alternative directly out of middle-class domestic ideology: keeping a clean house at home in England.[27] Part of what the novel solves in its conclusion is the problem of contamination from abroad. Rochester's mutilation keeps him at home, and thus within the space of the values the novel codes as English and domestic: in response to Jane's anxious questions, the innkeeper tells her, "Aye—aye—he's in England; he can't get out of England, I fancy—he's a fixture now" (548). Clean and unclean, healthy and unhealthy environments form a central symbolic structure in the novel, and what is clean is represented as intrinsically English. In *Shirley*, Caroline's illness is anticipated by a passage about the arrival of "the yellow taint of pestilence, covering white Western isles with the poisoned exhalations of the East, dimming the lattices of English homes with the breath of Indian plague" (*Shirley*, 421). Similarly, in *Jane Eyre* Brontë associates unhealthy, plague-ridden, contagious environments with other peoples and with the unjust distribution of power—a phenomenon, the novel suggests, that is itself a "poisoned exhalation of the East," not native to "white Western isles."

When Rochester decides to leave Jamaica, where he has participated in slavery and taken a dark wife whom he will treat as a slave, the novel poses the opposition between oppressive Jamaica and pure England in terms of atmosphere. As Rochester recounts it:

> It was a fiery West-Indian night; one of the description that frequently precede the hurricanes of those climates: being unable to sleep in bed, I got up and opened the window. The air was like sulphur steams—I could find no refreshment anywhere. Mosquitoes came buzzing in and hummed sullenly round the room ... the moon was setting in the waves, broad and red, like a hot cannon-ball—she threw her last bloody glance over a world quivering with the ferment of tempest. I was physically influenced by the atmosphere.... I meant to shoot myself....
>
> A wind fresh from Europe blew over the ocean and rushed through the open casement: the storm broke, streamed, thundered, blazed, and the air grew pure. I then framed and fixed a resolution. (392–93)

Under the influence of "the sweet wind from Europe" Rochester resolves to return to England, to "be clean in [his] own sight" (392) by leaving this place, which is, Brontë's imagery suggests, the locus of colonial oppression.

In a very similar passage Jane associates freedom and oppression with healthy and unhealthy environments. After she has fled Thornfield and settled at Morton she reprimands herself for repining: which is better, Jane asks herself (459), "to be a slave in a fool's paradise at Marseilles—fevered with delusive bliss one hour—suffocating with the bitterest tears of remorse and shame the next—or to be a village-schoolmistress, free and honest, in a breezy mountain nook in the healthy heart of England?" Jane here imagines the gender and class slavery she would endure as Rochester's mistress as a feverish, suffocating, southern atmosphere, while the alternative is the free, healthy, and rigorous atmosphere of England.[28]

The damp pestilential fog of Lowood charity-school is one of the novel's most drastically unhealthy environments; the atmosphere at this orphan institution where Jane thinks of herself as "a slave or victim" is the direct result of cruel economic inequities. After so many students die of the typhus fever fostered by the unhealthy environment, "several wealthy and benevolent individuals in the county" transform it into a less oppressive institution by the act of cleaning: a new building is erected in a healthier location, and "brackish, fetid water" (98) is no longer used in preparation of the children's food.

Creating a clean, healthy, middle-class environment stands as the novel's symbolic alternative to an involvement in unjust oppression. As Rochester is engaging in his most manipulative attempt to assure himself of Jane's love, by bringing home an apparent rival, he also orders that his house be cleaned. A great fuss is made over cleaning the house Jane had innocently thought to be "beautifully clean and well-arranged" already (205). "Such scrubbing," Jane says, "such brushing, such washing of paint and beating of carpets, such taking down and putting up of pictures, such polishing of mirrors and lustres, such lighting of fires in bedrooms, such airing of sheets and featherbeds on hearths, I never beheld, either before or since" (205). Yet despite all the cleaning, the presence remains in Thornfield that makes Rochester call it "a great plague-house" (175). What Rochester needs to have cleaned out of his house as he is trying to attain Jane's love is the black-faced wife in his attic, that wife whose "breath (faugh!) [once] mixed with the air [he] breathed" (392), and who represents his sullying, inegalitarian colonial past. All that he can do with the "plague" in his house is to hire someone to clean her away into a remote locked room. To remind the reader of that plague, Grace Poole periodically emerges amidst all the cleaning from the third story, "damping" Jane's cheerfulness and causing her "dark" conjectures, in order, as both the most expert cleaner and as evidence of the great stain in the house, to give advice to the other servants: "just to say a word, perhaps ... about the proper way to polish a grate, or clean a marble mantlepiece, or take stains from papered walls" (206).

The other great cleaning activity in the novel occurs as Jane decides to "clean down" Moor House, and it marks a more successful attempt at washing away injustice than the one at Thornfield. Jane cleans the house to celebrate the egalitarian distribution of her newly acquired legacy, which will enable her to live there happily with her new-found family. Brontë writes of Jane's egalitarian division of her fortune using the rhetoric of a revolution against inequalities of class, although this revolution symbolically represents a redistribution of wealth in favor of only a limited group of people, the lower middle class. When St. John tells Jane that he, Diana, and Mary will be her brother and sisters without this sacrifice of her "just rights," she responds, with a tone of passionate conviction Brontë obviously endorses (494): "Brother? Yes; at the distance of a thousand leagues! Sisters? Yes; slaving amongst strangers! I, wealthy—gorged with gold I never earned and do not merit! You, pennyless! Famous equality and fraternization! Close union! Intimate attachment!" This sort of redistribution of wealth, Brontë suggests, giving Jane the language of the French revolution—"Liberté! Egalité! Fraternité!"—will right the wrongs of the lower middle class, and clean from it the dark mark of oppression. Its women will no longer have to "slave" among strangers like people of other races; its men will no longer have to venture into the distant, dangerous environment of other races in the colonies. In celebrating the equal distribution of wealth, the novel offers an implicit rebuke to the upper class, for had Rochester's father been willing to divide his estate equally between his sons, Rochester, the younger brother, would never have become sullied by the contaminating environment of the West Indian colonies. With Jane, from the perspective of the middle class, Brontë redefines the claims of brotherhood, as her plot redistributes wealth: truly acknowledged fraternity, the novel suggests, requires distributing wealth equally, not, with an injustice that emanates from the upper class, letting a middle-class brother or sister remain a penniless "slave."

But to only a limited group among those who might ask, "Am I not a man and a brother?" does the novel answer, "Yes." The plot of *Jane Eyre* works toward a redistribution of power and wealth, equalization and an end to oppression just as Jane herself does, but its utopia remains partial; its "revolution" improves only the lot of the middle class, closing out both the working class and those from whom the figure of slavery has been appropriated in the first place. As Jane phrases her "revolution," it is one that specifically depends on erasing the mark of the "dark races."

To signify her utopian end to economic injustice, Jane creates a clean, healthy environment, free of plague: her aim, she tells St. John, is "to *clean down* (do you comprehend the full force of the expression?) to *clean down* Moor-House from chamber to cellar" (498). Jane works literally to set her own house in order, creating a clean, healthy, egalitarian, middle-class, domestic environment as the alternative to inequality and injustice. This environment is not, however, to the taste of St. John, who wants to force Jane into an inegalitarian marriage and to take her to the unhealthy atmosphere of British India (both of which she says would kill her) to help him preach to dark-skinned people his rather different values of hierarchical subordination. Jane recognizes this difference in mentality and their incompatibility when St. John does not appreciate her house cleaning, her cleaning of the "plague" of inequality out of the domestic space of England. "This parlour is not his sphere," she realizes, "the Himalayan ridge, or Caffre bush, even the plague-cursed Guinea Coast swamp, would suit him better" (502).

St. John's association with plague-cursed colonial environments rather than with England, cleanliness, and home reveals his preference, within the novel's symbolic framework, for domination rather than equality, that is, for values precisely at odds with those affirmed by both Jane and the novel itself. There has been virtual consensus, among those who touch on the issue of imperialism in the novel, that St. John is the voice of the novel's own imperialist ideology.[29] But to read him in this way is to elide all the ways in which the novel calls this character into question. And the novel's critique of

St. John is hard to overlook: Jane insistently describes him as stony, dominating, and heartless. In an article on the novel's ending, Carolyn Williams attends in detail to the novel's intertextual last words, in which Jane quotes St. John quoting the last words of the Bible, the section of the novel most repeatedly cited by other critics as evidence of Brontë's endorsement of St. John's imperialist missionary activity. In her reading of these last paragraphs, Williams argues convincingly that the novel protests against the "coercive mediation" represented by St. John, who claims to speak for Nature and for God, "a protest that is at once Protestant ... and feminist in its force."[30] The novel represents St. John as presumptuously assuming the voice of God in relation to Jane. Williams focuses on St. John's mediating relation to Jane, and only briefly mentions his relation to the Indians whom he sails off to civilize, but the implicit parallels drawn by the novel between Jane and the Indians suggest that St. John intends to take on an equally dubious mediating role in relation to the Hindus, learning their language the better to assume the voice of God toward them as well. The novel's critique of St. John's dubious mediations is thus also intrinsically a critique of his missionary imperialism: his desire to "hew down" others" "prejudices of creed" (578).

Indeed, from the moment St. John is first physically described, he is associated with an icy racial superiority implicitly condemned by the novel, as Jane is its first target. St. John himself has the Grecian physiognomy considered by nineteenth-century racial taxonomy the highest exemplar of racial type. Charles White's influential account of racial gradation, for example, describes the racial hierarchy using facial angles, as follows: "The facial line of a monkey makes an angle of 42 [degrees], with the horizontal line; that of an orang-outang, 58; that of a negro, 70; of a Chinese, 75; of an European, 80 or 90. The Roman painters preferred the angle of 95; the Grecian antique, 100."[31] But St. John's description in the novel is less than appealing. Although, as Jane notes, "it is seldom, indeed, an English face comes so near the antique models as did his" (440), St. John is (chillingly) more like a statue or a painting representing a racial archetype than he is like a human being. When St. John reveals his disinclination toward domesticity, Jane describes his forehead as "still and pale as a white stone" (501); he has "blue, pictorial-looking eyes" (440). And when Jane first looks at him she finds him as easy to examine as if he had been "a statue instead of a man" (440). She continues:

> He was young—perhaps from twenty-eight to thirty—tall, slender; his face riveted the eye: it was like a Greek face, very pure in outline; quite a straight, classic nose; quite an Athenian mouth

> and chin.... His eyes were large and blue, with brown lashes; his high forehead, colourless as ivory, was partially streaked over by careless locks of fair hair.
>
> This is a gentle delineation, is it not, reader? Yet he whom it describes scarcely impressed one with the idea of a gentle, a yielding, an impressible, or even of a placid nature. Quiescent as he now sat, there was something about his nostril, his mouth, his brow, which, to my perceptions, indicated elements within either restless, or hard, or eager. (440)

From his position at the apex of the white race, St. John offers as his first commentary on Jane a declaration of her physical inferiority. Against his sister's protestation to the contrary, and within Jane's hearing, he declares Jane to be "plain": "the grace and harmony of beauty are quite wanting in those features" (433). As Jane puts it, after her first description of him, "he might well be a little shocked at the irregularity of my lineaments, his own being so harmonious" (440). Later Jane experiences St. John's insistent tutelage, precisely the sort he intends to exercise on the Hindus, as an impossible demand for her physical transformation, for her ascent on the racial scale: "He wanted to train me to an elevation I could never reach: it racked me hourly to aspire to the standard he uplifted. The thing was as impossible as to mould my irregular features to his correct and classic pattern, to give to my changeable green eyes the sea blue tint and solemn lustre of his own" (509).

Recent critics have claimed that while Brontë condemns the way in which St. John treats Jane, she approves of his intentions with regard to the Indians, that the parallel we see between the two was one she herself could not have seen.[32] Yet in passages like those I quote above in which she invokes (and challenges) the idea of a racial scale in which all should aspire to attain St. John's forehead of white stone, it is Brontë herself who draws the parallel between Jane's position in relation to St. John and that of the Indians whom he sails off to civilize with the derogatory gaze of his "sea blue" eyes. Indeed, at one point St. John himself draws a parallel between Jane and the natives of India. In doing so, St. John resembles the other self-righteous minister to whom Jane has been like a Hindu: the Reverend Brocklehurst. When St. John tells Jane that should she refuse to come to India with him she may be "numbered with those who have denied the faith and are worse than infidels!" (522), he echoes Brocklehurst's declaration that the child Jane, although "the native of a Christian land," is "worse than many a little heathen who says its prayers to Brahma and kneels before Juggernaut" (76–77). The echo hints that St. John's fervent quest to convert the infidels is as misguided, and as destructive, as Brocklehurst's charitable missions.

In the final pages of the novel, Brontë again compares Jane to the natives of India. When Jane taunts Rochester after they reunite at Ferndean, by evoking his suspicions that she may be in love with St. John, whose fair "Grecian profile" she has just described for him, she perceives that jealousy has stung him. That sting is good for him, she comments, adding, "I would not, therefore, immediately charm the snake" (565). This final description of Jane as a snake charmer, in an image again associating her, although in an indubitably orientalist fashion, with the natives of India, once more suggests that the novel by no means unambiguously endorses St. John's Indian mission.

It is crucial as well that Jane refuses to accompany St. John to India as a missionary. Instead of deciding that it is her vocation to enter St. John's environment of plague, dark-skinned people, and hierarchical oppression, Jane experiences an alternative call to return to a house which, being larger than Moor House and more stained by inequality and injustice, it will be considerably more difficult to "clean down"—Rochester's Thornfield. But of course when she gets there she finds that this home Rochester once described as a plague-house has already been cleaned down. Brontë's plot participates in the same activity as Jane—cleaning, purifying, trying to create a domestic, English world free of oppression. The plot works precisely in the terms of Jane's French-inflected rhetoric of revolution. It redistributes wealth and the power of gender, and it does so both through the agency of Bertha, and then by cleaning her, as the staining woman of the "dark races" who has represented oppression, out of the world of the novel.

In the ending of the novel, Brontë has created the world she can imagine free of the forms of oppression against which the novel most passionately protests, inequalities of gender and economic injustice toward the lower middle class. The energies that made the novel's contemporary readers anxious lie in its utopian closure: the ending, as the echo of the French revolutionary slogan suggests, symbolically enacts Brontë's conception of a social revolution on behalf of women and the lower middle class. The mutilation of Rochester and the loss of his property in Thornfield redistributes power between him and the newly propertied Jane. Jane tells her former master emphatically that she is now both independent and rich: "I am," she says, "my own mistress" (556). In the last chapter Jane explicitly describes their marriage as egalitarian, unlike most: "I hold myself supremely blest—blest beyond what language can express; because I am my husband's life as fully as he is mine" (576).

The ending of the novel severely punishes Rochester both for his figurative enslavement of women and for his acquisition of colonial wealth. The blinding of Rochester recalls a passage from David Hume's essay "Of Love and Marriage" in which Hume recounts an anecdote told of the Scythian women, who, tired of their subordination in marriage, conspired to surprise the men "in drink, or asleep; bound them all fast in chains; and having called a solemn council of the whole sex, ... debated what expedient should be used to improve the present advantage, and prevent their falling again into slavery."[33] Despite their former enslavement, the women do not relish the idea of killing the men, and "it was, therefore, agreed to put out the eyes of the whole male sex, and thereby resign in all future time the vanity which they could draw from their beauty, in order to secure their authority. We must no longer pretend to dress and show, said they; but then we shall be free from slavery. We shall hear no more tender sighs; but in return we shall hear no more imperious commands."[34] For Jane, who has never had beauty, and for whom the obligation of elaborate dress, the obligation to make herself into a showy visual object for Rochester, has itself made her feel like a slave, the blinding of Rochester is liberating: it takes from him any power of male visual evaluation of her. As the servant Mary says at the end of the sightless Rochester, and his feelings for Jane, "i' his een she's fair beautiful, onybody may see that" (575). Fulfilling Rochester's own allusion to the accursed wealth wrongfully stolen by Achan, Brontë's ending enacts also a purifying destruction of Rochester's ill-gotten colonial wealth, like that of Achan who is "stoned with stones and burned with fire" (Joshua 7:25) for bringing the "accursed thing" into the camp of Israel. Rochester, unlike Achan, survives, but his "tent of Achan," the luxurious, oppressive plague-house to which he has brought his colonial fortune, is destroyed as his misbegotten wealth is symbolically exorcised from the novel.

But the symbolic revolution against both inequalities of gender and the economic injustices suffered by the middle class, and even the purifying away of the ill-gotten wealth of empire, are made possible in the novel by another sort of oppression and suppression. This symbolic revolution is initiated by the dark woman who has been imported from the colonies to signify both the oppressed and the oppressor. Bertha institutes the great act of cleaning in the novel, which burns away Rochester's oppressive colonial wealth and diminishes the power of his gender, but then she herself is cleaned away, burned and as it were purified from the novel. Brontë creates a character of the nonwhite races to use as the vividly embodied signifier of oppression in the novel, and then has this sign, by the explosive instability of the situation it embodies, destroy itself.

Jane Eyre ends with the purified, more egalitarian world created by this figurative sacrifice of the "dark races," Brontë's complex modification of available metaphors. But the novel does not end as peacefully as we might expect after this act of annihilation. The ending of the novel betrays Brontë's uneasiness about her own figurative tactics, about the way in which her metaphorical use of race involves erasing the humanity of those of other races. This uneasiness becomes evident in the way the spectre of the racial "other" remains to haunt the ending of the novel, refusing to be fully erased, although evaporated into the "dank" and "insalubrious" mist that hovers over Ferndean, where Jane and Rochester settle after the cleaning down of Thornfield (55051). The dank and unhealthy atmosphere of Ferndean is reminiscent of other oppressive, unhealthy environments in the novel, and, in particular, of Grace Poolen's periodical emergences from the attic, "damping" Jane's spirits. It disrupts the utopian elements of the ending, indicating that the world of the novel is still not fully purified from the unhealthy atmosphere of unjust hierarchy. And the unjust inequality that the insalubrious atmosphere signifies, now that it no longer refers to class or gender oppression, must be the original form of oppression that the novel has tried so hard to displace and repress: the oppression of the various nonwhite races by the British.

The atmosphere of Ferndean recalls the fact that, even if Rochester's tainted colonial wealth has been burned away by the ending of the novel, as the Achan allusion strongly suggests, the very wealth Jane is able to bring him, which enables her to meet him on more equal terms and which she distributes with such a scrupulously egalitarian spirit, has a colonial source. It comes from her uncle in Madeira, who is an agent for a Jamaican wine manufacturer, Bertha's brother. The location of Jane's uncle John in Madeira, off Morocco, on the West African coast, where Richard Mason stops on his way home from England, also indirectly suggests, through Mason's itinerary, the triangular route of the British slave traders, and suggests that John Eyre's wealth is implicated in the slave trade. The resonant details of the scene in which Brontë has Jane acquire her fortune mark Jane's financial and literary implication in colonialism as well. St. John announces Jane's accession to fortune by pulling the letter out of a "morocco pocket-book" (483), and he is able to identify Jane as the heiress because she has written her name, on a white sheet of paper, in "Indian ink" (486).

In this way the novel implicates in colonialism not only Jane's finances (the leather of the wallet has a colonial provenance) but the act of writing itself, for the pigment in which Jane has absently traced her name, with its startlingly colonial appellation, has such a provenance as well.[35] The words Jane writes in Indian ink are both her own name and the novel's title. Specifically writing "Jane Eyre," the passage suggests, creating one's own triumphant identity as a woman no longer oppressed by class or gender inequalities at home in England—or writing *Jane Eyre*, the fiction of a redistribution of wealth and of power between men and women—depends on a colonial ink. Whether advertently or not, Brontë acknowledges that dependence in the conclusion of *Jane Eyre*. Like imperialist trade itself, bringing home the spoils of other countries to become commodities in England, such as Indian ink, the use of the racial "other" as a metaphor for class and gender struggles in England commodifies the dark-skinned people of the British empire as they exist in historical actuality and transforms them into East or West Indian ink with which to write a novel about ending injustices within England.

The eruption of the words "Indian ink" into the novel at this telling moment hints at Brontë's uneasiness about the East Indian ventures to which England was turning in 1848, as well as about the West Indian colonies that were by then clearly becoming unprofitable after the abolition of slavery. St. John, who is given the last words in the novel, writes them from India as he is dying. He is killed off by the insalubrious atmosphere of domination in British India, where he undoubtedly has made the Indians feel, as he did Jane, the inferiority of their non-Grecian features. With the same retributive poetic justice Rochester is nearly killed when his West Indian plague-house collapses on him. Brontë's anxiety about British imperialism is everywhere apparent in the ending of *Jane Eyre*. The novel is finally unable to rest easily in its figurative strategy and its Anglocentric anti-imperialist politics: its opposition to colonial contact, which it portrays as contaminating and self-destructive for the English people, and its advocacy of a middle-class English domesticity freed from some of the most blatant forms of gender and class inequality. *Jane Eyre* is thus a fascinating example of the associations—and dissociations—between a resistance to the ideology of male domination and a resistance to the ideology of imperialist domination.

The critique of imperialism that the novel promises to make through its metaphorical yoking of forms of oppression finally collapses into uneasiness about the effects of empire on domestic social relations in England. That disquietude is the only remnant of Brontë's potentially radical revision of ideas about the similitude of white women and colonized peoples, and it is the only incomplete element in the ideological closure of the novel. The insalubrious mist that suggests British contact in the empire with other races, diffused throughout the ending of the novel, betrays Brontë's lingering anxiety about British imperialism and about her own literary treatment of other races, about the way in which, through her figurative tactics, she has tried to make the world of her novel "clean."

NOTES

1. Charlotte Brontë, *Shirley*, ed. Herbert Rosengarten and Margaret Smith (Oxford: Clarendon Press, 1981), 613.

2. In *The Isle of Devils*, a thinly disguised verse-narrative about race relations in the British West Indies, Monk Lewis creates a horrible monster, "black as the storm," who rapes a beautiful white virgin after her ship is wrecked near his island during a tempest. See Matthew Lewis, "The Isle of Devils" (1815), in *Journal of a West India Proprietor* (London: John Murray, 1834), 261–89. In Harriet Martineau's antislavery novel, *Demerara*, a West Indian hurricane enacts the rage the slaves themselves cannot: the slaves in her novel exult at the ravages the storm commits on their master's property, cry out with "horrid yells" as they watch their overseer drowning, and seem "like imps of the storm." Harriet Martineau, *Demerara*, in *Illustrations of Political Economy* (London: Charles Fox, 1834), II: 109–12. Brontë herself uses similar imagery in her juvenile Roe Head journal when a wild storm evokes in her the vision of Africans in revolution against white British colonists. See Chapter 1 above and Charlotte Brontë, "Well, here I am at Roe Head", ed. Christine Alexander, in Richard J. Dunn, ed. *Jane Eyre: A Norton Critical Edition*, 2d ed. (New York: Norton, 1987), 410–12.

3. Charlotte Brontë, *Villette*, ed. Herbert Rosengarten and Margaret Smith (Oxford: Clarendon Press, 1984), 456. For a discussion of the abolition of slavery in the French West Indian colonies, see F. R. Augier, S. C. Gordon, D. G. Hall, and M. Reckord, *The Making of the West Indies* (London: Longmans, 1960), 200–201; J. H. Parry and P. M. Sherlock, *A Short History of the West Indies* (New York: Macmillan, 1957), 218–19. Parry and Sherlock note that "the events of 1848–49, which marked the end of slavery, foreshadowed also the end of white political supremacy ... in Martinique and Guadeloupe".

4. Charlotte Brontë, *The Professor*, ed. Margaret Smith and Herbert Rosengarten (Oxford: Clarendon Press, 1987), 14. Subsequent references are included in the text.

5. Every slave plantation colony in the West Indies had its "maroons," roaming communities of runaway slaves who had banded together and survived in the uncultivated areas of the colony. The Jamaican maroons were particularly successful and particularly threatening to the British colonists. See Michael Craton, *Testing the Chains: Resistance to Slavery in the British West Indies* (Ithaca: Cornell University Press, 1982), especially 61–67.

6. Charlotte Brontë, "Emma," appended to *The Professor*, ed. Smith and Rosengarten, 322–23. Subsequent references are included in the text. Ellin's "joke" becomes even less amusing when we recall that the schoolmistress would have been prevented from selling Matilda as a slave not because black slavery no longer existed in Virginia—slavery in the United States lasted through the end of the Civil War in 1865—but simply because England had abolished the slave trade in 1808. See Michael Craton, *Sinews of Empire: A Short History of British Slavery* (Garden City, N.Y.: Anchor Books, 1974), 239–84, for an account of the abolition and emancipation movements in England.

7. Charlotte Brontë, *Jane Eyre*, ed. Jane Jack and Margaret Smith (Oxford: Clarendon Press, 1969), 63, 78. Subsequent references are included in the text.

8. Gayatri Chakravorty Spivak, "Three Women's Texts and a Critique of Imperialism", *Critical Inquiry* 12 (1985): 243–61. Two previous critics have made brief allusions to the significance of race in *Jane Eyre*. R. J. Dingley notes in his Rochester as Slave: An Allusion in *Jane Eyre*," *Notes and Queries* 31 (1984): 66, that Rochester uses the phrase "a man and a brother" in speaking to Jane. Dingley interprets the phrase as Rochester's impulsively premature declaration that the intensity of his passion makes him

Jane's slave. Patricia Beer frames the chapter on Charlotte Brontë, in her *Reader, I Married Him: A Study of the Women Characters of Jane Austen, Charlotte Brontë, Elizabeth Gaskell and George Eliot* (New York: Barnes & Noble, 1974), 84–126, by suggesting that the novel draws an analogy between women and slaves and noting that Brontë, unlike Jane Austen, made "serious ... comment" on this form of the "slave trade" (84), but she goes no further in exploring the analogy. Since the first publication of an earlier version of the present chapter under the title "Colonialism and the Figurative Strategy of "Jane Eyre" in *Victorian Studies* 33 (1990): 247–68, reprinted in Jonathan Arac and Harriet Ritvo, ed., *Macropolitics of Nineteenth-Century Literature: Nationalism, Exoticism, Imperialism* (Philadelphia: University of Pennsylvania Press, 1991), three subsequent critics have taken up the treatment of race relations in the novel. See Jenny Sharpe, *Allegories of Empire: The Figure of Woman in the Colonial Text* (Minneapolis: University of Minnesota Press, 1993), 27–56; Elsie Michie, "From Simianized Irish to Oriental Despots: Heathcliff, Rochester, and Racial Difference", *Novel* 25 (1992): 125–40; Suvendrini Perera, *Reaches of Empire: The English Novel from Edgeworth to Dickens* (New York: Columbia University Press, 1991), 79–102.

9. Here Spivak may be alluding to Homi Bhabha's notion of a unified "colonial subject" that encompasses both the colonizer and colonized. Homi K. Bhabha, "The Other Question ... The Stereotype and Colonial Discourse", *Screen* 24 (1983): 19. Abdul R. JanMohamed ably takes issue with this notion in "The Economy of Manichean Allegory: The Function of Racial Difference in Colonialist Literature", *Critical Inquiry* 12 (1985): 59–87. Criticizing the general lack of attention to political history in writing on colonialist literature, JanMohamed writes: "While otherwise provocative and illuminating, [Bhabha's] work rests on two assumptions—the unity of the 'colonial subject' and the 'ambivalence' of colonial discourse—that are inadequately problematized and, I feel, finally unwarranted and unacceptable. In rejecting Edward Said's 'suggestion that colonial power and discourse is possessed entirely by the coloniser,' Bhabha asserts, without providing any explanation, the unity of the 'colonial subject (both coloniser and colonised).' I do not wish to rule out, a priori, the possibility that at some rarefied theoretical level the varied material and discursive antagonisms between conquerors and natives can be reduced to the workings of a single 'subject'; but such a unity, let alone its value, must be demonstrated, not assumed" (59–60).

10. See, for example, Adrienne Rich's reference to Bertha's "dark sensual beauty," in "Jane Eyre: The Temptations of a Motherless Woman" (1973), reprinted in her *On Lies, Secrets, and Silence: Selected Prose 1966–1978* (New York: Norton, 1979), 99, or Sandra Gilbert and Susan Gubar's description of Bertha as "a Creole—swarthy, 'livid,' etc.," in *The Madwoman in the Attic: The Woman Writer and the Nineteenth-Century Literary Imagination* (New Haven: Yale University Press, 1979), 680n.

11. See Winthrop Jordan, *The White Man's Burden: Historical Origins of Racism in the United States* (New York: Oxford University Press, 1974), 70–73, and Craton, *Sinews of Empire*, 176, 181–86, 223–26, for the practices of and attitudes toward interracial sex and manumission in the English colonies.

12. John Malcolm Forbes Ludlow, *A Sketch of the History of the United States* (Cambridge: Macmillan, 1862), 316. This passage is quoted in *The Oxford English Dictionary*, 2d ed. (Oxford: Clarendon Press, 1989), IV:7.

13. For the association of the racial "other" with madness, see Sander Gilman, *Difference and Pathology: Stereotypes of Sexuality, Race, and Madness* (Ithaca: Cornell University Press, 1985), especially chap. 5, "On the Nexus of Blackness and Madness", 131–49. A more lengthy discussion of the ambiguity of the word "creole" appears in

Christopher Miller, *Blank Darkness: Africanist Discourse in French* (Chicago: University of Chicago Press, 1985), 93–107.

14. The West Indian Controversy, *Blackwood's Edinburgh Magazine* 14 (October 1823): 442.

15. Q. D. Leavis, notes to *Jane Eyre*, by Charlotte Brontë, ed. Q. D. Leavis (New York: Penguin Books, 1984), 487–89.

16. Terry Eagleton, *Myths of Power: A Marxist Study of the Brontës* (New York: Barnes & Noble, 1975), 4, 16.

17. Jina Politi, "*Jane Eyre* Class-ified", *Literature and History* 8 (1982): 66. See also Kathryn Sutherland, "*Jane Eyre*'s Literary History: The Case for Mansfield Park", *ELH* 59 (1992): 409–40. Sutherland contends of Jane Eyre that "the political dimension is one that the heroine successfully outgrows.... All Jane's anger, symbolic and real, we finally see, has been directed against those social structures which refused her admittance" (429–30).

18. Carol Ohmann, "Historical Reality and 'Divine Appointment' in Charlotte Brontë's Fiction", *Signs* 2 (1977): 757–78; Igor Webb, *From Custom to Capital: The English Novel and the Industrial Revolution* (Ithaca: Cornell University Press, 1981), especially 70–86.

19. Ohmann, 762.

20. Webb, 86.

21. See Patricia Meyer Spacks, *The Female Imagination* (New York: Knopf, 1972), 64–65; *Rich*, 97–99; Gilbert and Gubar, 336–71, especially 359–62.

22. Robert Knox, *The Races of Men: A Fragment* (Philadelphia; Lea & Blanchard 1850), 151.

23. For a treatment of the European fear of "going native" in the colonies, which includes a discussion of Kurtz in Conrad's *The Heart of Darkness*, see Patrick Brantlinger, "Victorians and Africans: The Genealogy of the Myth of the Dark Continent", *Critical Inquiry* 12 (1985): 166–203, especially 193–98. Brantlinger argues that "the potential for being 'defiled'—for 'going native' or becoming 'tropenkollered'—led Europeans again and again to displace their own 'savage' impulses onto Africans" (196).

24. I thank Katherine Snyder for referring me to this passage.

25. See Charles White, *An Account of the Regular Gradation in Man, and in Different Animals and Vegetables* (London: C. Dilly, 1799), 51n. Or compare the well-known essay by the American physician Samuel Cartwright, "Natural History of the Prognathous Species of Mankind," in which he cites Cuvier to explain, succinctly, that the word "prognathous" "is a technical term derived from *pro*, before, and *gnathos*, the jaws, indicating that the muzzle or mouth is anterior to the brain. The lower animals, according to Cuvier, are distinguished from the European and Mongol man by the mouth and face projecting further forward in the profile than the brain.... The typical negroes of adult age, when tried by this rule, are proved to belong to a different species from the man of Europe or Asia ... their mouth and jaws projecting beyond the forehead containing the anterior lobes of the brain. Moreover, their faces are proportionally larger than their crania." *New York Day-Book*, November 10, 1857; reprinted in Eric L. McKitrick, ed., *Slavery Defended: The Views of the Old South* (Englewood Cliffs, N.J.: Prentice-Hall, 1963), 139–40.

26. At the novel's end, St. John goes to India to "hew down like a giant the prejudices of creed and caste that encumber it," although the novel has made clear that such energy is better spent attempting to obliterate this sort of prejudice in England.

27. See Leonore Davidoff's analysis of the relationship between the upper-middle-class Victorian writer A. J. Munby and his servant Hannah Cullwick in "Class and Gender in Victorian England", in *Sex and Class in Women's History*, ed. Judith L. Newton, Mary P.

Ryan, and Judith R. Walkowitz (Boston: Routledge & Kegan Paul, 1983), 17–71, and Peter Stallybrass and Allon White, "The City: The Sewer, the Gaze, and the Contaminating Touch", in *The Politics and Poetics of Transgression* (Ithaca: Cornell University Press, 1986), 125–48, for two discussions of the nineteenth-century bourgeoisie's equation of dirt and pollution with the "lower orders."

28. Patricia Beer also notes that "the fresh air and the open countryside remain for [Jane] symbols of personal freedom and independence" which she opposes to the thought of suffocation as Rochester's "slave." Patricia Beer, 126.

29. Francis G. Hutchins writes in *The Illusion of Permanence: British Imperialism in India* (Princeton: Princeton University Press, 1967), 32, that while Jane rejected St. John's "tyranny for herself", she (and, he implies, Brontë with her) "warmly rejoiced to see it exercised in India where she felt its sternness would be beneficial." Politi similarly contends that "the text will conceal the complicity of the Church with Imperialism and will present St. John as the disinterested missionary" (Politi, 59). Spivak also sees "the unquestioned idiom of imperialist presuppositions" in the novel's concluding description of St. John (Spivak, "Three Women's Texts", 249). Parama Roy, "Unaccommodated Woman and the Poetics of Property in *Jane Eyre*," *SEL* 29 (1989): 721, finds "a reflexive endorsement of patriarchalism in the chapters on St. John and his vocation to convert the heathen," and claims that Brontë has "the most unambiguous respect for the missionary's job" (723). Michie claims that the novel represents missionary work as "pure" (Michie, 138), and Sharpe argues that "the grand narrative" of the colonial "civilizing mission," voiced by St. John, legitimates and creates a space for Jane's creation of her autobiographical self (Sharpe, 38). David Bromwich, responding to Spivak, differs from the prevailing reading not by questioning the valuation of Rivers as the voice of the novel's ideology, but by claiming, without textual elaboration, that "the novel identifies Rivers as belonging to an evangelical sect that fought hard for the abolition of slavery: his parentage, though at a distance, includes men like Zachary Macaulay. If described as imperialist, it ought to be described carefully." David Bromwich, *A Choice of Inheritance* (Cambridge: Harvard University Press, 1989). 267.

30. Carolyn Williams, "Closing the Book: The Intertextual End of Jane Eyre", in *Victorian Connections*, ed. Jerome J. McGann (Charlottesville: University Press of Virginia, 1989), 80–81.

31. White, 51n.

32. See for example Roy, 723.

33. David Hume, Of Love and Marriage, in Essays: *Moral, Political, and Literary*, ed. Eugene F. Miller (Indianapolis: Liberty Classics, 1985), 559.

34. Ibid.

35. According to the *OED2*, Indian ink, also and more accurately known as China ink, is "a black pigment made in China and Japan, sold in sticks; understood to consist of lampblack made into a paste with a solution of gum and dried."

SUSAN OSTROV WEISSER

Thornfield and 'The Dream to Repose on': Jane Eyre

> The paths of vice are sometimes strewed with roses, but then they are forever infamous for many a thorn.
>
> John Cleland, *Fanny Hill*, 1748

Though I have said that the meanings of desire cannot be separated out from historical context, the reader of Charlotte Brontë's novels must engage with fictional texts which present Desire precisely the opposite way. In *Jane Eyre*, Desire is originary to the search for a psychologically contained 'self'—one's own or other—powerful enough to fulfil or restrain it. For Charlotte Brontë both sexual love and the art of creating fiction itself are figured as 'dreaming', acts of imagination which represent virtual survival. 'The dream' is, in fact, almost the only resistance—the other is anger—against the condition of 'vacancy', the emptiness and smallness of the female self in a society in which there is no place for meaningful work or social gestures. Through the love she both espouses and exposes as a fiction, and the fictions she writes about sexual love, the very blankness of existence is transformed by the author: the 'vacancy' of womanhood becomes the creatively open, blank slate of the imagination, on which can take shape the story of what can be done with a woman's life.

In this sense sexual love to a Brontë heroine is an assertion of her mastery and strength, a felt power. Yet it also contains its own contradiction:

From *A "Craving Vacancy": Women and Sexual Love in the British Novel, 1740–1880*. © 1997 by Susan Ostrov Weisser.

it is represented as an overwhelming force in its own right, one which subordinates and contracts female identity to the strictures of social conventions of femininity. By casting Desire as a state of craving vacancy, a reification of the traditional idea of feminine absence and passivity, Brontë reconceptualizes sexual love as a 'power' which *must itself be resisted.*

In this and the following chapter, Charlotte Brontë's two best-known novels will be examined as an evolving attempt to represent, and by reaching towards an accommodation, resolve these contradictory positions, i.e. sexual love as both liberatory and oppressive. To do so, love must be presented fictionally and then re-presented as a fiction, which is to say first mystified and then clarified as an ideology. It is very important, therefore, that all Brontë's novels, as well as those of her sister Emily, begin with a realization of the conditions of oppression, the overwhelming estrangement of the heroine from her society as the one radical fact of her existence. But whereas novels about besieged young sexual innocents from *Clarissa* to *Tess of the D'Urbervilles* begin by depicting a stable, seemingly ideal social world, then slowly build an atmosphere of injustice, suspicion and danger caused by the unchecked male will marauding in virgin territory, the plots of Charlotte and Emily Brontë, by contrast, frequently begin with images of helpless, rebellious or suffering children in an oppressive adult world.

The children bereft of protective parents who appear in *Jane Eyre*, *Villette* and *Wuthering Heights* represent a sense of estrangement from the bonds of nurturing love, presaging the powerlessness, vulnerability and social injustice which are the conditions of falling in love for the heroines in these novels.[1] A sense of the loss of traditional community, with its ties of morality and economic interdependence, precedes the Brontë heroines' sojourn in the Carlylean Lodging House, that site of commercial, self-interested relations between humans, or more to the point, between men and women. Charlotte's heroines, especially, are literal Lodgers—either in homes where they are not at home, like the Gateshead of *Jane Eyre*, in boarding schools or in foreign lands. It is from this starting point—the inability to find a meaningful place in the social community—that the Brontë heroine is impelled to find an alternative home in sexual love.

The relationship of sexual love to the anger caused by the heroine's isolation from society is an especially complex one in Charlotte Brontë novels. Unlike the paradigm of Moral Femininity, with its saint-like resignation and calm, Jane Eyre, Lucy Snowe and Catherine Earnshaw are decidedly not 'sweet'. Matthew Arnold's famous characterization of Charlotte Brontë's writing as full of 'hunger, rebellion and rage', could equally well be applied to both Jane Eyre and Catherine Earnshaw, furious and rebelling from the first scene in which we are introduced to them, while

Lucy Snowe's apparent calm is relentlessly dissected and found to be utterly false.

From 1835–7, Charlotte Brontë, in the adult world for the first time as a very young teacher at the girls' boarding school Roe Head, kept a remarkable journal in which she articulated that sense of estrangement from 'insipid' society which was to fill an important function in her novels.[2] Early in 1836 she notes that her ability to detach herself imaginatively from her surroundings sets her apart from the others at the school. When 'the school room is quiet' she can

> assume my own thoughts; my mind relaxes from the stretch on which it has been for the last 12 hours, and falls back onto the rest which nobody in this house knows but myself.... It is strange I cannot get used to the ongoings that surround me. I fulfil my duties strictly and well [but] it is the still small voice alone that comes to me at eventide ... which takes up my spirit and engrosses all my living feelings, all my energies which are not merely mechanical.[3]

Similarly, in a letter from Charlotte Brontë to her very conventional best friend, she cries, '*I am not like you*', by which she means 'my thoughts, the dreams that absorb me, and the fiery imagination that at times eats me up, and makes me feel society, as it is, wretchedly insipid'. These are 'qualities which make me very miserable, some feelings you can have no participation in, that few, very few people in the world can at all understand ... they burst out sometimes, and then those who see the explosion despise me.'[4] The heroines of her novels, it should be noted, are also not merely outside and superior to society, but also inadequate to it in some way. This difference is the permanent Byronic limp of the potential artist.

By the summer of 1836, Brontë's dreamy detachment reveals itself as a secret contempt for the stupid conventionality of the 'ladies' around her. After 'toiling for an hour with Miss Lester, Miss Marriott and Ellen Cook, striving to teach them the distinction between an article and a substantive', she explodes,

> Am I to spend all the best part of my life in this wretched bondage, forcibly suppressing my rage at the idleness, the apathy, and the hyperbolical and most asinine stupidity of these fat-headed oafs, and on compulsion assuming an air of kindness, patience and assiduity?[5]

She 'longs to write', but again and again a distinctly inferior reality intrudes: 'Miss W. came in with a plate of butter',[6] or 'the ladies were now come into the room to get their curl-papers';[7] when a 'dolt came up with a lesson', interrupting her fantasies, she writes, 'I thought I should have vomited ...'[8]

The constant humiliation and rage that Charlotte Brontë recorded resulted from her secret sense of inner superiority and frustrated capabilities, combined with a strong suspicion of persecution: repeatedly, as the journal progresses, the others are 'talking about her',[9] or 'staring, gaping', while she is lost in the 'divine unseen land of thought'.[10] As Charlotte admitted in a letter of 1836, 'things that nobody else cares for enter into my mind and rankle there like venom'.[11] Yet the scorn she evinced towards the 'ladies' was often mixed with a covert envy of their smooth air of assurance and strength of self-will. Her own sense of social incompetence only added to her humiliation and led her to the admission in a letter to Ellen Nussey that 'I have a constant tendency to scorn people who are far better than I am.'[12]

In Brontë's journal we can see the development of the persona of the Lodger, the female boarder, as it takes on its characteristic elements: the feelings of secret superiority to and contempt of others, the rejection by others in turn, the consequent humiliating necessity for mask and disguise: 'It is the living in other people's houses—the estrangement from one's real character—the adoption of a cold frigid apathetic exterior that is painful,'[13] she writes of her experience as a governess in 1841. The idea that there is a self more 'real' than the social persona was extremely important to her and would pervade both Charlotte and Emily's work. This 'real' identity is conceived as an experiential self, living deeply 'inside' superficial physiognomy or determinate social behaviours and yet 'outside' the conditions of oppression: the self that experiences Desire.

Just as she had '*assumed* an air of kindness and patience' at Roe Head, the estranged heroine is shut out from ordinary 'feminine' virtues and must act a role continually. The 'real character' of which Charlotte spoke does not—*cannot*—fit either of the prescribed conventional roles for women: she is *neither* the type of Moral Femininity—passively self-denying, kind, pious and patient—nor successful in the role of the cold but socially adept Lady.

More and more in Charlotte Brontë's journal, the so-called 'real' self exists only in her inward capacity to plunge with dizzying boldness into the empirically *unreal*, to connect with the buried imaginative life she had fashioned as a bulwark against her estrangement. Eventually Charlotte herself feared that the increasing reliance of her 'real' self on the inner life for its identity was becoming a source of further social isolation. In 1839, when she made a conscious decision to abandon the melodramatic fantasies which had grown to 'a system strange as some religious creed',[14] she noted that she felt 'as if I stood on the threshold of a home and were bidding farewell', while the concrete world of which she intended to write was 'a distant country where every face was unknown'.[15] The *literal* search for a home in this 'distant country' was, of course, to become the theme of her two best novels, which were to use the materials of her 'dream world', an imaginative social order which was a projection of this internal 'real' self, integrated with the demands of novel-writing in the actual social world of mid-Victorian England.

Yet Brontë's heroines are not conventional orphan-victims who will make good and enter the society from which they were excluded, after teaching it or being taught a lesson or two. They are not, in other words, either alternative forms of Dickens' Oliver Twist or Pip with the gender reversed, nor even a nineteenth-century version of Richardson's Pamela, but are, in some elemental sense, *different* from others of both genders—at once superior and inadequate to the role of Lady to which every woman around them aspires, both forcibly excluded and deliberately aloof from the solid rewards of conventional society. The innovative mysteriousness of a Charlotte Brontë heroine is that though there is so much more to her than meets the eye, in terms of her imaginative and emotional capacities, there is virtually no bodily self to speak of. So often is she described as small, thin and plain, that the heroine seems about to disappear entirely, were it not for the enormous strength of her desire and imagination.

Charlotte's adolescent writings already reveal the imaginative fusion of sexual and social metaphors that is characteristic in her major novels, where her rendering of 'sympathy', for example, acquires ever-widening circles of emotional, social and moral connotation. The juvenilia are wonderfully lurid: in 'Caroline Vernon', for example, one of the last of the early novelettes, and probably written soon after the Roe Head journal in 1835 or 1839, we may see how the primitive armature of a love-fantasy provided the material for tying together Charlotte's concerns with artistic superiority and female humiliation, identity, will and self-interest, albeit in immature and rough, form. Caroline Vernon, the heroine, small in size like Charlotte herself, is nobly born: 'distinguished', 'patrician', 'ladylike' by nature. Yet she is not a conventional Lady: like the Brontë persona of the journal, 'something might remain behind which she did not choose to tell or even to hint at ... she'd sensations somewhere that were stronger than fancy or romance.' Caroline is different from the start by virtue of this mysteriousness, her superior capacity for feeling and her strong will, which is signalled by 'impetuousness of manner'.[16]

When the tale begins, Caroline's father has come to release her from the virtual captivity in which he had placed her, 'where she had been reared like a bird'. In Brontë's later novels the caged bird image comes to represent an important conflict between the prison of feminine selflessness and the demands of the desiring will. When Caroline, the bird poised for flight, is told about the romantic, 'powerful' Zamorna, with his 'vicious, passionate past', and his 'feelings stronger than his reason' (p. 323), the pattern is set for the wild, strong father-figure to arouse great feeling in the young girl seeking her 'real' self.[17] The man who will fill the vacancy that craves is also 'different' and unconventional. In fact, Caroline almost seems attracted to him for what he is not. Like Rochester, he does not appear 'good, kind or cheerful'; like M. Paul, he is neither witty nor 'complimentary' (p. 337).

Unlike Jane Eyre or Lucy Snowe, however, Caroline Vernon acts purely because 'her Will urged it' (p. 341); her feeling for Zamorna is said to be 'restless' and 'devouring' (p. 349). Sexual love is frankly depicted as a form of the aggrandizement of the devouring will, devoid of the altruism of Jane Eyre's love for Rochester or the intellectual admiration of Lucy Snowe's for M. Paul.[18] The passionate nature of this love story seems to derive from its strongly familial setting. Caroline 'wished her sister [Zamorna's wife] dead and herself his wife' (p. 349), while her own father, angered by their affair, wishes Zamorna a 'withered hand and foot' (p. 357), in an interesting anticipation of Rochester's fate.

Here, then, in very rough and juvenile form, is the love-myth of Charlotte Brontë's later novels, with one notable distinction: its entire lack of concern with questions of morality. Caroline Vernon does not judge; she has no conscience. There are no moral issues in the imaginary Angrian world of Charlotte's apprenticeship because there is no society, only pure passion and will thwarted or fulfilled, whereas in actual society, as Charlotte perceived it, passionate feeling was castigated, while moral restraint was not necessarily rewarded. Conversely, the 'strong will', while clearly the only means for the uprooted individual to survive, had to be hidden behind the mask of feminine passivity at all costs. We recall that at the formative time of her apprenticeship writing, Charlotte began with a negative definition of self: 'I am not *like you*', i.e. *not* calm, restrained, 'moral', passive—or conventional.

In her novels, Charlotte attempted to forge a heroine of the negative materials of this estrangement of the so-called 'real' self from social recognition or power. Emptied of definition, the female outsider will successively try on all the roles available to women: the wilful Lady, the Moral Feminine who renounces her own will, child/mother, pupil/teacher, slave/mistress/wife. The novels rise above these sentimental models because they evolve into the means through which to re-evaluate social definitions of womanhood by imagining a strong female selfhood capable of uniting desire, power and morality.

In only the second paragraph of the novel, Jane draws the reader's attention to her 'physical inferiority' (p. 39) to these proto-gentlemen and ladies, her young cousins. This very plainness is symbolic of her utter unfitness for conventional Ladyhood. Nor can Jane be successful in the role of submissive femininity: her aunt finds her repugnant precisely because of her strong will. In sum, Jane Eyre at Gateshead is 'not one of them', as was said of Richardson's Clarissa, the outsider in her family. 'I was a discord in Gateshead Hall,' she tells us, 'I was like nobody there.'[19]

The same 'no-win' attitude dominates the emotional worlds of the early family scenes in both *Clarissa* and *Jane Eyre*. Just as Clarissa's attempts to propitiate her mother cause her further rejection on the grounds of hypocrisy, Jane's very act of questioning why she has been excluded from fireside and family love becomes further proof of *her* unworthiness to be loved because of an unbecoming forwardness. Yet Jane contends at all costs against putting on a pretence of resignation, which represents to her literal self-obliteration. Imprisoned in this vicious circle, Jane sees that asserting the will which is the only means to survival causes her oppressors, as it did Clarissa's, to wilfully misinterpret her as a monster of self-interest, a projection in fact of themselves.

In such a home, only lying, role-playing and calculating would overcome Jane's reputation for dishonesty. The double point of view of this section—the Jane as others see her as opposed to the person she thinks she is—establishes the particular nature of Jane's estrangement in this novel. Jane's tenacious clinging to a belief in a 'real' self, lying dormant until 'discovered', i.e. affirmed, by others, is her chief strength. This kernel of elemental self, protected from social oppression, is kept alive for Jane only by the sheer heat of her anger. When Mrs Reed judges her 'not worthy of notice' (p. 59), Jane's sudden reckless cry of protest, 'They are not fit to associate with me', emerges 'without her will consenting', from a voice over which she 'has no control' (p. 60). So important is Jane's passionate anger to her sense of selfhood that when she next engaged in a violent argument with Mrs Reed, 'shaking from head to foot, thrilled with ungovernable excitement' (p. 68), her soul is said to 'expand, to exult' (p. 69), as it later does in sexual exaltation. Anger, like sexuality, is viewed as an expression of the necessary will to individuation; yet like sexual love, it is also dangerous to a self conceived as an essential nature, prior to the creation of others or the pressures of the social order. Both anger and sexual love consume and eventually obliterate the will because they are 'ungovernable' once let loose (as Jane is said to be by Mrs Reed), and therefore self-devouring if not imprisoned.[20]

In this plight, her schoolmate Helen Burns' potent calm under suffering is meant to offer an alternative point of view to Jane, but it is a stance that is presented as highly problematic. Helen's is the role of Moral Femininity, which seems to create a self-contained meaning and humanness by an individual spirit of submission in a haven apart from the self-seeking ethos of society. By contrast to Jane, Helen flies in the face of power and its ethos of self-interest by her saint-like trust in goodness. Her absolute rejection of anger, like Jane's submission to it, is considered a rebellion in itself: thus, when Helen calmly allows herself to be unjustly whipped, the cruel Miss Scatchard is doubly infuriated and calls her 'a hardened girl' (p. 86).

Helen's creed of universal forgiveness and salvation makes the universe, and even death, a 'mighty home' (p. 91) for her so that she can bear the world's evil. But neither she nor the kind Miss Temple, who spreads goodness by small acts of personal benevolence, are the models of behaviour for Jane that some critics have contended.[21] In part this is because neither can be ultimately effective, since Miss Temple's power in the school community is very limited and Helen, though armed with a coherent vision of selfhood, is soon literally extinguished as an individual amidst the oppression and deprivation against which she struggles. More importantly, this critical portion of the novel, while sympathetic to Helen as an individual, at the same time bitterly parodies the very concept of self-denial as a useful social or ethical category and reveals it as potentially self-interested through the character of Mr Brocklehurst and the principles of Lowood School.

While accompanied by overdressed and pampered ladies, Mr Brocklehurst expostulates on the virtue of allowing as little food, clothing and pleasure as possible in order to 'mortify in these girls the lusts of the flesh' (p. 96). Again and again, the dignity of the individual and of physical need is asserted in this part of the novel, as is the absolute necessity for human love. While Helen wins their rhetorical argument with the conventionally religious speech that begins, '"Hush Jane! you think too much of the love of human beings"', her success in calming Jane's turbulent emotion is quickly undercut by a surprising qualification. 'In the tranquillity she imparted,' notes Jane, 'there was an alloy of inexpressible sadness' (p. 100). It is significant that Jane questions Helen's religious beliefs virtually until the latter's death; she never verbally accepts them. What Jane most seems to absorb from Helen and Miss Temple is the nourishment of their affection, and the importance of an *appearance* of feminine calm.

When we next see Jane, she is on the verge of womanhood and still seeking 'liberty', which is the release of the imprisoned 'real' self into the social world. From the beginning of Jane's experience at Thornfield, where she takes up her new role of governess, the doubleness of Jane's character is emphasized.[22] As she herself advises us when she has arrived at her destination, 'Reader, though I *look* comfortably accommodated, I am not very tranquil in my *mind*' (p. 125, my italics).

Thornfield itself is a place of the imagination, an old Gothic mansion, whose name derives from its 'mighty old thorn trees, strong, knotty, and broad' (p. 131); this image is a wonderfully connotative fusion of masculine sexual energy and imaginative power. When Jane meets Rochester, her new master, on the road, he is 'puzzled to decide what I was' (p. 146). Through Rochester, in other words, we are able to see Jane as a self not yet generated (or even, given the use of 'what' instead of 'who', gendered). The heart of the matter (so to speak) has been reached: the reader is observing Brontë in the act of creating a male character who, as the product of her own imagination, will empower her to do what imagining itself is a trope for: the creation of a female identity out of sheer desire.[23] Jane begins to live as a woman because Rochester does not know how to fix and imprison her in a social context. She is nameless, new, unformed, not yet placed in a genre: is she the Rose among the Thorns, the romantic heroine she feels she could be, or the plain, calm, romance-debunking 'servant' she is at pains to appear to be? Does she, in other words, both literally and metaphorically, belong to Thornfield, or not?

Rochester himself is described by the narrator again and again, as though Charlotte Brontë were struggling to pin down the exact qualities which will do their work on the as yet unexpressed 'real' self of Jane Eyre. We are told he is like a 'mass of crag' or 'a great oak' (p. 143); 'dark, strong and stern' (p. 147), like God the Father, but 'cynical' and 'self-willed' (p. 174). His eyes are 'irate and piercing' (p. 152), his features are 'all energy, decision, will', his look one of 'genuine power' (p. 204). The strength of desire and will which is the primary characteristic of Rochester's 'masculine' sexuality calls to mind the image of the thorn trees surrounding the mansion, in which physical size and 'might' evoke imaginative and sexual power.

Even before Rochester appears on the scene, Jane was told that he is 'peculiar' by the down-to-earth housekeeper, who has only a vague sense that 'you cannot always be sure whether he is in jest or earnest, whether he is pleased or the contrary: you don't thoroughly understand him in short' (p. 136). It is absolutely essential to Rochester's sexual attractiveness that he is moody, hard to 'read', an intensely private and convoluted hero who presents no surface smoothness or conventional blandness on which to depend: he constitutes a secret. Like the thorn trees on his property, he is, we may say, knotted; in his own characterization, he is 'hard and tough like an india rubber ball; pervious, though, through a chink or two still' (p. 163). Rochester is penetrable: There is a private, even a 'female', entrance to this secret, available to the adventurer willing to undertake the risk of enduring the full power of masculine sexuality. And Jane, as we know, is ready for 'vividness'.

At their first meeting, Jane is 'set at her ease' (p. 145) by Rochester's physical ugliness, ill-humour and total lack of gallantry. They are the emblems of his own estrangement from conventional society: under no other circumstances could she trust him. Jane feels 'no fear' (p. 145) of the angry, frowning Rochester because no *conventional* romance seems possible under such conditions.[24] If the stranger is not playing the Gentleman, Jane feels no challenge to rise to the role of the Lady. Whereas the conventional Lady would see the polite formalities of society as a protection from unwarranted sexual intimacy, this vulnerable and guarded heroine presents them as hypocritical pretexts for self-interest and exploitation.

Though a good deal of their early conversations turn on the theme of hierarchy and power—his 'claim to superiority' and 'right to be a little masterful' (note the qualifier) versus Jane's status as 'a paid subordinate' (p. 165)—this parody of the customary master/servant relation is itself part of the sexual game. Here the issue is introduced early in order to declaw the potentially dangerous difference in class power; it is exposed as a joke rather than as part of the sexual appeal of the situation. Similarly, Rochester's irrational ill-humour parallels the attitude of the Reeds towards Jane as a child, but the anger is here reduced to the delicious tyranny of love, rendered innocuous by the promise of a 'real' kindness underneath. Yet it is this promise of kindness, this hope of a relation of trust, which the next part of *Jane Eyre* proposes to examine. In the love relation of Jane and Rochester we will see the hope and promise of sexual love stripped away to reveal the dangers, as well as pleasures, of individual gratification in a self-interested society.

Jane recognizes that she is in love when she feels understood: Rochester, she says, can 'dive into her eyes' (p. 164), 'read [her] glance' (p. 166) and 'interpret its language' (p. 167). She is named and therefore created in a new private social order: 'I felt at times as if he were my relation rather than my master ... [so] that I ceased to pine after kindred.... The blanks of existence were filled up; my bodily health improved; I gathered flesh and strength' (p. 177). She willingly becomes Rochester's 'diary' (p. 167), and believes she 'understands the language of his countenance and movements' because she is 'akin' to him, 'assimilated' (p. 204) to him.

In identifying with the assertive will and defiant individualism of the male who can act on desire, Jane's 'real self', constituted by the desire confined behind a conventional representation of calm, is released like the bird from the cage in which Rochester imagines her: were the 'restless, resolute captive' but free, he says, 'it would soar cloud-high' (p. 170). Not least important for Jane's sense of selfhood is the opportunity for aggression conferred by her 'assimilation' with her masculine counterpart. But like the tyranny of Jane's oppressors, the quality of Jane's own aggression has been altered by the corrective of love. The uncontrollable and impotent rage of Jane's childhood is replaced with Jane's metaphorically 'stick[ing] a sly penknife under my ear' (p. 162), as Rochester laughingly complains, and keeping her lover at bay with this 'needle of repartee' (p. 301). The impotent anger that was a problem in childhood is thus reduced to a part of coy sex-play: role-playing phallic self-assertion *and* feminine submission 'by turns', as Jane knows 'the pleasure of vexing and soothing by turns' (p. 187), trying her skill in argument by keeping Rochester on the verge of retaliation.

During the period of the growth of her love for Rochester, Jane is also given the opportunity to define herself partly through comparison with other women. In Blanche Ingram, the Lady as Bitch, Jane observes female self-assertion in the service of self-interest: 'I must have my will' (p. 221), cries Blanche coldly and imperiously. Significantly, the only wedding Blanche can have with Rochester is in the form of charades, the game in which one assumes another's identity. Blanche has no 'real' female self, because her 'will' is not dictated by the uncontrollable emotions of sexual love.

Jane's visit to Gateshead with her now grown cousins, Eliza and Georgiana Reed, frames a contrast between the two which is still more significant to Jane in defining herself as a woman who spurns the ideal of Ladyhood. The younger of Jane's former oppressors, Georgiana, who was always the beauty, has become 'weak, puffy and useless', existing to be stylish, enter society and marry a 'prospect' (p. 264); the sight of her 'full-blown' figure 'fallen asleep on the sofa over the perusal of a novel' (p. 265) is a comic portrait of vapid and self-indulgent Ladyhood.

Eliza, on the other hand, is the type of Moral Femininity gone wild: she would 'seek a retirement where punctual habits would be permanently secured from disturbance, and place safe barriers between herself and a frivolous world' (p. 263). Eliza takes Moral Femininity to its logical extreme—namely, to a nunnery, where she will 'take the veil' (p. 270). Whereas the Moral Feminine restrains her sexual feelings, Eliza rejects the importance of feeling entirely; and whereas the ideal of Moral Femininity seeks to inspire order in a chaotic moral world by renunciation, Eliza seeks a rigid celibacy out of a desire for selfish isolation, which she calls being 'independent of all efforts, and all wills, but your own' (p. 264). Eliza's is a type of isolation from society which Jane inevitably must compare unfavourably to the sympathetic communion of lovers, who at least live with and for the other. If Georgiana is the super-feminine, '*craving*, whining and idling' (p. 264, my italics), Eliza represents the dangers of frigid self-control, where celibacy is another name for self-will.

Jane Eyre builds, then, through the invocation of *Bildungsroman* and the emphasis on the search for a positive female identity, to an apparent assertion of the innate, lawful power and dignity of sexual love. The argument from nature—that the 'natural' self, with its necessary urges, should be the 'real' self—underlies Rochester's pronouncement to Jane, that 'I think you will be natural with me, as I find it impossible to be conventional with you' (p. 170). Similarly, to think of Rochester as only her 'paymaster' would be, according to Jane, 'blasphemy against nature' (p. 204); passion sets the natural at war with the merely commercial, the relation of trust with the relation of self-interest.

Consequently, when Rochester proposes marriage to Jane, the 'nightingale's song', the song of passionate love, 'was then the only voice of the hour' (p. 282). Jane, formerly the caged bird, is now happy in her imprisonment. But the freedom conferred by the release of a confined sexuality proves a deception, just as the power of the individual lover is qualified by the submergence of the lover's will into the beloved's. Rochester's features are 'full of an interest, an influence that quite mastered me', says Jane, 'that *took my feelings from my own power and fettered them in his*' (p. 204, my italics). Particularly for a woman, presumed to own the weaker will, 'real' passion is constructed as involuntary—'I *must* love him' (p. 204, my italics), declares Jane. It is in this sense only 'a new servitude', like her work.

Jane has experienced two self-defining aspects of sexual love: one is a wish for a father-like figure who will punish and master with cruelty, render one will-less, swallow one's identity up, and the other a kind of mother-longing, in which the lover creates, nurtures and props the self with kindness, so that one can 'repose on what I trust'.[25] Such trust is the final hedge against the heroine's life-long loneliness. But the protection of Rochester's love requires, as Jane will find, the absolute dependence of a child, an image which will recur with new significance.

Rochester's 'kindness', in which she trusts, proves oppressively paternalistic. Just as his tyranny was sexually provocative rather than threatening because it was based on loving desire, the 'power' to make 'unheard-of-rules' (p. 169)—i.e. to make Jane his mistress—should be his, according to Rochester's dictum, because it too is based on right motives, 'to guard, cherish and solace her' (p. 284). His passionate pronouncement to Jane, '"Let it be right"' (p. 169), stands alongside the argument from nature as the credo for self-gratification and the importance of individual desire.

Once again, Jane's identity is revealed as unstable and fluctuating as she is forced to try on one of the roles available to women with her 'new name'. To her dismay, Rochester, in his 'kindness', attempts to mould her into a Lady, 'dressed like a doll' (p. 297), on whom he may bestow jewels and lavish money. During their engagement she is variously called a fairy, a 'peer's daughter', or an angel, all of which she deflates, Pamela-like, with the self-deprecating remark, '"Don't address me as if I were a beauty; I am your plain, Quakerish governess"' (p. 287). But Jane perceives her new status as a fall from the dignity of honest self-employment to the dependence of the Lady who parasitically feeds from the material wealth of her host. The reality of the Lady is that she is a well-kept courtesan, 'slave' of a fond sultan.

As Jane finds herself losing 'the sense of power over him' (p. 294), the restraining influence which is the essence of Moral Femininity, she again takes up the weapon of sarcasm which served her during their first encounters as both sexual defence and allure. But she now has a new enemy: her own desire for the submergence of her self, as Rochester becomes to her 'my whole world; and more than the world; almost my hope of heaven' (p. 302). Whereas the heroines of Pamela and Clarissa, or numerous Gothic novels, were literally imprisoned by their lovers, Jane Eyre has stepped willingly into the prison of love, and will pay the price of further diminishment.[26]

Dressed for her wedding morning, Jane is forced literally to look her own departure from her 'real' self in the face: the mirror reflects only 'a robed and veiled figure, so unlike my usual self that it seemed almost the image of a stranger' (p. 315). Exactly who is this 'stranger'? Significantly, Jane has recounted to Rochester, the day before, disturbing dreams in which she is on an 'unknown road' or in the 'dreary ruin' of Thornfield Hall, 'burdened with the charge of a little child' (pp. 309–10), which shivers and wails as she half attempts to comfort it, half wishes to lay the burden down. The symbology of this pining, protesting child has naturally been the subject of a good deal of critical speculation.[27] Yet all along, one of the most vibrant metaphors animating the novel is that of a dependent, powerless child set against a selfish but powerful woman. Repeatedly, we are told that Jane, who even in maturity looks 'almost like a child' (p. 453), is attractive to Rochester partly *because* he perceives her as vulnerable and childlike.

Rochester is attracted, not only to Jane's dependence on him, but also to the uncorrupted integrity associated with her pre-sexual self. Jane, on the threshold of consummation of a highly sexual love, carries the burden of this helpless yet necessary childishness in her role as the Moral Feminine. She must, she believes, be childishly innocent in order to counteract the immoderation of Rochester's own sexuality. Moreover, Jane has been asked to abandon this unresolved identity for the role of the Lady, who is also dependent, like a child, but with disturbing overtones of the wilful self-seeking inherent in sexuality. Caught between these two roles or definitions of self—the childishly 'helpless', i.e. ineffectual, Moral Feminine, and the forceful but self-willed Lady—Jane has become a stranger to the 'real' sexual self she thought she had just discovered.

In the catastrophe that follows, the promise of sexual love to create a viable identity will prove to be a 'mere dream', as Jane prophetically terms her lover, despite the solidity of the 'rounded, muscular and vigorous hand' and 'long, strong arm' (p. 307), he laughingly—and provocatively—holds before her. The strength in that masculine hand is not nurturing as Jane has hoped, but potently destructive, like the secret strength of Rochester's mad wife, Bertha, the hidden impediment to their marriage, whose fiery rampages follow each mention of Jane's wailing-child dreams. Bertha, 'savage' like Rochester's look when he proposes, is the dark self of *both* Jane and Rochester. In the 'vampire'-like Bertha, the lust for aggrandizement, whether for material or sexual acquisitions, is horribly revealed as the corollary of the desire for self-creation.

Jane's abortive false marriage has removed the pretext which conveniently prevented her from confronting the central problem she has avoided: how to create a strong female identity in an oppressive social world. She can no longer be a Lady, thereby merging the components of sexuality, ennobling romantic love and social respectability in one legally and morally sanctioned union. Her alternatives are now bifurcated into a Victorian woman's other essential roles: as Rochester's mistress, she may become the purely sexual being she has thus far denied and evaded, or by leaving him entirely, she may choose to create meaning through the self-sacrifice of the Moral Feminine.

In her last turbulent scene with Rochester, Jane is the bird in the cage again, as Rochester sees in her eyes a 'resolute, wild, free thing looking out of it'. But the cage is now self-protective and of her own making: '"Whatever I do with its cage,"' groans Rochester, '"I cannot get at it"' (p. 344). Passion has moved her as its passive victim, and Jane sees that her only chance of selfhood lies in opposing Rochester's 'frenzy' and 'wild licence' with her own inward power. But although she is now 'honest', she is not at all certain what she is 'free' to do. She and Rochester do not speak the same moral language; therefore, Jane has become once more the Lodger, the inarticulate stranger in a foreign land. Having left Thornfield, wandering without money or connections of any sort, Jane is also the helpless and starving child of her dream, a nightmare repetition of her own childhood state.

In the passages which describe Jane's homeless wanderings, we are aware of a community all around which is closed to her. This exclusion is all the more poignant to Jane because she is conscious, as she says, of 'having no claim to ask—no right to expect interest in my isolated lot' (p. 354). In an era when individual charitable solutions to social problems were popular, Jane affirms the true ethic of a commercial society: 'As to the woman who would not take my handkerchief in exchange for the bread, why, she was right, if the offer appeared to her sinister or the exchange unprofitable' (p. 355). The mistrust Jane has learned from her encounter with sexual love is writ large in society as a whole, where it is only necessary and proper precaution to be suspicious of the Lodger who comes and goes in one's Lodging House.

Familial adoption becomes Jane's mediated state between the utter estrangement from an unnatural/impersonal society and the perilous ecstasy of belonging in a bond of sexual love with a man. It is St John Rivers, the clergyman she meets at the cultured home into which she is adopted, who becomes the means through which Jane will complete her search for self-definition.[28] He does so by harking back to an earlier stage in Jane's quest, her struggle against Mr Brocklehurst, another clergyman whose rigid ethic of anti-sensualism and renunciation enforces the self-sacrificing values of Moral Femininity.

St John, a devout Christian like Helen Burns, the Angel in the boarding school, castigates Jane, as she did, because 'human affections and sympathies have a most powerful hold on you' (p. 382); like Helen's, his message of conscious renunciation of passion and self-will leaves Jane with 'an inexpressible sadness' (p. 378).[29] But there the resemblance ends. While both Helen and St John resolutely control their own strong wills, Jane senses that the core of St John's passionate renunciation of passion is another kind of urge towards gratification: 'It seemed to me... that the eloquence to which I had been listening had sprung from a depth where lay turbid dregs of disappointment, where moved troubling impulses of insatiate yearning and disquieting aspirations' (p. 378). In his ambitious will and repressed 'impulses', in his 'restlessness' and need to fulfil special 'faculties' (p. 382), St John clearly resembles an aspect of Jane herself, pacing passionate and restless for 'a new servitude' in her chamber at Lowood.

The servitude St John chooses, however, is not the service of romantic love, but like Jane's convent-entering cousin Eliza's, a logical extension of the values of Moral Femininity into the foreign arena of the 'primitive': a life of personal renunciation spent morally influencing and restraining passionate natives as a missionary. Like Eliza Reed, St John would purposefully isolate himself from 'human affections', because he is incapable of seeing earthly love in any terms but the carnal, a 'mere fever of the flesh' (p. 400), as he calls his feelings for Miss Oliver. St John is like a 'guardian angel', as Jane says later, ever watchful, restraining and purifying, and he thus plays the same role to Jane as Jane herself, the womanly Angel of Moral Femininity, has played to Rochester.

St John's demand that Jane follow him to be 'a wife: the sole helpmeet I can influence efficiently in life, and retain absolutely till death' (p. 431), provokes another crisis. Jane is challenged to live out the values of Moral Femininity just as she begins to comprehend that the renunciation of passion necessary to this social ideal will signify 'abandon[ing] half myself' (p. 430). St John wishes to 'retain' Jane, to form her to his tastes as absolutely and selfishly as the most possessive lover. In a parody of self-definition through sexual love, Jane sees that St John would create a new selfhood for her, 'give to my changeable green eyes the sea-blue tint and solemn lustre of his own' (p. 424). But unlike Rochester's, St John's despotism is not sexually attractive. His is the self-will and urge to possession of romantic love, without its 'sympathy' and mutuality. Thus, if Rochester's masculinity was imaged in a thriving mighty tree, St John is 'a cold cumbrous column' (p. 419), as the more malignant Rev. Brocklehurst was perceived by the child Jane as a 'black pillar', oddly phallic in the way it is said to stand 'erect on the rug' with a 'grim face at the top ... like a carved mask above the shaft' (p. 63).

In the last remarkable scene between the two, St John attempts to force Jane's decision by 'claiming' her. Like Rochester, St John sees himself as a 'pastor recalling his wandering sheep' (p. 443). In a close parallel between religious and sexual ecstasy, this and other metaphors from Jane's last passionate scene with Rochester are repeated in her desire to lose herself in St John's will to absolute renunciation. Jane had responded to the temptation to submit to a purely sexual gratification by navigating the flood like 'the Indian in his canoe'; now Jane is 'tempted ... to rush down the torrent of his will into the gulf of his existence, and there lose my own' (p. 443). The referent of 'my own' could be either 'will' or 'existence', and the interchangeability of terms is telling: without will there is no Self and no life.

Jane's 'real' self emerges as she physically and metaphorically breaks from St John's grasp: 'My powers were in play and in force,' she tells us. Desire has literally willed Selfhood into existence. Jane's 'faculties', by which she seems to mean both an imaginative/intellectual capability and the life of the senses, including sexual desire, must somehow be incorporated into a definition of what is possible for women. In a sense, the imaginative production of the narrator Jane's novelistic story becomes her halfway house.

Two alternative modes of being for women have been measured and found wanting: the loss of social supports in abandoning the sexual morality of the traditional community, and the loss of selfhood in restraining or renouncing private will and sexual passions. But the balance is not perfectly equal, for sexual love has come to be seen as a necessary source of strength for a woman if she is to preserve herself in a social context that wants to obliterate her into self-sacrifice.

When Jane returns to Thornfield Hall as she resolved, she finds that both Bertha, the impediment to her marriage, and the mansion itself have been destroyed, self-devoured in a conflagration, the 'natural' end of unrestrained (i.e. 'natural') desire. Rochester is living in near-total isolation, cut off from all community, having lost his left eye and hand in a selfless effort to save others, including his mad wife, from the fire. In an ironic variation of earlier female caged-bird imagery, Jane compares him to a 'fettered wild beast or bird', a 'caged eagle' (p. 456), a 'royal eagle chained to a perch' (p. 464) in his woman-like helplessness and passivity. Certain of the strength and validity of her own impulse, Jane sets out, in her own words, to 'rehumanize' Rochester (p. 461) by liberating his will as he earlier did hers.

But Jane Eyre's own description of her love clearly abjures the conventional catchwords of Moral Femininity, its 'nobility' and 'selflessness'. Jane vigorously denies Rochester's analysis of her motive for loving him as 'delight in sacrifice' (p. 470) for its own sake; indeed, as she herself emphasizes, her new economic independence as her 'own mistress' (p. 459) gives her the ability to pursue her own will and pleasure. Though she soothes him, her own 'spirits' are said to be 'excited': with him, there is 'no harassing restraint, no repressing of glee' (p. 461). Her usefulness to him, so far from signifying the noble self-restraint of Moral Femininity, frees her to express sexual excitement because it brings their relation to terms of equality in power at last.

'Humanizing' Rochester has meant taking the infectious 'frenzy'—i.e. the tyranny and greed for possession—from his sexuality. It cannot be denied, therefore, that the nature of this sexual love is transformed.[30] Rochester is diminished but certainly not entirely emasculated or asexual in his helplessness; he seizes Jane with his 'muscular hand' as soon as he knows her, and she pointedly alludes to him as a 'green and vigorous tree' (p. 469). The masculinity which, as the housekeeper said, 'you do not thoroughly understand' is rendered coherent, however, and therefore narratable: you do thoroughly understand him by the novel's end, in short.

Rochester is tamed into a narrative with closure, but the point is that Jane has not only reformed a rake (the Byronic rather than eighteenth-century version) and won a husband, but also has achieved something for herself: the fulfillment of her own sexuality. Rochester's sexual desire and appeal are altered in quality, not quantity, in order to ensure the fulfillment of Jane's own desire. Charlotte Brontë thus makes use of the paradigm of Moral Femininity, in which the crown is refused so that it may in the end 'be yours', while deforming and reforming it to her own purposes. We can see the difference in emphasis from an author like Richardson when Brontë has Jane herself use the same argument for individual fulfillment pleaded by Rochester during their last feverish meeting before separation: 'Nor did I refuse to let him, when seated, place me on his knee. Why should I, when both he and I were happier near than apart?' (p. 464). But this scene of physical intimacy can take place only after Jane has 'led him out of the wet and wild woods into some cheerful fields' (p. 464); when 'nature', whether the physical world or man's intrinsic character, is accepted as beneficent as well as 'wild'. This is, after all, sexuality in the context of 'real' love, i.e. courtship leading to marriage.

Sexual love, then, is seen by Brontë as properly a form of life, not the 'real' and essential thing; an affirmer, not the creator, of the female self. But in their oneness after reunion, in which 'in his presence I thoroughly lived; and he lived in mine' (p. 461), sexuality has a definite, if controlled, place as part of 'thoroughly living'. The observation about St John which closes the novel is filled with admiration for a near impossibility, a remote ideal: 'His is the exaction of the apostle, who speaks but for Christ, when he says "Whosoever will come after Me, let him deny himself"' (p. 477). To deny the self and the desire for sexual love is to be like Jesus, but in the end it is not an ideal for a woman of feeling and imagination.

At an emotional moment early in their relationship, Rochester cried out to Jane, 'My little friend! I wish I were in a quiet island with only you' (p. 232). At the conclusion of *Jane Eyre*, Jane does not so much take her place *in* society, radiating influence all around as does Richardson's Pamela or Austen's Fanny in *Mansfield Park*, or find certain values in rejection of society, like Clarissa, as form an isolated strong bond in the midst of society, a 'quiet island', on the order of Dickens' Little Dorrit. Threatened by the growing power of self-interest as an ethic in a commercial society, only an individual solution seems possible to Charlotte Brontë.

Jane Eyre, in spite of its religious-mystical vocabulary, is an attempt at a private morality, in which one 'cares' for the sake of one's selfhood, as Jane cried, 'I care for myself' (p. 344).[31] Sexual passion is found to have a dignity of its own, but it seems valid only for the unconventional, socially estranged individual with special needs and 'faculties', not in the context of a society of self-indulgent Ladies or aggrandizing males. By the end of *Jane Eyre*, some of the passionate energy of the sexual imagination must be ritually sacrificed through the act of fiction to gain a greater good: that of membership in a microcosmic 'moral economy', whose peculiar conditions allow one, in Jane's words, 'to repose on what I trust' (p. 470), in 'the dream' of sexual love, a pure connection beyond social power.

Notes

1. See Chapter 3, n. 15.

2. See Winifred Gerin, *Charlotte Brontë: Evolution of a Genius* (Oxford: Clarendon Press, 1967); and Fannie Ratchford, *The Brontës' Web of Childhood* (New York: Russell and Russell, 1964).

3. Ratchford, *ibid.*, pp. 108–9. See also Thomas Wise and J.A. Symington, eds., *The Brontës: Their Lives, Friendships and Correspondence* (Philadelphia: Porcupine Press, 1980) I, p. 123.

4. Letter of 10 May 1836 to Ellen Nussey, in Wise and Symington, I, p. 319; the second quotation is on p. 141.

5. Ratchford, *Web of Childhood*, pp. 109–10. See also Gerin, *Brontë*, pp. 103–4.

6. Ratchford, *Web of Childhood*, p. 114.

7. Gerin, *Brontë*, p. 106.

8. *Ibid.*, p. 104.

9. *Ibid.*, p. 106.

10. *Ibid.*, p. 103. See also Ratchford, *Web of Childhood*, p. 109.

11. Wise and Symington, *The Brontës*, I, p. 146.

12. *Ibid.*, p. 143.

13. Letter of 7 August 1841 in *ibid.*, p. 241.

14. *Ibid.*, p. 110.

15. *Ibid.*, p. 148.

16. C. Brontë, *Five Novelettes*, ed. Winifred Gerin (London: The Folio Press, 1971), p. 311. Subsequent references will appear in the text.

17. See Dianne Sadoff, *Monsters of Affection*, for an analysis of father-figures in, Brontë's writing.

18. I disagree here with Helene Moglen, who in *Charlotte Brontë: The Self Conceived* (New York: Norton, 1978) discusses Charlotte's juvenilia in terms of her 'masochism', and her early heroines as 'submissive'. See Terry Eagleton, *Myths of Power: A Marxist Study of the Brontës* (London: Macmillan, 1975), pp. 29–30: 'The novels dramatise a society in which almost all human relations are power struggles'; the same may be said of the sexual world of the juvenilia.

19. Charlotte Brontë, *Jane Eyre* (Harmondsworth: Penguin, 1966), p. 47. Subsequent references appear in the text.

20. Jane's time at Gateshead, and particularly the episode of the imprisonment in the Red Room, has been effectively analysed by Elaine Showalter, *Literature of Their Own*, pp. 114–15, and Gilbert and Gubar, *Madwoman in the Attic*, pp. 339–41, who all emphasize the symbolic sexual imagery. Nancy Pell, 'Resistance, Rebellion and Marriage: Economics of *Jane Eyre*', *Nineteenth Century Fiction* 31 (1977): 397–420, concentrates on the aspects of rebellion in the text.

21. Helene Moglen, for example, says: 'Miss Temple and Helen Burns provide her with role models ... a new universe of values and the opportunity to excel', p. 114.

22. The doubleness of the Victorian governess's status in the household and in the culture in general has been explored by M. Jeanne Peterson, 'The Victorian Governess: Status Incongruence in Family and Society', in *Suffer and Be Still: Women in the Victorian Age*, ed. Martha Vicinus (Bloomington: Indiana University Press, 1972); and Mary Poovey, 'The Anathematized Race: The Governess and *Jane Eyre*', in Richard Feldstein and Judith Roof, eds., *Feminism and Psychoanalysis* (Ithaca, NY: Cornell University Press, 1989), among others. The role of governess was constructed by two conflicting discourses: they

were Ladies and they were maternal figures, policing the sexual desire of their charges yet potentially tempting upper-class men to desire themselves, thus providing a link between views of gender and class.

23. For an innovative reading of the meaning of 'desire' in Victorian fiction, see John Kucich, whose *Repression in Victorian Fiction* locates the repression of passion as a means to representing interiority.

24. Karen Chasé observes in *Eros and Psyche: The Representation of Personality in Charlotte Brontë, Charles Dickens and George Eliot* (New York: Methuen, 1984) that a 'saving distance' is the 'stringent requirement of romantic love' for Brontë, p. 90.

25. Janice Radway's analysis of popular romance in *Reading the Romance*, which emphasizes the heroine's quest for mother-nurturance, is based to a large extent on the work of Nancy Chodorow, *The Reproduction of Mothering: Psychoanalysis and the Sociology of Gender* (Berkeley: University of California Press, 1978); Adrienne Rich noticed Jane's mother-longing in 'Jane Eyre: Temptations of a Motherless Woman', *Ms* 2 (1973).

26. Michelle A. Masse, *In the Name of Love: Women, Masochism, and the Gothic* (Ithaca, NY: Cornell University Press, 1992), treats the Gothic as a kind of narrative therapy for women to work through the trauma created by the ideology of romance. She is most interesting on Jane Eyre's ability to resist the calls of masochism by her status as rational narrator.

27. See, for example, Gilbert and Gubar, *Madwoman in the Attic*, p. 358, who see the dream-child as the 'part of [Jane Eyre] which resists a marriage of inequality'; more recently, Mary Poovey has analysed these dreams as 'psychological gestures' which seek to 'eroticize economics' and overcome social difference, in 'The Anathematized Race', pp. 242–6.

28. Jean Kennard discusses what she calls the 'convention of the two suitors' in the British novel, of relevance particularly in *Jane Eyre*, *Villette*, *Wuthering Heights* and *Mill on the Floss* in *Victims of Convention* (Hamden, CT: Archon Press, 1978), especially pp. 10–20; see also H.M. Daleski, *The Divided Heroine: A Recurrent Pattern in Six English Novels* (New York: Holmes and Meier, 1983) for an account of how the heroine pulled between two kinds of lovers embodies the Pauline dichotomy of flesh and spirit.

29. These are the exact words used on p. 101 to describe Jane's reaction to Helen's admonition. Also compare Helen's 'you think too much of the love of human beings' (p. 101).

30. See, for example, Richard Chase, 'The Brontës: A Centennial Observance', *Kenyon Review* IX (1947), as representative of this point of view, as well as extremely influential in later Brontë criticism; Carolyn Heilbrun, in *Toward a Recognition of Androgeny* (New York: Knopf, 1973) offered an important political interpretation based on Jane's demand for autonomy and Rochester's necessary suffering in giving up his own; Maurianne Adams sees the resolution in terms of Jane's return to her psychic and spiritual 'estate' in '*Jane Eyre*: Woman's Estate', in *The Authority of Experience: Essays in Feminist Criticism*, ed. A. Diamond and Lee R. Edwards (Amherst: University of Massachusetts Press, 1977), pp. 137–59; Rachel Brownstein, *Becoming a Heroine*, sees the ending of the novel as affirming 'not the heroine's transformation but her remaining herself', p. 156; Dianne Sadoff has an unusual view in her lengthy argument in favour of interpreting the closure as a wish for castration on Brontë's apart; Shirley Foster, *Victorian Women's Fiction: Marriage, Freedom and the Individual* (London: Croom Helm, 1985) reads the ending two different ways, trying for a balanced view: Charlotte Brontë is neither 'conventional nor militantly feminist', p. 92. Some recent critics such as Pat MacPherson tend to a more flexible

analysis of Brontë's relation to the feminist agenda of the present day, in *Jane Eyre* (London and New York: Routledge, 1989).

31. My reading here is similar to that of Rosemarie Bodenheimer, *The Politics of Story in Victorian Social Fiction* (Ithaca, NY: Cornell University Press, 1988), which sees novels as social texts reflecting the irresolvable contradictions of the nineteenth-century sex/gender system.

SANDRA M. GILBERT

Jane Eyre and the Secrets of Furious Lovemaking

Wild Nights—Wild Nights!
Were I with thee
Wild Nights should be
Our luxury! ....

Rowing in Eden—
Ah, the Sea!
Might I but moor—Tonight—
In Thee!

—Emily Dickinson, #249

In the spring of 1975, I found myself, rather to my own surprise and for the first time, theorizing about a novel. To be sure, I'd produced fiction myself, including not only a few published short stories, but also a vaguely experimental novel, the typescript of which was still rather hopelessly circulating among New York editors. But in the professional life as teacher and critic on which I had fairly recently embarked, I really considered myself a "poetry person." I'd been writing poems since I was a child and had studied mostly poetry—especially Romantic and modernist verse but the theory of the genre, too—in college and graduate school. My dissertation was on the poetry of D. H. Lawrence, and after I'd expanded, "booked," and in 1973

From *Novel* 31, no. 3 (Summer 1998). © 1998 by Novel Corp.

published it, I planned an intensive study of "death as metaphor" in nineteenth and twentieth-century poetry. As a product of sixties radicalism, moreover, I'd sworn only to write, on the one hand, Meaningful Books and, on the other hand, literary journalism (Meaningful Reviews and Significant "Think-Pieces"), and never, never to start grinding out academic hack articles like what Henry James once called "an old sausage mill." But now I *was* writing what would ordinarily be defined as an article, though I thought of it as an essay ultimately destined to become part of a book. And that article was about the novel *Jane Eyre*.

What had intervened to change my supposedly well-laid plans? Lots of intangibles, no doubt, but the proximate causes, so far as I could see, were, first, my youngest child, and second, the women's movement. When she was eight or nine, my daughter Susanna had begun devouring nineteenth-century novels, especially such female-authored standards as *Little Women*, *Jane Eyre*, and *Wuthering Heights*. (My other two children read voraciously too, but had different literary tastes.) Nostalgically—for the books Susanna read were the ones I myself had loved best when I was growing up—I reread along with her, and as we discussed the books we often tried to explain to each other our feelings about episodes or settings each of us found particularly compelling. Susanna especially loved what she called "the wonderful tea" featuring seed cake and sympathy with which stately Miss Temple nourishes Jane and Helen amidst the desolation of Lowood. I was drawn over and over again to the sanctuary in the attic where, "wild and savage and free" as the young Cathy in *Wuthering Heights*, obstreperous Jo pens her blood-and-thunder Gothics, far from the pieties of superegoistic Marmee and long before meeting censorious Professor Bhaer. And, too, as I'd been when as a teenager I read *Jane Eyre* for the second time, I was delighted by the illicit glamour of the romance between Charlotte Brontë's "poor, plain, little" governess and her brooding master. When the so-called second wave of feminism crested in the seventies, I was more than ready—was indeed desperately eager—to understand the manifold ways in which not only is the personal the political (as the famous movement motto had it) but the literary is, or can be, both the personal *and* the political.

That we bring ourselves to what we read—that, as Emerson put it, our "giant" goes with us wherever we go—is hardly a new insight. In an era of cultural studies, new historicism, and gender theory, such a notion seems self-evident. Yet for those of us raised on the austere dicta of the New Criticism (Beware the extra-textual! Never look an author in the intentions! One ambiguity is worth a thousand histories!), it was profoundly exhilarating to find myself, as I had in the fall of 1974 at Indiana University, team-teaching what I sensed was a largely undiscovered literary tradition in the context of a history—the history of *women*—that I'd never myself been taught. In response to departmental needs, Susan Gubar and I were that term offering a course we called "The Madwoman in the Attic," so in my daily professional life I frequently found myself reflecting with considerable intellectual passion on books that in my personal life I'd lately been exploring far more naively. For indeed, though in some part of myself I must have understood even then that no reading is altogether innocent, the readings I'd begun doing with my nine-year-old daughter felt both innocent and sentimental, if only because they were not only outside my disciplinary "field," but they were also rereadings and rememberings, hence, recapturings, of experiences I'd had when I myself was at least a more innocent reader.

And, a more innocent movie-goer! For surely my memories of such classics as *Jane Eyre*, *Little Women*, and *Wuthering Heights* were colored not just by my almost kinetic recollections of the fat gold armchair in Queens where, romantic and dreamy, I'd curled up to read them but also by the Hollywood versions of these books I'd seen in my growing up years, versions that amounted to a series of pop-culture exegeses of the nineteenth-century novel. If Jo was always already a tomboy played by Katharine Hepburn, Heathcliff was perpetually Laurence Olivier, stalking apart in a fit of Byronic "joyless reverie," while Rochester was inevitably an even more Byronically glowering Orson Welles. That Jane and Cathy were more dubiously identified with, on the one hand, the timid prettiness of Joan Fontaine and, on the other hand, the come-hither elegance of Merle Oberon testifies to a tension between page and screen that would prove productive for feminism—for weren't Fontaine and Oberon just the kinds of socially sanctioned female figures the Brontë heroines were struggling *not* to become? I didn't quite realize this when I first began my researches into books and movies past, but it would become clear soon enough, as I gained sophistication in the new field of women's studies.

What I *did* realize was that there was a commonality among these (and other) female-authored novels—as well as, very differently, among their film redactions—that went beyond the Gothic elements about which Jo March writes and among which Jane and Cathy live. In my first critical efforts at defining this commonality, I saw it as a shared discomfort with *houses* that issued in repeated and, to me, quite charismatic acts of defiance by all the heroines. Jo flees to the attic in order to escape the moralizings of the parlor, where she is obliged to act like a "little woman." Jane suffocates in the red-room where Aunt Reed imprisons her, then grows up to pace the battlements at Thornfield, brooding on social injustice. Cathy oscillates discontentedly between the oppressive squalor of Wuthering Heights and the bourgeois constraints of Thrushcross Grange. Soon the women's movement would provide me with a vocabulary through which to define these "patriarchal strictures and structures" that fostered what Matthew Arnold, writing of Charlotte Brontë, called "hunger, rebellion and rage" in so many of the heroines (and novels and authors) my daughter and I admired. But my uncertainty about the issues at hand was probably reflected in the first title I proposed to give the class Susan and I were planning for the fall of 1974: "Upstairs/Downstairs," after the popular television series.

That I was rather taken aback when Susan quite reasonably objected to my title as not only vulgar but misleading shows, I think, how much I had to learn about the subject we were soon going to teach. Yet the replacement on which we quickly settled—"The Madwoman in the Attic"—was from my point of view, anyway, merely a more precise formulation of the argument I wanted to make about neighboring fictional spaces inhabited by turbulent spirits. Thus, when Susan and I decided that the course to which we'd given that name had been so illuminating, indeed, so intellectually transformative for both of us that we had to write a book based on what we'd been learning as well as teaching, it fell to me to write an article (out of which we'd develop a chapter) through which the madwoman of Thornfield Hall resonantly wanders, with her mystery breaking out "now in fire and now in blood, at the deadest hours of night" (239). And inevitably, of course, my article was both infused with and shaped by the extraordinary feminist excitement of the season in the mid-seventies that had inspired me to abandon my sixties snobbery about "articles," along with my bias toward poetry rather than fiction. Bliss was it in that spring to be alive, but to be embarking on a feminist analysis of one of the greatest and most influential novels in the female literary tradition was very heaven!

My analysis was a product of its historical moment, and so it obviously emphasized just those aspects of *Jane Eyre* that dramatized issues to which we in the women's movement had begun to awaken with special passion in those years: the "hunger, rebellion and rage" fostered in both Charlotte Brontë and her heroines by a coercive cultural architecture; the subversive strategies through which author and characters alike sought to undermine the structures of oppression; and the egalitarian sexual as well as social relationships toward which the novel strove. That Brontë's earliest readers had themselves been struck by these elements in her work seemed to me evident, not only from Arnold's well-known phrase, but also from other remarks made by nineteenth-century reviewers. Not surprisingly, I was particularly fond of Elizabeth Rigby's 1848 assertion that "Jane Eyre is throughout the personification of an unregenerate and undisciplined spirit" (Gilbert and Gubar 173–4), of Anne Mozley's 1853 comment that the book seemed to have been written by "an alien ... from society [who was] amenable to none of its laws" (423), and of Margaret Oliphant's 1855 observation that "the most alarming revolution of modern times has followed the invasion of *Jane Eyre*" (Oliphant 557).

There were, however, a few Victorian responses to which I paid less attention. I don't think, for instance, that I quite knew what to make of the clause that preceded Mrs. Oliphant's description of the "alarming revolution" that ensued after "the invasion of *Jane Eyre*": "Ten years ago we professed an orthodox system of novel-making. Our lovers were humble and devoted." And still less was I certain how to treat her further description of the book's distinguishing characteristic as its portrayal of "furious lovemaking"—a kind of lovemaking that she thought constituted "a wild declaration of the 'Rights of Woman' in a new aspect." To be frank, seventies feminism was uneasy in the presence of the erotic, torn between Erica Jong's notorious celebration of the "zipless fuck" and Kate Millett's not unrelated claim that "there is no remedy to sexual politics in marriage" (147). Commenting on the writings of two contemporaries she much admired, Sylvia Plath and Diane Wakoski, Adrienne Rich noted in her influential "When We Dead Awaken" that "in the work of both ... [the] charisma of Man seems to come purely from his power over [woman] and his control of the world by force, not from anything fertile or life-giving in him," and this because of "the oppressive nature of male/female relations" (35–6). Within a decade, Andrea Dworkin would declare that (hetero)sexual intercourse virtually by nature entails a tyrannical master/slave relationship between male and female, with the man "communicating to her cell by cell her own inferior status ... shoving it into her, over and over ... until she gives up and gives in—which is called *surrender* in the male lexicon" (Dworkin 100). And such a diagnosis of desire would seem to have been a logical outcome of Plath's embittered "Every woman adores a Fascist, / The boot in the face, the brute / Brute heart of a brute like you" (Plath 223).

"*Furious* lovemaking" in *Jane Eyre*? Well, the oxymoronic phrase could be at least in part understood if one factored in the ferocity with which the novel urged "the 'Rights of Woman' in a new aspect." But from the born-again perspective of seventies feminism that new aspect had more to do with Jane's declarations of independence *from* Rochester than with expressions of erotic feeling *for* him. To be sure, I saw Jane's story as ending with a vision of egalitarian marriage that was a consummation devoutly to be wished, if only a utopian one. But how were we to understand the complex, at times tyrannical or even sadistic "lovemaking" that led to a fantasy of such bliss? When in moments of what sociologists call "introspection" I analyzed my own earlier responses to the relationship between Jane and her "master," I had to admit to myself that in my teens I'd wanted more than anything for her to run off with him to the south of France, or even indeed to the moon, where at one point he had playfully promised to bring her to "a cave in one of the white valleys among the volcano-tops" (295). And why, after all, shouldn't politically astute readers wish that she and her lover had at least eloped, if not to the moon, to France? Such real-life literary heroines as George Sand and George Eliot had done as much! Why did feminist critics, of all people, have to accept the marriage-or-death imperatives built into what Nancy Miller called "the heroine's text"?

In those days, however, there seemed to be no middle ground between the banal rhetoric of the pulp novelist who declared that "*Jane Eyre* is one of the most passionate of romantic novels" because "it throbs with the sensuality of a woman's growing love for a man; there is the deep longing of the lonely heart in its every line" (Nudd 140) and Adrienne Rich's stern insistence that "we believe in the erotic and intellectual sympathy of [Jane and Rochester's] marriage because it has been prepared by [Jane's] refusal to accept it under circumstances which were mythic, romantic or sexually oppressive" (Nudd 140). Indeed, to many of us the "deep longing" of a woman's "lonely heart" for the "brute, / Brute heart of a brute like" a *man* appeared to be a radical weakness—a neurotic flaw—in the otherwise talented and politically correct Charlotte Brontë. Hadn't such feverish yearnings for the love of a (bad) Byronic hero left her vulnerable to Thackeray's rude ruminations on the "poor little woman of genius! The fiery little eager brave tremulous homely-faced creature! I can read a great deal of her life as I fancy in her book, and see that rather than have fame, rather than any other earthly good or mayhap heavenly one she wants some Tomkins or another to love and be in love with" (Lerner 199).

Rich's classic (and still brilliant) essay on *Jane Eyre* is entitled "The Temptations of a Motherless Woman," and it focuses on the moment, not long after Rochester's seductive plea to Jane that she flee with him to France, when the maternal moon rose to reveal a "white human form" gazing at the tormented governess and gloriously admonishing "'My daughter, flee temptation!'" Brontë herself had had to flee temptation (though she had done so with considerable ambivalence) when she left Brussels and her adored M. Heger. And as a feminist critic in the seventies, I knew that I too had to flee temptation. I had to rigorously repress my own desire for Jane's and Rochester's "furious lovemaking" to reach a romantic—and more specifically a sexual—climax and undertake instead a weary journey across the moors to a political position where, along with Charlotte Brontë and Adrienne Rich, I could rejoice in our heroine's new life as "a village schoolmistress, free and honest, in a breezy mountain nook in the healthy heart of England" (386).

Still, wasn't there an element of bad faith in this reading? If as Judith Fetterley so persuasively argued, we women readers had long been acculturated to identify against ourselves when we perceived the world (and in particular our own gender) from a patriarchal, male perspective, weren't we identifying against ourselves in another way when we refused to acknowledge the rebellious sexual passion driving Jane's assertion to Rochester that "if God had gifted me with some beauty and much wealth, I should have made it as hard for you to leave me, as it is now for me to leave you" (281)? Though we might quite properly scorn the clichés of those who saw the novel as primarily a romance that "throbs with sensuality" and a book that "only the lonely" could have written, oughtn't we to have conceded that something about the "furious lovemaking" in the book was what made it ragingly popular in the first place? Or at least that the "'Rights of Woman' in a new aspect" had as much to do with something about the lovemaking as did the more obviously feminist striving toward equality?

Since Brontë first published her bestseller in 1847, there have been at least forty dramas (several of them musicals), nine television versions, and ten movies based on the book, most of them focused on the complexities of its "lovemaking."[1] And when the writer herself was told of the first of these adaptations, a play staged in London just a few months after the novel's appearance, her instant reaction was to wonder "What ... would they make of Rochester?" and then to fear that what "they [would] make of Jane Eyre" would be "something very pert and very affected" (Nudd 137). Clearly she sensed the charisma of the interactions between her hero and her heroine, and she may have sensed, too, that along with Jane's feminist insubordination, her sexual aggressiveness—the indecorous demeanor with which she confesses her feelings to Rochester while rebuking what she considers his indifference ("Do you think I am an automaton?—a machine without feelings?" [281])—might be represented as "pert" or even "affected" in a setting where the personalities of the characters had been "woefully exaggerated and painfully vulgarized by the actors and actresses" (Nudd 137). What (in another context) one feminist critic rather dismissively called "romantic thralldom" may have been Brontë's problem in her frustrated relationship with Heger, but her fantasy of fulfillment liberated Jane into erotic as well as linguistic assertion.[2] For this reason, the novel in which this "poor, plain, little" governess unabashedly tells her story very likely seemed scandalous to its earliest readers not just because its narrator was uppity and "pert" but also—perhaps more importantly—because she was uppity and frankly desirous.

* * *

Let me make it quite plain that I don't in any way want to repudiate earlier claims I've made about *Jane Eyre*. Rather, I want to elaborate, complicate, and enrich them by speculating that the perpetual fascination of this novel arises at least in part from its ambivalent obsession with "furious lovemaking," that is, from its impassioned analyses of the multiple dramas of sexuality. Like so many other (yes) *romance* writers, Charlotte Brontë created a heroine who wants to learn what love is and how to find it, just as she herself did. Unlike most of her predecessors, though, Brontë was unusually explicit in placing that protagonist amid dysfunctional families, perverse partnerships, and abusive caretakers. Unlike most of her predecessors, too, she endowed her main characters—hero as well as heroine—with overwhelmingly powerful passions that aren't always rational and often can't be articulated in ordinary language. This sense of unspeakable depth or fiery interiority imbues both Rochester and Jane with a kind of mystery that has always been charismatic to readers. But it was almost certainly the startling, even shocking intensity with which Jane publicly formulates unladylike eroticism as well as indecorous social resentment that struck so many Victorians as revolutionary. Here, therefore, Mary Oliphant's association of Brontë's book with Mary Wollstonecraft's *A Vindication of the Rights of Woman* "in a new aspect" was not just accurate but perhaps unnervingly so. For even while Jane formulates a traditional feminist creed when she argues that "women feel just as men feel; they need exercise for their faculties, and a field for their efforts as much as their brothers do ... and it is narrow-minded in their more privileged fellow-creatures to say that they ought to confine themselves to making puddings and knitting stockings" (141), her narrative dramatizes a "furious" yearning not just for political equality but for equality of desire.

That *Jane Eyre* introduced audiences to the "wild declarations" and egalitarian strivings of an unprecedentedly passionate heroine certainly explains why the novel has always had a special appeal for women, who tend to identify—and want to identify—with this compelling narrator's powerful voice. For the same reason, the work has often elicited different, at times less enthusiastic, responses from male readers, with some dismissing Jane as priggish (for refusing to succumb to her desires) and others disparaging her ferocity (in articulating those desires).[3] Yet of course Brontë's novel broods as intently on the mysteries of male sexuality as it does on those of female eroticism, transcribing the fantasies of both sexes with uncanny clarity and (for its period) astonishing candor. To men as well as women, in other words, *Jane Eyre* tells a shifting almost phantasmagoric series of stories about the perils and possibilities of sexual passion. For indeed, as Elaine Showalter observed some years ago, a "strain of intense female sexual fantasy and eroticism runs through [even] the first four chapters of the novel and contributes to their extraordinary and thrilling immediacy" (Showalter 115).

To be sure, Brontë was working with plots familiar to many of her readers, who would have known, among other significant precursors, the Cinderella story Samuel Richardson told in *Pamela* and the Bluebeard tale of Anne Radcliffe's *Mysteries of Udolpho*. But the author's genius in *Jane Eyre* consisted in the fervor with which she defamiliarized such received plots by putting them together in a new way. In fact, as a number of comparatively traditional analyses have long since suggested, it's possible to summarize this novel's narrative with a *National Inquirer* headline: CINDERELLA MEETS BLUEBEARD! More particularly, a "poor, obscure, plain and little" but notably rebellious stepchild/orphan becomes the servant of a princely master, falls in love with him, and desires him intensely, even while finding herself used and abused by him. In fact, this not very acquiescent Cinderella sees her Prince Charming turn into Bluebeard, the jailor (and murderer) of wives, while she herself simultaneously toys with fantasies of seducing him and rebels against his sway by struggling to subvert his power. Brontë's book thus asks a number of crucial questions. For example, what if instead of wielding her broom Cinderella rages against (and amidst) the cinders? And what if Prince Charming is not just a charming aristocrat but a Bluebeard who elicits passionate desire in Cinderella? And at the same time, what if Bluebeard feels he has exonerating reasons for locking up his sexual past? Can, or *should*, a Cinderella like this one live happily ever after with such a Bluebeard?

To say that Jane Eyre "is" Cinderella and that Rochester "is" Bluebeard is of course to imply that they embody ideas of the feminine and the masculine in a particularly resonant way: an impoverished and orphaned dependent in a hostile household, Cinderella is, after all, condemned to a life of humiliating servitude from which she can only hope to escape through the intervention of an imperious man, and significantly, in the old tale, she finally achieves release through diminution. The ancient plot stresses not just her modesty (and the modesty of her needs), but also her physical daintiness—notably the tininess of her feet compared to those of her arrogant stepsisters, both of whom are literally as well as figuratively swollen with pride and ambition. As for Bluebeard, in the old tale he is depicted as a mysteriously predatory, dark ("blue"), even swarthy figure whose beard signifies an animal physicality frighteningly associated with his femicidal erotic past, and, more particularly, with the bloody chamber in the attic where he keeps the ghastly relics of past sexual conquests.

From one of the perspectives of the Victorian culture whose myths and anxieties Charlotte Brontë so eerily transcribed in *Jane Eyre*, then, to embody the feminine in Cinderella is to call attention to the physical, financial and emotional deprivation—in a sense, the diminution—endured by married as well as single women in a society where the "second sex" was politically, economically, legally, and erotically disempowered, a culture in which, according to the famous if apocryphal advice Victoria is said to have given one of her daughters, on her wedding night a good woman was supposed to "close her eyes and think of England!" Similarly, to embody the masculine in Bluebeard is to call attention not just to the public power but also to the often fatal private knowledge of sexuality attributed to men in a society that often claimed men were beasts—insisting that, as one of the post-Darwinian heroines of Gilbert and Sullivan's *Princess Ida* put it, "a man is only a monkey shaved." And perhaps, in fact, because such images of the feminine and the masculine were both so pervasive and so troublesome for Brontë and her contemporaries, there is a sense in which all the female characters in the novel can be seen as variations on the theme of Cinderella, with special emphasis on the problem fleshly desire poses for that heroine, while all the men can be considered variations on the theme of Bluebeard's sexuality.

In this reading, then, the styles of what we now call "the feminine" available to Jane Eyre are variously represented in the stories told about a range of other female characters. The possibilities these subplots explore extend from extreme resignation to equally extreme rebelliousness, from suicidal self-abnegation to murderous passion.[4] The angelic Helen Burns, for instance, is a kind of Cinderella who was abandoned, in effect "orphaned," when her father remarried. But her solution to what we might call the Cinderella problem deviates radically from the fairy tale ending. Opting for absolute repudiation of desire in the physical realm of the present, Helen consumes her own body (dying, indeed, of "consumption") for the sake of a spiritual afterlife. Similarly, though in a twist on the Cinderella plot that more closely evokes the traditional story, Miss Temple manages to escape the hardships of her job at Lowood through marriage to a Prince Charming. Yet her self-abnegation requires a rigidity that virtually turns her body to marble: by implication, indeed, she is repressing desire as well as rage when, in one famous scene, her mouth closes "as if it would have required a sculptor's chisel to open it" (95).

But there is yet another, even more disturbing mode of "the feminine" that Jane encounters on her desirous pilgrimage, and it is quite literally embodied in the slavish flirtatiousness that characterizes little Adèle (Rochester's ward), as well as the hardheaded ***quid pro quo*** eroticism of the child's mother Celine (Rochester's French mistress), and even the practiced charm of Blanche Ingram (his supposed fiancée). As Jane clearly sees, each of these characters is eager to overcome her sexual helplessness in a male-dominated society by selling herself to the highest bidder. Prancing and flouncing like a living doll, Adèle is plainly in training for the career of polished coquetry that in different ways shapes the destinies of Celine and Blanche, since if Celine openly prostitutes herself, Blanche is perfectly willing to sell herself on the marriage market. To Jane, who vehemently declares that "I am a free human being with an independent will" (282), all these modes of sexual slavery represent a degradation far more radical than the self-abnegation of the consumptive and the self-represSion of the governess.

But if, taken together, many of these minor characters demonstrate to Jane the problems Cinderella faces in a male world, the "eccentric murmurs" our heroine hears echoing in her mind and in the corridors of her Bluebeard's chambers—the "low, slow ha! ha!" she herself associates with Grace Poole, but which Brontë also connects with Jane's own self-defined "restlessness"—suggest that, whatever form it takes, female desire may breed dissatisfaction, resentment, and even madness. I have argued elsewhere that the intensity of this Cinderella's own anger at the inequalities she has had to face throughout her life is ultimately embodied in the source of the "eccentric murmurs" and "low slow ha! ha!" that haunt the third story of her master's mansion, for Rochester's mad wife, Bertha Mason Rochester, might be said to represent a kind of "third story" about Jane-as-Cinderella, a tale in which, instead of practicing unearthly renunciation or gaining earthly reward, the hapless heroine gives way to rage. Specifically, as I've also argued, Jane's own incendiary "hunger, rebellion and rage" are theatrically enacted by Bertha when the madwoman sets Rochester's bed on fire, when she attacks her own brother like a vampire, when she rips up Jane's bridal veil, and finally, most dramatically, when she torches the central symbol of Rochester's power, his ancestral mansion.[5]

At the same time, however, even while Bertha enacts Jane's rebellious rage at servitude, she may also be said to dramatize the sexual "hunger" that all the women in this novel either repress (in the hope of spiritual reward) or pervert (for financial gain)—sexual hunger that (as Showalter also noted in the seventies) some Victorian physicians thought could drive a woman to madness. The beautiful but dissolute daughter of a "Creole" (probably French and Spanish) mother, Bertha is most likely of European descent, although her upbringing in the hot West Indies has led to a tradition of critical speculations that she is racially mixed.[6] Whether or not this is the case, she certainly appears to be "other" than Brontë's small, pale, outwardly austere and self-controlled heroine. Rochester himself describes her as a "fine woman, in the style of Blanche Ingram: tall, dark, and majestic" (332) at the time of their first meeting, and like Blanche, she is a woman who has willingly offered herself as a sexual trophy on the marriage market.

Unlike any of the Englishwomen we encounter in *Jane Eyre*, however, Bertha is the product of a symbolic as well as literal tropic in which desire flourishes, or so Rochester claims. After marriage, he tells Jane, "her vices sprang up fast and rank ... and what giant propensities [she had]!" (333–4). Although his language is guarded (he is after all talking to a supposedly pure English virgin), Victorian readers would certainly have been able to decode what Rochester is saying when he describes such "giant propensities" as causing his wife to be "at once intemperate and unchaste," noting that her nature was "gross, impure, depraved," and adding that "her excesses had prematurely developed the germs of insanity" (334). Even if she is not, in his phrase, "a professed harlot" (335), Rochester is explaining to Jane that Bertha's virtually nymphomaniac abandonment to excesses of desire—to the heat of lust—has "sullied [his] name" and "outraged [his] honor," while driving *her* to madness (336).

Significantly, too, the "third story" of Bertha's desire-driven madness has both masculinized and, as it were, *animalized* her (a not-so-surprising phenomenon in a culture professing that "men are beasts"). Thus, when Jane, Rochester, and the other members of the interrupted wedding party finally view the madwoman in the attic at Thornfield, she is described as a sort of beastly "it": "at the farther end of the room, a figure ran backwards and forwards. What *it* was, whether beast or human being, one could not, at first sight tell: *it* grovelled, seemingly, on all fours; *it* snatched and growled like some strange wild animal: but *it* was covered with clothing, and a quantity of dark, grizzled hair, wild as a mane, hid *its* head and face" (321; emphasis added). A minute later, as Rochester strives to subdue her, she is revealed as "a big woman, in stature almost equalling her husband, and corpulent besides," who shows "virile force in the contest" (321) while the contest itself, taking place "amidst the fiercest yells and the most convulsive plunges" (322), is cast in terms that simultaneously evoke mud-wrestling and sexual intercourse.

Considered as a scene of instruction, this episode—with its overtones of what Mrs. Oliphant called "furious lovemaking"—would seem at the very least darkly monitory to a Cinderella who experiences herself as utterly enthralled by her Bluebeard. Shortly before the disrupted marriage, after all, Jane had struggled to check not only Rochester's desires but her own. In one of the novel's more explicit love scenes, the heroine's "master"—now her fiancé—sits down at the piano and sings meltingly to her, but she quails when he "rose and came towards me, and I saw his face all kindled, and his full falcon-eye flashing, and tenderness and passion in every lineament" (301). My "task," she goes on to explain, "was not an easy one; often I would rather have pleased than teased him," for "[m]y future husband was becoming to me my whole world; and more than the world.... He stood between me and every thought of religion.... I could not, in those days, see God for his creature: of whom I had made an idol" (302). Sunk in the abyss of desire, this apparently decorous and dainty Cinderella may well be in danger of yielding to the same "giant propensities" that (as we will soon learn) turned her Bluebeard's first bride into a beast monstrously swollen or bloated ("corpulent"!) with intemperate sensuality. For from one Victorian perspective, the pious position that would seem to have been official dogma, it's not just rage and rebellion, but sexual hunger that threatens to leave a woman gibbering the "eccentric murmurs" and "low slow ha! ha!" of an animal imprisoned in an attic. At the same time, however, from a less officially pious point of view, it may have been, even pre-Freud, *unsatisfied* sexual hunger that could turn a lady into a tiger (or, as *Jane Eyre* later puts it, a "clothed hyena").

I return to, and meditate on, "official" and less official positions because I want to claim, following Mrs. Oliphant's insight into the charisma of this novel's "furious lovemaking," that in her role as Jane's as well as Bertha's author and alter ego Charlotte Brontë was far more ambivalent toward female sexual hunger than has usually been conceded. Elaine Showalter's influential analysis of Bertha's sexuality, for example, depends heavily on Dr. William Acton's notion (articulated in his 1857 textbook on the "reproductive organs") that strong sexual appetite in women might lead to "moral insanity," to "nymphomania [as] a form of insanity" (Showalter 120). But more recent commentators—beginning most notably with Peter Gay—have significantly complicated our picture of Victorian attitudes toward the erotic, allowing us a more nuanced understanding of the "giant propensities" of desire that drive Jane as well as Bertha toward "furious lovemaking."[7] In his incisive *The Education of the Senses*, Gay devotes a chapter to the sexually charged diaries of Mabel Loomis Todd, a woman only a generation or two away from the Brontës who was not only the mistress of Emily Dickinson's brother Austin but also one of the (notoriously insensitive) editors of Dickinson's poetry. Noting Todd's frequently and fervently expressed delight in the erotic, he argues that her experience was exemplary rather than exceptional—a joy in the kinds of "Wild Nights—Wild Nights!" of sexual "Rowing in Eden" for which Dickinson herself also expressed a passionate, if more obliquely formulated, desire. Indeed, Gay observes, by the 1880s, the Scottish gynecologist J. Matthews Duncan was insisting that "Desire and pleasure ... may be ... *furious*, overpowering, without bringing the female into the class of maniacs" (Gay 134; emphasis added), while Elizabeth Cady Stanton (with a candor rather like Jane Eyre's) was announcing "I have come to the conclusion that the first great work to be accomplished for women is to revolutionize the dogma that sex is a crime" (Gay 119).

Thus, yes, on the one hand, Jane herself—along with Charlotte Brontë, Dr. Acton, and Mrs. Oliphant—would second Rochester's contention that in imprisoning the snatching, growling, and groveling Bertha, Thornfield guards a heart of darkness no proper virgin should confront. Stanton had not yet, after all, revolutionized "the dogma that sex is a crime." "This girl," declares Rochester to the bemused Reverend Wood (who would have married the pair but now cannot) "knew no more than you ... of the *disgusting secret*" (320; emphasis added) in the attic. But on the other hand, like Stanton herself, Jane knows all too well the intricacies of that secret. Defining herself as "an ardent expectant woman" (323), she has to battle the desire that mounts in her even as she exerts her will to renounce Rochester. Just as "the clothed hyena [that was Bertha] rose up, and stood tall on its hind-feet" (321) before falling on Rochester in what he feared would be "the sole conjugal embrace I am ever to know" (322), so Jane responds to her master's seductive pleas by considering herself "insane—quite insane, with my veins running fire, and my heart beating faster than I can count its throbs" (344). Her project throughout the novel, indeed, will be not (as most critics have thought) to eradicate but to accommodate and decriminalize this fiery and desirous animal self that marks her as a most unusual Cinderella: the mate rather than the prey of Bluebeard.

In the light of recent work on Victorian sexuality, what makes this point especially important is that after all, from Bluebeard's point of view the problem of the conjugal embrace—that is, how, when, where, and with whom desire should be satisfied—was also difficult to resolve. Was a "disgusting secret" about masculinity imprisoned in the virtually official sexual double standard of the age? If so, Rochester's story implies that it was not easy for men themselves to come to terms with the erotic "beastliness" that could easily drive a woman mad, despite the fact that an animal nature was supposedly part and parcel of their own sexual structure. Thus, just as Brontë rings changes on a number of Cinderella stories in order to investigate the life possibilities available to Jane, she offers virtuoso variations on the theme of Bluebeard to represent the life options available to Rochester. In particular, through the subplots she spins around a range of minor and major male characters, she comments on the choices made by the man Jane calls her "master" and specifically about what it would mean either to give in to beastliness or to try conquering it altogether. Unlike as the wealthy owner of Thornfield and the supposedly poor plain governess who tends his ward may seem, in fact, Brontë suggests that Jane and Rochester face comparable dilemmas. Just as Jane seems to have been forced toward either extreme resignation or equally extreme rebelliousness, Rochester appears to be confronted with the alternatives of masochistic self-abnegation or sadistic passion, even though the mystery of male sexuality inevitably plays itself out differently from that of female sexuality.

To be sure, at least the first of the beastly men Jane encounters as she moves toward adulthood is in fact the virulently anti-erotic clergyman Brocklehurst, whose wolfish countenance—"What a face he had ...! what a great nose! and what a mouth! And what large, prominent teeth!" (64)—demonstrates "the horror! The horror!" of repression, even while (or perhaps especially because) this sanctimonious villain does act like a Bluebeard when in a grotesque parody of Christianity he punishes the bodies of the girls at Lowood with the ostensible goal of saving their souls, in the process murdering a number of them en masse. But an even more obviously beastly male character appears earlier in the book. Brontë depicts young Master John Reed as virtually a paradigm of the Victorian bad boy, wallowing in gluttony, sadism, and a host of other deadly sins. Even at fourteen, the boy Jane reviles as a murderer, a slave-driver, and a Roman emperor "gorged himself habitually at table, which made him bilious, and gave him a dim and bleared eye and flabby cheeks" (41). And after he has left Gateshead, we learn that he has become so degraded that even his mother, herself Jane's wicked stepmother, dreams that she sees "him laid out with a great wound in his throat, or with a swollen and blackened face" (261).

At the same time, however, Mrs. Reed's dreams of the most depraved and vicious of *Jane Eyre*'s male characters seem curiously to evoke an opposite extreme. As Susan Gubar has cogently observed, the suicidally submissive Richard Mason, Bertha Mason Rochester's ingenuous brother, is laid out at the center of the narrative with a great wound in his throat and a "corpse-like face" (238). In a sense, then, if Brocklehurst and Master Reed demonstrate exactly how unattractive the role of Bluebeard is, the feminized Mason appears more like one of the fairytale villain's bloody victims. After having gone to visit the attic's inhabitant, Mason—who looks pale and feeble, "like a child" (240) and a sickly one at that—moans over the "trickling gore" (239) that flows from a hideous bite on his shoulder, reduced to whimpering terror of the sister who "sucked the blood: she said she'd drain my heart" (242). Can it be that some men are so horrified by the aggressiveness implicit in the equation of masculinity with bestiality that they attempt to repress even their own instincts of self-defense? Are some so distressed by their own animal potential to wound that they would rather be wounded? Or does

Mason represent a male anxiety about being drained of vital masculine fluids?[8]

St. John Rivers, one of the most complex characters in the book, suggests that Brontë may have been toying with the last of these three alternatives. Rather than become a bestial Bluebeard or one of his drained emasculated victims, Rivers renounces desire altogether, at great cost and pain to himself. Admitting that he loves Rosamond Oliver "wildly—with all the intensity ... of a first passion" (399), he scorns this rapture as "a mere fever of the flesh," incommensurate with the "convulsion of the soul" (400) that convinces him to dedicate his life to missionary work in India. Yet when he attempts to coerce Jane into a loveless marriage that would, as she herself insists, "kill" her, it becomes clear that even the most apparently renunciatory of men may incarnate the femicidal threat symbolized by Bluebeard. Describing her "ecclesiastical cousin's ... experiment kiss[es]" as "marble kisses or ice kisses," Jane defines each as "a seal affixed to my fetters" (424) and fears that as St. John implores her to marry him an "iron shroud" (429) is contracting round her, especially because as his wife she would have to "endure all the forms of love (which I doubt not he would scrupulously observe)" though "the spirit" would be "quite absent" (430).

But if the consequences of male sexual repression are represented by the "cold cumbrous column" into which the river of St. John Rivers's passion has frozen, the problems of unchecked male eroticism are most vividly dramatized in this novel by its Ur Bluebeard, Edward Rochester himself, for just as the mystery of female sexual hunger is incarnated in Bertha Mason Rochester, the mystery of male sexuality resides in her tormented husband. But while Bertha's lustful madness masculinizes her, Rochester's response to it feminizes (that is, disempowers) him in curious ways, or at least threatens to. Indeed, it is arguable that if in this Victorian psychodrama unfeminine sexual hungers may leave a woman gibbering like a corpulent animal in an attic, such inappropriate and unwomanly appetites are equally dangerous to men, reducing even a powerful "master" to a terrifying awareness that unless he asserts mastery over the female animal she may tear him apart. Does Bluebeard murder his wives because he fears that their inordinate desires might unman him? Do the possibilities of female sexuality imperil male passion? Although Rochester effectively represses whatever explicitly bloodthirsty impulses he may have, his confessions to Jane, after the wrestling scene in which his wife displays "virile force in the contest," emphasize his dread of feminization on several counts.

To begin with, as a second son who could not inherit property in a patrilineal culture where wealth passes automatically to the first-born male, Rochester believes himself to have been used by his father and brother as a tool to enable *them* to gain a fortune. Like Blanche Ingram, indeed, Rochester himself was commodified on the marriage market: his father (like Blanche's mother) arranged for him to be "provided for by a wealthy marriage" (332) that would also profit his relatives. Just as painfully, during the charade of his courtship in the West Indies, he was tricked by *Bertha's* family (who kept secret his bride's five year seniority as well as her mother's madness) because they wished to secure a man "of a good race." Like Queen Victoria's daughter, Rochester was supposed to sacrifice his youthful body to this marriage of convenience, and, if necessary, on his wedding night he was supposed to "close his eyes and think of England." At the same time, to further complicate the matter, the language with which he describes his earliest responses to Bertha reveals that her eroticism had at first "stimulated," "excited," and "besotted" him, even turning him into a "gross, grovelling, mole-eyed blockhead" (332–3). The symbolically foreign and beastly, "impure, depraved" nature he associates with his madly sexual wife remains "a part of me," he admits. That after consigning Bertha to Thornfield's attic he has indulged in erotic adventures with a series of foreign (and thus metaphorically alien and beastly) mistresses lends substance to this confession. What, Brontë seems to wonder, if female desire is simultaneously debilitating and contagious (to men), even while it is maddening (to women)?

In one sense, then, through its portrayal of "furious lovemaking" and its meditation on the dangers of desire, *Jane Eyre* investigates the problem that even a closely guarded wish for such lovemaking posed to both sexes in Victorian society. From this perspective, the secret in the attic is not simply Brontë's rebellion and rage against the subordination of women, but also her intuition that the social enforcement of such subordination was grounded in widespread fears of yearnings that, if not properly controlled, could turn into insatiable and deadly sexual hungers. Certainly, the novelist's Bluebeard is as frightened of beastly Bertha as is her Cinderella: if the madwoman at Thornfield instills in Jane a dread that she will turn into a grovelling, intemperate harlot besotted with desires of "giant propensities" for her "master," she also evokes in Rochester an anxiety that either his own virility will be found wanting in a sexual contest or that he will be turned into an instrumental "blockhead" who is himself subordinated to—destined merely to service!—a growling, snatching wild animal. In another sense, however, *Jane Eyre*'s (and Jane Eyre's) preoccupation with "furious lovemaking" represents an unusually candid rejection of Victorian moral constraints. Indeed, it is arguable that an implicit repudiation of sexual double standards was a major source of the novel's power, for ultimately Brontë allowed her heroine to acknowledge, accommodate, and articulate her own as well as her mate's "giant propensities" without becoming either a clothed hyena or a sacrificial lamb.

Throughout the novel, indeed, Jane's gaze turns voraciously, even at times voyeuristically, toward Rochester, as she catalogs his bodily parts and properties in what amounts to a series of female-authored *blazons*. His "broad and jetty eyebrows, his square forehead, made squarer by the horizontal sweep of his black hair ... his decisive nose ... his full nostrils, denoting, I thought, choler; his grim mouth, chin, and jaw" (151) and "his great dark eyes" (162) all receive her close scrutiny, along with his "unusual breadth of chest, disproportionate almost to his length of limb," the "unconscious pride in his port" (164) and his hand that is "a rounded, supple member, with smooth fingers, symmetrically turned" and "a broad ring flash[ing] on the little finger" (231). When he confides to her what from any conventional Victorian perspective are the sexual improprieties in his past, she "hear[s] him talk with relish ... never startled or troubled by one noxious allusion" (177). Indeed, she explains, "my bodily health improved; I *gathered flesh and strength*" (177; emphasis added) while his face becomes "the object I best liked to see" (178). Growing ever less ethereal, more physical, she becomes ever more easily intimate with him, so much so that after she wakes him from his burning bed in chapter fifteen, she rather boldly remains in his presence while he gets "into some dry garments" (180), then huddles in his cloak for half the night in his smoky chamber while he goes to deal with "Grace Poole." And that at first he himself explicitly associates the ostensibly pale, pure governess with the ungovernable elements of fire and water that have engulfed him in his sleep—first inflaming, then flooding—surely has erotic resonance. "'In the name of all the elves in Christendom, is that Jane Eyre?' he demand[s], 'What have you done with me, witch, sorceress?'" (180). Nor is the significance of this interaction lost on Jane, who delightedly records the "[s]trange energy ... in his voice, strange fire in his look," then repairs to her bed, trying to "resist delirium" and "warn passion" though she is too "feverish to rest" (182).

Interestingly, while many of us seventies feminists concentrated on Jane's "wild declaration of the 'Rights of Woman'" in their *old* aspect, Brontë bestows on the ice-encrusted St. John Rivers the same awareness of her sexual intensity that informed Mrs. Oliphant's identification of the "alarming revolution" fostered by the novel's commitment to a "new aspect" of the "'Rights of Woman'" that would condone a female desire for "furious lovemaking." Though Jane never confesses to St. John her fear that "as his wife ... [she would be] forced to keep the fire of my nature continually low, to compel it to burn inwardly and never utter a cry, though the imprisoned flame consumed vital after vital" (433), he nevertheless intuits her ineradicable passion. "'I know where your heart turns and to what it clings,'" he declares, adding censoriously, "'[t]he interest you cherish is lawless and unconsecrated. Long since you ought to have crushed it: now you should blush to allude to it. You think of Mr. Rochester?'" (439). But indeed, Jane doesn't merely "think" of Mr. Rochester. Rather, in a moment of mystically orgasmic passion she virtually brings him into being. As St. John prays over her, reading (tellingly) from the Book of Revelation inscribed by his namesake—a sacred text in which female sexuality, figured as the Whore of Babylon, is banished to the desert so that a new heaven and new earth can be constituted from the blood of the lamb—the "May moon shin[es] in through the uncurtained window" (442), as powerfully as the July moon had shone on the night at Thornfield when a glorious maternal figure bade Jane to "'flee [*from*] temptation.'" Now, however, the same moon silently advises the heroine to flee *to* temptation, in a moment whose erotic charge is unmistakable:

> *All the house was still; for I believe all, except St John and myself, were now retired to rest. The one candle was dying out: the room was full of moonlight. My heart beat fast and thick: I heard its throb. Suddenly it stood still to an inexpressible feeling that thrilled it through, and passed at once to my head and extremities. The feeling was not like an electric shock, but it was quite as sharp, as strange, as startling: it acted on my senses as if their utmost activity hitherto had been but torpor, from which they were now summoned, and forced to wake. They rose expectant: eye and ear waited while the flesh quivered on my bones.* (444)

In fact, what Jane discovers through this climax of impassioned epiphany is that the paradise for which she longs is not St. John's heaven of spiritual transcendence but rather an earthly paradise of physical fulfillment. And it is at this instant, of course, that she hears her "master's" voice and declares that she is "coming" to him. Her saintly—and sanctimonious—cousin had prayed "for those whom the temptations of the world and the flesh were luring from the narrow path" (442), had "claimed the boon of a brand snatched from the burning" (442–3). But although she had briefly seen "death's gates opening, show[ing] eternity beyond" and toyed with the notion that since "safety and bliss [were] there, all here might be sacrificed in a second" (444), she now, definitively, chooses "the burning" of her own desire for gratification "here" rather than "there": "My powers were in play and in force," she declares, explaining that she now willingly "fell on my knees; and prayed in *my way—a different way to St John's, but effective in its fashion*" (445; emphasis added).

That this "way" of prayer is defiantly different must have been, again, as clear to Mrs. Oliphant as it had been to St. John Rivers himself, for Brontë's heroine was quite frankly replacing a Christian theology of renunciation with a more hedonistic theology of love. Importantly, she does not know at this point that Rochester has been freed to marry her by Bertha's death. Instead, she determines to return to him with a lucid consciousness of the "temptation" he constitutes. The "spirit, I trust, is willing, but the flesh, I see, is weak" (446), comments the cousin whose "iron shroud" of morality she has experienced as a deadly—a "killing"—superego, but the ambiguity of her response to his warning hints that a deep skepticism toward received morality is driving her back toward the "furious lovemaking" she had only temporarily rejected: "'My spirit,' I answered mentally, 'is willing to do what is right; and my flesh, I hope, is strong enough to accomplish the will of Heaven, *when once that will is known to me*'" (446; emphasis added).

To be sure, those of us who know the story realize, as Jane does not, that the will of Heaven is for her to fulfil her desire within the bounds of lawful matrimony—but there is surely a sense in which that will (indistinguishable from the will of the narrative, after all) has chosen to reward her precisely for the acquiescence in temptation that underlies her challenge to the clerical custom St. John so frostily incarnates. Thus while there is no doubt justice in Adrienne Rich's claim that "we believe in the erotic and intellectual sympathy of [Jane and Rochester's] marriage because it has been prepared by [Jane's] refusal to accept it under circumstances which were mythic, romantic, or sexually oppressive," that assertion must be qualified by a recognition of the powerful Romanticism (with a capital "R") that shapes not just Jane's but Brontë's refusal of circumstances that are drearily quotidian, anti-romantic, or morally oppressive. (105). In a proud denial of St. John's insulting insistence that she is "formed for labor, not for love" (428), Jane chooses—and wins—a destiny of *love's* labors.

As seventies feminism (rightly) saw it, of course, given the inequality of the sexes in nineteenth-century England if not in Brontë's imagination, the Bluebeard in Rochester had in some sense to be diminished, even mutilated, in order for the Cinderella in Jane to become whole. And the redeemed pair had to retreat into a world outside history so as to construct a personal story of fulfilled desire. Yet if the Rochester of Ferndean appears at first to be a "sightless Samson" who is "desperate and brooding" as "some wronged and fettered wild beast" (456), Jane's yearning gaze discerns in him still the physical properties that had first aroused her desire, and once more she lingeringly catalogs them. "His form was of the same strong and stalwart contour as ever: his port was still erect, his hair was still raven black," she tells us, confessing that she longs to "drop a kiss on that brow of rock, and on those lips so sternly sealed beneath it" (456).

There can be no question, then, that what Jane calls the "pleasure in my services" both she and Rochester experience in their utopian woodland is a pleasure in physical as well as spiritual intimacy, erotic as well as intellectual communion. "[E]ver more absolutely bone of [Rochester's] bone and flesh of his flesh," Jane has reconstructed herself as literally part of her husband's body—"his right hand"—in a postlapsarian Eden where she is also the "apple of his eye" (476), and he is her audience, fit though few. In the meantime, St. John Rivers—the quintessentially anti-erotic Bluebeard of self-denial—has been banished from an England where wild nights are now not the torment but the luxury of Jane and Rochester. It is no doubt to emphasize this point that the novel ends with an otherwise puzzling focus on the unmarried missionary's anticipation of death in faraway India ("My Master ... has forewarned me. Daily He announces more distinctly, 'Surely I come quickly!' and hourly I more eagerly respond, 'Amen; even so, come, Lord Jesus!'" [477]). With the exorcism of both the id-like Bertha and the superegoistic St. John from the plot, repression can be repressed, sacrifice sacrificed. Jane has come to Rochester, and St. John is coming to God.

That Jane and Rochester have built their bower of bliss in a "nowhere" kind of place, however, has generic as well as theological significance, reminding us yet again that despite the richly observed texture of, say, the Lowood episode, *Jane Eyre* is more a romance in the mode of such diversely Gothic descendants as *The Turn of the Screw*, *Rebecca*, and *Wide Sargasso Sea* than it is a "realistic" novel in the mode of *The Mill on the Floss* or *Middlemarch*. In a sense, Rochester *has* brought "Mademoiselle" to the "cave in one of the white valleys" of the moon where he had fantasied to Adèle that he would bring his bride—or at least he has lured her to the *Minnegrotte*, the sacramental Cave of Love where Tristan and Isolde consummate their love in the medieval romance.[9] For it's arguable, indeed, that *Jane Eyre's* "furious lovemaking" participates as much in the mystical Romanticism of Wagner's nineteenth-century re-visioning of the Tristan plot as it does in the genres of fairytale, Gothic, and feminist polemic. Hard as it is to imagine a happy ending to the adulterous affair of Wagner's tortured lovers (could Isolde ever have said "Reader, I married him"?), the merging that Jane and Rochester achieve at Ferndean, as they become bone of each other's bone and flesh of each other's flesh, recalls the desire of "Tristan *und* Isolde" to eradicate the *und* and become "TristanIsolde" or, better, "nicht mehr Isolde! / nicht mehr Tristan! / Ohne Nennen, / ohne Trennen."[10]

Of course, if I return in conclusion to the comparisons of *Jane Eyre*-the-novel and *Jane Eyre*-the-movie that I attempted earlier in this revisionary enterprise, I'd certainly have to concede that none of the many screen translations of Brontë's novel are especially Wagnerian. On the contrary, the two best-known versions—the 1944 film directed by George Stevenson and the recent (1996) film directed by Franco Zeffirelli—generally speaking "read" the book as a paperback romance that "throbs with the sensuality of a woman's growing love for a man" because "there is the deep longing of the lonely heart in its every line." The proposal scene in the Zeffirelli movie is particularly banal. True, it offers erotic intensity. Indeed, the soulful kiss with which Charlotte Gainsbourg rewards the avowals of William Hurt was classed as one of the "ten best movie kisses of the year" in a 1996 film roundup. But, neither "furious" nor Romantically mystical, the lovers' embraces are determinedly healthy in a "sensitive" postmodern sort of way, as if Jane and Rochester had separately been taking lessons from Dr. Ruth. And even the madwoman in this film seems trendily sedated, less like "some strange wild animal" than a doped-up housewife in a neatly starched nightgown from a *Victoria's Secret* catalog.

Rather more appropriately, the proposal scene in the 1944 movie does feature a kind of operatic melodrama, with Jane (Joan Fontaine) cringing before a swaggeringly Byronic Rochester (Orson Welles) and the pair's confessions of love punctuated by Welles's wildly glittering eyes and counterpointed by a howling wind that suggests the onset of tempestuous desires, as well as a ferocious streak of lightning that cleaves the novel's infamous "great horse-chestnut" in one fell swoop. But there's hardly any "wild declaration of the 'Rights of Woman'" in either an old or a "new aspect" here, much less the sort of "furious lovemaking" that would have shocked Victorian audiences. What I think must have impressed me as a teenager, however, was the voyeuristic fixity of Jane's gaze at Rochester, a gaze that (as current film theory would have it) gave Joan Fontaine's otherwise incorrectly timid Jane a compelling epistemological authority.[11] Equally impressive to me, also, must have been the extraordinarily powerful moment when, as if to convey the dangers presented by the "furious lovemaking" that might constitute an "alarming revolution," Stevenson's film positions us—its viewers—in the shadows with the unseen, howling madwoman, while Welles and Fontaine stand in a lighted doorway as if confronting the forces of (sexual) darkness only tentatively contained in the attic. In a brilliant stroke, Stevenson exploits a cinematic reticence comparable to Brontë's narrative secrecy: we never see the madwoman as Jane and Rochester see her; instead, we see the lovers as *she*—raging with pain and desire—sees *them*. Finally, perhaps, that fierce gaze of darkness is what Jane and Rochester, similarly riddled by desire, assimilate into themselves. And perhaps, too, their defiant acceptance of such darkness makes the "wild nights" of their Romanticism so compelling to me that once again, to my own surprise, here I am, theorizing about the novel in which they star.

Notes

1. Indeed, if *Jane Eyre* dramatizations are added to *Wuthering Heights* dramatizations and Brontë family history dramatizations, they constitute such a major industry that one "Wilella Waldorf" once wrote a comic editorial calling for a "National Society for the Suppression of Plays about the Brontës" (Nudd 137).

2. On "romantic thralldom," see Rachel Blau Du Plessis.

3. See, for example, Bret Harte's "Miss Mix by Ch-l-tte Br-nte" (1867), in which the smugly virtuous heroine leaves her childhood home at "Minerva Cottage" forever to enter the service and the arms of "Mr. Rawjester," the polygamous master of "Blunderbore Hall."

4. In reviewing these stories, along with those implicit in Brontë's representations of her male characters, I am drawing heavily on a talk entitled "Plain Jane Goes to the Movies" that I coauthored and delivered with Susan Gubar at the University of South Carolina in the spring of 1997. For the contribution that work has made to this section of my essay, as well as the part her incisive thinking has played throughout this piece, I am (as I have so often been throughout my career) deeply indebted and very grateful to my longtime collaborator.

5. See my "Plain Jane's Progress"; and Gilbert and Gubar.

6. For "postcolonial" readings of *Jane Eyre*, see (among others) David 77–117, Donaldson, Meyer 69–95, Perera, Sharpe 26–53, Spivak, and Young.

7. In *The Education of the Senses*, Gay rejects as "derisive" and "little-challenged," the "tenacious misconceptions ... of Victorian culture as a devious and insincere world in which middle-class husbands slaked their lust [with mistresses and prostitutes] ... while their wives ... were sexually anaesthetic" (6).

8. I am particularly indebted to conversations with Susan Gubar for these observations about the textual function of Richard Mason as well as for a number of other points about the ways in which Brontë represents and interrogates received notions about male sexuality.

9. For a brief discussion of the *Minnegrotte* as an implied trope in *Jane Eyre*, see Lerner 190.

10. Act II, Scene II: "*Isolde*: No more Isolde! / *Tristan*: No more Tristan! / *Both*: No more naming, / no more parting" (Wagner 19–20). For a further comment on this phenomenon (and the darkness of the *Liebestod* it often entails), see Bataille: "Only the beloved, so it seems to the lover ... can in this world bring about what our human limitations deny, a total blending of two beings, a continuity between two discontinuous creatures .... For the lover, the beloved makes the world transparent. Through the beloved appears ... full and limitless being unconfined within the trammels of separate personalities, continuity of being, glimpsed as a deliverance through the person of the beloved" (20–1). The rhetoric of mystical communion that marks the orgasmic moments when Jane and Rochester "hear" each other's calls is best explained in this context, as is Rochester's declaration in chapter twenty-three that "My bride is here ... because my equal is here, and my likeness" (282).

11. For a different perspective on the authority (or lack of it) associated with Jane's/Joan Fontaine's gaze in the 1944 Stevenson movie, see Ellis and Kaplan: "Cinematically, Jane is placed as Rochester's observer .... We retain [her] point of view, but her gaze is fixed on Rochester as object of desire, an odd reversal of the usual situation in film where the male observes the woman as object of desire in such a way that the audience sees her that way too. Interestingly, the reversal of the look does not give Jane any more

power: Rochester comes and goes, commands and manages, orders Jane's presence as he wishes. Jane's look is of a yearning, passive kind as against the more usual controlling male look at the woman" (89). (I should confess, in response to this comment, that I have trouble understanding the distinction between a "yearning" look and a "controlling" look.)

WORKS CITED

Bataille, Georges. *Erotism: Death and Sensuality*. Trans. Mary Dalwood. San Francisco: City Lights Books, 1986.

Brontë, Charlotte. *Jane Eyre*. Harmondsworth: Penguin, 1986.

David, Deirdre. *Rule Britannia: Women, Empire, and Victorian Writing*. Ithaca: Cornell UP, 1995.

Dickinson, Emily. *The Poems of Emily Dickinson*. Ed. Thomas H. Johnson. Cambridge: Harvard UP, 1955.

Donaldson, Laura E. *Decolonizing Feminisms: Race, Gender and Empire Building*. Chapel Hill: U of North Carolina P, 1992.

Du Plessis, Rachel Blau. "Romantic Thralldom in H.D." *Signets: Reading H.D.* Ed. Susan Stanford Friedman and Rachel Blau Du Plessis. Madison: U of Wisconsin P, 1990. 406–29.

Dworkin, Andrea. *Intercourse*. New York: Free Press, 1987.

Ellis, Kate and E. Ann Kaplan."Feminism in Brontë's Novel and Its Film Versions." *The English Novel and the Movies*. Ed. Michael Klein and Gillian Parker. New York: Frederick Ungar, 1981. 93–84.

Fetterley, Judith. *The Resisting Reader: A Feminist Approach to American Fiction*. Bloomington: Indiana UP, 1978.

Gay, Peter. *The Education of the Senses*. New York: Oxford UP, 1984.

Gilbert, Sandra M. "Plain Jane's Progress." *Signs* 2.4 (Summer 1977): 779–804.

Gilbert, Sandra M. and Susan Gubar. *The Madwoman in the Attic: The Woman Writer and the Nineteenth-Century Literary Imagination*. New Haven: Yale UP, 1979.

Harte, Bret. "Miss Mix by Ch-l-tte Br-nte." *The Luck of Roaring Camp and Other Stories and Sketches*. Boston: Houghton Mifflin, 1921. 103–112.

Jong, Erica. *Fear of Flying*. New York: New American Library, 1973.

Lerner, Laurence. *Love and Marriage: Literature and its Social Context*. London: Edward Arnold, 1979.

Meyer, Susan. *Imperialism at Home: Race and Victorian Women's Fiction*. Ithaca: Cornell UP, 1996.

Miller, Nancy K. "Emphasis Added: Plots + Plausibilities in Women's Fiction." *PMLA* 96.1 (1981). 36–48.

Millett, Kate. *Sexual Politics*. New York: Avon, 1969.

Mozley, Anne. *The Christian Remembrancer* 25 (June 1853): 423–43.

Nudd, Donna Marie. "Rediscovering *Jane Eyre* through Its Adaptations." *Approaches to Teaching Jane Eyre*. Ed. Diane Long Hoeveler and Beth Lau. New York: MLA, 1993. 139–47.

Oliphant, Margaret. "Modern novels—great and small." *Blackwood's Magazine* 77 (May 1855): 544–68.

Perera, Suvendrini. *Reaches of Empire: The English Novel from Edgeworth to Dickens*. New York: Columbia UP, 1991.

Plath, Sylvia. "Daddy." *The Collected Poems of Sylvia Plath*. New York: Harper & Row, 1981. 223.

Rich, Adrienne. "When We Dead Awaken: Writing as Revision." *On Lies, Secrets, and Silence: Selected Prose, 1966–1978*. New York: W. W. Norton, 1979. 33–49.

———. "Jane Eyre: The Temptations of a Motherless Woman." *On Lies, Secrets, and Silence: Selected Prose, 1966–1978*. New York: W. W. Norton, 1979. 89–106.

Sharpe, Jenny. *Allegories of Empire: The Figure of Woman in the Colonial Text*. Minneapolis: U of Minnesota P, 1993.

Showalter, Elaine. *A Literature of Their Own: British Women Novelists from Brontë to Lessing*. Princeton: Princeton UP, 1977.

Spivak, Gayatri Chakravorty. "Three Women's Texts and a Critique of Imperialism." *Critical Inquiry* 12 (1985): 243–261.

Stoneman, Patsy. *Brontë Transformations: The Cultural Dissemination of Jane Eyre and Wuthering Heights*. Hemel Hempstead: Prentice Hall, 1996.

Wagner, Richard. *Tristan and Isolde: Opera in Three Acts*. Trans. Stewart Robb. New York/London: G. Schirmer, n.d.

Young, Robert. *Colonial Desire: Hybridity in Theory, Culture, and Race*. New York: Routledge, 1995.

MARIANNE THORMÄHLEN

The Enigma of St John Rivers

Some ten years ago, Laurence Lerner undertook to remind people with an interest in *Jane Eyre* that the madwoman in the attic is not in fact a major character in Charlotte Brontë's novel. In a piece of suave polemics, he pointed out that nobody who insists on having someone play the role of Jane Eyre's double will be short of candidates. Lerner's review of the options includes the following possibility:

> Is not Rivers a double for Jane? More insidiously and more dangerously than Helen [Burns], he represents the urge toward duty from which she needs to free herself in order to act out of pure love. Rivers quite consciously represses his sexuality, knowing his love for Rosamund Oliver, and putting it aside in order to be a missionary and demand a wife toward whom he feels no sexual attraction. Jane similarly repressed her own sexuality in placing duty before her love for Rochester.[1]

While this tongue-in-cheek suggestion does not look very promising, it should be pointed out that St John Rivers, unlike Bertha Rochester, plays a literally dominant role throughout a sizeable part of the novel. It is surprising that generations of readers have found St John so 'unmemorable', to quote a

From *The Brontës and Religion.* © 1999 by Marianne Thormählen recent writer on Charlotte Brontë.[2] Adapters of the novel for film or television have obviously not thought him particularly interesting either, and yet he is arguably the most important person in the story after Jane and Rochester: he saves Jane's life, provides her with the affectionate blood relatives she always longed for, nearly persuades her to marry him (in consequence of which action she would probably have lost her life for real relatively soon)—and anticipation of his demise concludes the novel.

St John's functions as a counterpart to Brocklehurst and Rochester were observed from the first. For instance, Mary Taylor pronounced 'I do not believe in Mr Rivers. There are no *good* men of the Brocklehurst species' and told Charlotte she had met a nincompoop who felt that Jane should have married St John instead of Rochester.[3] But although commentators on *Jane Eyre* traditionally observe that both St John and Brocklehurst are forbidding, column-like Calvinists and both St John and Rochester attempt to break down Jane Eyre's integrity, late twentieth-century critics have usually found Bertha more absorbing than the man who is her complete antithesis. St John Rivers is a fastidious intellectual resolved to stifle every expression of physical appetite, uncontrolled emotion and animal spirits. The black-haired, vile-looking monster incarcerated in the top storey at Thornfield, a personification of unreason and animality, is at one extreme in the novel's thoroughgoing tension between reason and feeling; at the other we find the handsome, fair-haired parson who rules his household with quiet sternness and is a self-avowed champion of reason. It is odd that this pair of opposites does not seem to have been perceived as such.[4] The hero of the novel is tricked into marrying the former, and but for Divine intervention the heroine would have committed herself for life to the latter. In both cases, physical and spiritual death loomed as the consequences of these acts of folly.

Insofar as Brontë scholars have paid more than passing attention to St John, they have found him hard to come to grips with, and no wonder: the book seems to transmit a profoundly contradictory picture. The saviour at the door of Moor House becomes the merciless oppressor who comes close to 'killing' (III.ix.417) the girl, not yet twenty years old, who has just saved his sisters from a life of drudgery. If that transformation can be made to appear consistent and acceptable—and St John would always rather exert himself on behalf of a stranger than show consideration for a close relative—the ending of the novel poses a seemingly insoluble problem. Does that ending announce the imminent apotheosis of the man whose human and pastoral shortcomings have been so acutely portrayed in the hundred or so preceding pages? If so, why have readers not been told how he qualified himself for it—or have they?

Two of the finest analyses of St John Rivers in *Jane Eyre* criticism supply a basis for a consideration of these crucial questions. Judith Williams has demonstrated that St John, though according to Jane Eyre an exponent of 'evangelical charity' (III.iii.352), is in no sense truly charitable and that 'the greatest of these' is conspicuously lacking among the qualities he evinces as the end draws near.[5] More incisively than any preceding critic, Williams makes the essential point that St John's glorious ending is merely anticipated, and anticipated by himself rather than by Jane: it is not presented as an achieved consummation. Elisabeth Jay, equally aware of St John's imperfections, observes that no conversion has paved the way for his translation to the saints in Heaven and that other, less gifted contemporaries of Charlotte Brontë's would not have neglected to describe a change of heart in such a case.[6]

Less searching discussions of St John's functions have resolved the difficulty by maintaining that he is in fact an admirable character who deserves his crown, even if Charlotte Brontë 'cannot sympathize with him'[7] and the path he has chosen in life, a path which excludes earthly love. Several passages in the novel can be quoted in support of this view. St John is repeatedly said, by such fearless truth-tellers as Jane Eyre and Diana Rivers, to be a 'good' man. Why should the reader trust them less than St John himself, who maintains that he is a 'cold' and 'hard' one? (After all, we know that his self-characterisations cannot be taken at face value; for example, his claim to be 'humble' (III.viii.407–8) is patently ludicrous.) Should we as readers allow ourselves to be reassured by that 'goodness' and by Jane's evocation of Bunyan's Mr Greatheart to the point where we accept his confident expectation of a place among those who 'stand without fault before the throne of God' (III.xii.457)? The quotation from Revelation 14:5 (noted by several scholars) attributes the qualities of virginity and guilelessness to the 'hundred and forty and four thousand' who are 'redeemed from the earth'. It is easy to imagine that St John was never 'defiled with women' (Rev. 14:4),[8] and deceit is not one of his vices. But 'without fault'? That description cannot possibly be made to fit him. After a brief consideration of the implications of his name, this chapter presents St John's deficiencies, especially as a man of God, as well as the arguments that may be adduced in his defence. A review of relevant historical circumstances follows, with special emphasis on missionaries and their work in the early nineteenth century. Finally, the discussion turns to the question asked by so many Brontë students: why does *Jane Eyre* end with the impending death of this enigmatic man, rather than with the 'perfect concord' of the much more appealing Rochesters?

'St John Rivers'

Brontë critics have drawn attention to the cleansing, elemental force of the surname borne by Jane Eyre's 'good' cousins (as contrasted with the contemptible 'Reeds'), pointed out that St John's sisters are named after the greatest female deities of the classical world and Christianity respectively and reminded their readers of St John the Baptist,[9] St John the Evangelist and St John the Divine of the Revelation. All this is surely pertinent. Charlotte Brontë obviously took great care over the naming of people in her works and invested some of their names with characterising properties, though she was more subtle in this respect than many of her contemporaries. In respect of St John, however, the recapitulated relevancies do not constitute an exhaustive list.

The writer of the Gospel according to St John has traditionally been regarded as the same John who wrote the Apocalypse and the Epistles of St John, and as the John of the twelve disciples. In giving his name to Jane's 'good' as well as her 'bad' male cousin,[10] I think Charlotte Brontë was alluding to a quality associated with that apostle which both Jane's kinsmen lack. St John was the disciple whom Jesus loved and to whose filial care he recommended his mother. Neither John Reed nor St John Rivers is ever capable of genuine love for a fellow human being. The former indirectly kills his mother, and not even the latter shines as a son: his father's death is seen as the removal of an impediment to his plans for himself, and the idea that he could liberate his orphaned sisters from near-slavery by abandoning those plans and going in for an ordinary career in the Church never appears to occur to him.

The central texts on God's love in the New Testament are found in the first epistle of St John, which also urges human beings to love one another.[11] The prefix '(My) little children' which often heads the apostle's exhortations to his flock adds a note of familial tenderness to his injunctions: the members of the epistle-writer's audience are assured of their filial position in relation to God as well as to his apostle. Though not devoid of 'natural affection', as he states, St John Rivers regards it as part of the feelings that must be made subservient to that 'vocation' which is 'dearer than the blood in [his] veins' (III.vi.378). It is hard not to regard his 'kirstened name' (as Hannah calls it) as an implicit reminder of the quality which is so obviously lacking in him, a circumstance which lends a disturbing dimension to the fact that the sole stressed syllable in that name is pronounced 'sin'.

The Case Against St John

For a Christian, and especially a clergyman, to be deficient in sympathy for and love of his fellow creatures is a grievous fault. In the case of St John it is exacerbated by his untroubled acceptance of the fact: he admits that his sisters' warm compassion is a feeling he does not share, charitable action being all he is capable of (III.iii.353), and he takes pride in being—as he thinks—guided by reason, not by feeling (III.vi.379). Another worrying lacuna is the absence of any patent love for God and his Son. St John may be like Thomas à Kempis in urging others not to attach too much importance to human affections, but he has none of that compensatory devotion to Jesus as 'lover' which suffuses *The Imitation of Christ*—at least not at the time when he dispenses such advice. A 'follower of the sect of Jesus', he has adopted the doctrines of his Master and is pleased to contemplate the way in which religion has developed his much-vaunted faculties (III.vi.380); but nothing he says to Jane at Morton suggests that he has given his own heart to God, though he recognises that Jane's offer of hers is a crucial event (III.viii.412).

Indeed, few parsons could be less suitable for preaching Evangelical Christianity, 'the religion of the heart', than the apparently heartless St John Rivers. He acknowledges (and Jane sees that he is right) that his love for Rosamund Oliver is a physical passion only, though no less strong for that. It is not the least intriguing aspect of this extraordinary man that his sensual urges are so powerful and his aesthetic sensibilities so keen (the wording of his very first appraisal of Jane reveals him as a would-be connoisseur of beauty: III.iii.344).

The conversation during which St John tells Jane how his decision to be a missionary was formed is significant. Having spoken of his former desire for 'the active life of the world', for secular fame, glory and power, he continues:

> 'After a season of darkness and struggling, light broke and relief fell: my cramped existence all at once spread out to a plain without bounds—my powers heard a call from heaven to rise, gather full strength, spread their wings and mount beyond ken. God had an errand for me; to bear which afar, to deliver it well, skill and strength, courage and eloquence, the best qualifications of soldier, statesman and orator, were all needed: for these all centre in the good missionary.' (III.v.366)

It was thus St John's *powers* that received a summons, not his *heart*. His adoption of a missionary's calling was the outcome of a yearning to employ his faculties in a way that would satisfy his avid ambition; it was not the result of an ardent wish to transform the lives of other troubled and restless souls by bringing them the comfort of the Gospel. When he attempts to harness Jane's similarly unusual talents to his project, he tries to tempt her with 'a place in the ranks of [God's] chosen', an offer he is not authorised to make (III.viii.406). Jane is a better Evangelical-Protestant theologian than her learned cousin: she asks him whether the few who might be fit for such work should not be receiving the call to it in 'their own hearts'. When St John replies by demanding to know what *her* heart says, she answers, and repeats, 'My heart is mute'. St John's immediate rejoinder is a masterful 'Then I must speak for it'.

No Christian can govern another's heart, however, and in claiming control of Jane's, St John commits Rochester's arch-sin of '[arrogating] a power with which the divine and perfect alone can be safely entrusted' (I.xiv.139). St John appears to believe that the master's infallibility is somehow communicated to the servant. This is arrogance in a peculiarly literal sense, and St John cannot be absolved from the sin of spiritual pride.

The heinous nature of that sin in any Christian, but especially in a clergyman, is constantly hammered home by Anglican writers, from Henry Venn to F. D. Maurice.[12] The latter emphasised that spiritual pride 'is the essential nature of the Devil'. It is a terrible sentence to set up beside St John Rivers, but the imputation of infernal characteristics to him is no novelty. Judith Williams, for instance, claims that he is in some ways 'the demonic version of Helen Burns' and even calls him 'essentially Satanic'.[13] Williams has also observed that St John is attended by 'imagery of light', but she has not linked this circumstance to what would have been a natural extension of her argument.

St John Rivers may believe himself a man of reason, but he is in fact ruled by passionate ambition. For that ambition, only the greatest conceivable prize is exalted enough. The human format, earthly existence, will never content it; only a heavenly triumph will do. Insensible to the warnings of theological writers—including Simeon and Wilberforce—never to forget that Jesus Christ alone is the rightful wearer of the heavenly crown and that no man should let his thoughts roam beyond Christ and his atoning sacrifice, St John dreams of the highest honours; in this as in other respects, he differs from the famous American missionary David Brainerd, who had said 'I do not go to heaven to be advanced; but to give honour to God ... It is no matter where I shall be stationed in heaven'.[14] St John's Calvinist bias is apparent in his conception of the chosen few, and he never doubts that he is one of them (III.ix.422). The combination of his burning ambition with his ruthless bullying,[15] the images of light that surround him and his striking physical beauty recall the leader of the angels who fell by the sin of ambition: is St John, the man with the name of an angel and the face of a pagan god, some kind of Lucifer?[16]

While the resemblances seem too apparent to overlook, the answer must surely be 'no': St John is not a rebel; restless as he is, he is not driven by envy of or dissatisfaction with the stations of others, and he has no desire to overthrow God's rule and assume power in Heaven. All he wants is a front-rank position there. It is a sufficiently reprehensible wish, as any fellow Church of England clergyman could have told him; but it does not amount to challenging God.

The conclusion that the Apollonian divine with the saintly name is at least no Satan seems small comfort to anyone who prefers to view the ending of *Jane Eyre* as a case of religious virtue rewarded. There is a more positive case to be made for St John, too; but before its merits can be looked into, the 'con' side must be supplemented by a look at St John Rivers the preacher. This is Jane's attempt at describing the effect that his sermon in his Morton church has on her:

> The heart was thrilled, the mind astonished, by the power of the preacher: neither were softened. Throughout there was a strange bitterness; an absence of consolatory gentleness: stern allusions to Calvinistic doctrines—election, predestination, reprobation—were frequent; and each reference to these points sounded like a sentence pronounced for doom. When he had done, instead of feeling better, calmer, more enlightened by his discourse, I experienced an inexpressible sadness; for it seemed to me ... that the eloquence to which I had been listening had sprung from a depth where lay turbid dregs of disappointment—where moved troubling impulses of insatiate yearnings and disquieting aspirations. I was sure St. John Rivers—pure-lived, conscientious, zealous as he was—had not yet found that peace of God which passeth all understanding: he had no more found it, I thought, than had I; with my concealed and racking regrets for my broken idol and lost elysium[.] (III.iv.356–7)

Though St John is a model clergyman when it comes to visiting the sick and providing education for the young—those two essential parochial duties—he does little to comfort his parishioners' souls. The occurrence in his sermon of those Calvinist doctrines which were so abhorred by all the Brontës is telling in itself, made worse by the absence of 'consolatory gentleness' and the presence, at a deeper level, of the preacher's own inner disquiet. Contemporaneous manuals for clergymen insisted on the necessity of offering enlightenment and comfort in a spirit of love and tenderness, warning clerics against allowing personal concerns to mingle with their addresses from the pulpit.[17] In this vital part of his ministry St

John cannot but fail: he does not love his flock, and his own mind is far from serene.[18]

It may seem harsh to criticise a clergyman for the absence and presence of feelings of which he cannot be expected to be master. After all, love does not come to order, and a restless temperament cannot be wished away. But the policy of blanket repression of every human feeling save ambition which St John adopts does him as little credit from a religious point of view as from a romantic—secular one, and the same applies to the reason for his discontent: the conviction that his unique talents are wasted in a rural parish (III.iv.361). Any good-enough colleague would have told him to pray for the qualities he lacks, notably empathy for his fellow men and patience to serve them and God faithfully in a position where he would be able to support his sisters (as a well-educated brother was still expected to do in the early nineteenth century). When Jane grants him goodness and greatness, she adds, significantly, 'but he forgets, pitilessly, the feelings and claims of little people, in pursuing his own large views' (III.ix.421). That accusation comes close to charging St John with breaking Christ's most important commandment respecting the dealings of human beings with one another: 'Inasmuch as ye have done it unto one of the least of these my brethren, ye have done it unto me.' The implications of his neglect of 'little people' are sombre indeed; those who fail to succour 'one of the least of these ... shall go away into everlasting punishment' (Matthew 25:40, 45–6). By that token, his case is a desperate one—but there are other factors which may be held to redress the balance.

In Defence of St John

St John Rivers the missionary may not be inspired by love of his Indian converts, his 'race'; but his work on their behalf is carried out in a spirit of fidelity and devotion (III.xii.457). Jane's description of what St John accomplishes in India confirms his assessment of his abilities:

> He entered on the path he had marked for himself; he pursues it still. A more resolute, indefatigable pioneer never wrought amidst rocks and dangers. Firm, faithful, and devoted; full of energy, and zeal, and truth, he labours for his race: he clears their painful way to improvement; he hews down like a giant the prejudices of creed and caste that encumber it. He may be stern; he may be exacting; he may be ambitious yet: but his is the sternness of the warrior Greatheart ... His is the exaction of the apostle, who speaks but for Christ, when he says—'Whosoever

> will come after me, let him deny himself, and take up his cross and follow me.' (III.xii.457)

The comparison of St John to Mr Greatheart, Christiana's wise and valiant guide in the second part of *The Pilgrim's Progress*, and to one of the Evangelists makes the missionary appear in a different light from the discontented rural parson. However impure his motives may have been, his choice was doubtless the right one. An inability to evince tender feelings towards individuals matters less when one is faced with colossal obstacles to the welfare of multitudes. Here St John's forcefulness is put to good use, and his on-the-brink frustration back at Morton seems understandable. Jane's allusion to Mark 8:34 strikes a note of promise; Christ's exhortation to those that would follow him is itself followed by the assertion that whosoever shall lose his life for Christ's sake shall save it and by the question of what it shall profit a man if he shall gain the whole world and lose his soul (Mark 8:35–6). Applied to St John the missionary, who surrendered every worldly advantage and took the burden of crushing labour on himself, these Biblical passages do much to offset the grim implications of the fact that key New Testament texts on love and concern for 'little people' could not be applied to him.

In the context of the Christian individual's right and duty to turn his/her life to the best possible use, which were so keenly felt by the Victorians, St John's decision to dedicate himself to missionary work fulfils every conceivable demand. He may have chosen God's work on the theologically unsound understanding that a heavenly crown awaits him at the end; but choose it he did, and it is still God's work. The thought of what could have happened if he had joined his abilities to the forces of darkness is terrifying; Heathcliff's local evildoing would have seemed trivial in comparison to the large-scale disasters which gifts like St John's could have brought about. He is the only person who comes close to assuming control of Jane Eyre's fiercely independent spirit, a circumstance which is as good a testimony as any to his charismatic and persuasive powers, and his intellect is as sharp and vigorous as his zeal is inexorable. As Jane herself says, he is 'of the material from which nature hews her heroes—*Christian and Pagan*—her lawgivers, her statesmen, her conquerors: a steadfast bulwark for great interests to rest upon' (III.viii.397, italics added). Shortly before she draws this conclusion, understandably annoyed with St John for pointedly rejecting 'domestic endearments and household joys', '[t]he best things the world has' in Jane's view (III.viii.395), she called him 'pagan' to his face ('You would describe yourself as a mere pagan philosopher'). St John contradicts that imputation in cool, reasoned terms:

> 'No. There is this difference between me and deistic philosophers: I believe; and I believe the Gospel. You missed your epithet. I am not a pagan, but a Christian philosopher—a follower of the sect of Jesus. As his disciple, I adopt his pure, his merciful, his benignant doctrines. I advocate them: I am sworn to spread them. Won in youth to religion, she has cultivated my original qualities thus:—From the minute germ, natural affection, she has developed the overshadowing tree, philanthropy. From the wild, stringy root of human uprightness, she has reared a due sense of the Divine justice. Of the ambition to win power and renown for my wretched self, she has formed the ambition to spread my Master's kingdom; to achieve victories for the standard of the cross. So much has religion done for me; turning the original materials to the best account: pruning and training nature. But she could not eradicate nature: nor will it be eradicated "till this mortal shall put on immortality."' (III.vi.380)

This passage was alluded to above, as evidence that the call which St John experienced was not heart-felt and hence suspect in the eyes of an Evangelical Anglican. It can, however, be quoted in his defence, too. To start with, he asserts—and there is no reason to doubt his sincerity at this point—his belief in the Gospel. This is the first condition that must be fulfilled by those who would be saved; hardly any nineteenth-century writer on the problematics of salvation omits to emphasise that he/she who believes in Jesus Christ will have eternal life. And while St John is anything but a philanthropist—a lover of mankind—in the literal sense, he devotes all he has and is to the practical improvement of humanity under the auspices of Christianity, and he undertakes the commitment freely. It fits in perfectly with the nineteenth-century improvement ethos: St John's chosen path towards self-improvement entails clearing '[the] painful way to improvement' (III.xii.457) of others, people suffering from material distress and social oppression. As his sister Diana, the only person in his vicinity who is as strong-minded as he, admits in tears, his decision is 'right, noble, Christian' (III.iv.361).

Arguably, what goes for Jane should go for her cousin, too: he is surely as entitled as she to strive for improvement as best he can, unhampered by social convention (such as a gentleman's obligation to support his sisters). As Jerome Beaty points out in an excellent analysis which places God in the centre of *Jane Eyre*'s authorial world, 'St. John's way [is not] wrong or antilife, as many modern readers would have it'; it is just 'not Jane's way'.[19]

Missions and Missionaries

Philanthropy is usually defined in terms of concrete secular endeavour, and Jane's account of St John's efforts stresses their practical character. It is natural to doubt that St John does as well when it comes to winning souls for Christ, that primary duty of the Evangelical clergyman constantly reiterated in clerical manuals. He certainly has none of the warm, joyous spirituality that made the Moravians such successful missionaries.[20] In the early nineteenth century, however, British people with an interest in and knowledge of mission work in India maintained that the best approach to Christianising the Indians consisted in leading by example. There was less point in 'the public preaching of the Christian tenets' than in 'the ... gradual developement [*sic*] of the error of existing systems, by the promulgation of Christian morality ..., especially if done in schools'.[21] This kind of work suits St John perfectly: his moral superiority and consistency are beyond question, and his prodigious efforts must command universal respect.

It has been suggested that Charlotte Brontë chose India as St John's destination so as to balance an 'Eastern' colonial prospect against the 'Western' sphere which produced Bertha Mason and Uncle Eyre's wealth.[22] There were far less sophisticated reasons for that choice, though. Nineteenth-century Evangelicals took a particular interest in Indian missions,[23] and there is a related reason, too: Henry Martyn, often mentioned as a model for St John (though no comparative analysis has, as far as I am aware, been undertaken before), was a missionary to India, and Martyn was a man with a particular standing in the Brontë family.

Though four years younger than Patrick Brontë, Henry Martyn was a Fellow at St John's College when Patrick Brontë studied in Cambridge. He became something of a sponsor for the Irish sizar, persuading wealthy Evangelicals with Wesleyan affiliations to support Brontë financially.[24] Martyn was from Cornwall, like the Maria Branwell who was to become Mrs Patrick Brontë. A brilliant student (Senior Wrangler in 1801), Martyn was marked out for a distinguished academic career when he came under the influence of Christianity, partly as personified by Charles Simeon. The year of Patrick Brontë's arrival in Cambridge, 1802, was also the year of Martyn's spiritual crisis. As a scientist and mathematician, he had not taken a great deal of interest in religion before; but intense study of the Bible—the book of Isaiah especially, also a favourite of Charlotte Brontë's—brought about a conversion. A few years after becoming Simeon's curate, Martyn set sail for India as Chaplain to the East India Company. It was a natural choice for a disciple of Simeon's, the latter being particularly interested in missionary work on the Subcontinent. A superb linguist who 'read grammars as other men read novels',[25] Martyn is still known for his translations, among them Hindustani/Urdu versions of the New Testament and the Book of Common Prayer. Worn out by hard work in an unfavourable climate, Henry Martyn died of a fever in Persia, on his way home, in 1812.

The parallels to St John Rivers are clear and numerous. As some scholars have noted, St John bears the name of Martyn's, and Patrick Brontë's, Cambridge college.[26] As a Cambridge man with Calvinist sympathies and a belief in missionary work (not uncontroversial at the time), educated for the ministry just after 1800, St John must be envisaged as belonging to the Simeonite camp. Charlotte Brontë will have been aware of the circumstances pertaining to Martyn's life that were recapitulated above, and of others too, including the opposition of family and friends to Martyn's career choice and the fact that that choice cost him the love of his life (his fiancée refused to accompany him).[27] Charlotte is also likely to have known that the strongest influence on Martyn in 1802, after the Bible and besides Simeon, was the journal of the American missionary David Brainerd, already referred to above. Brainerd, whose missionary work was among the American Indians, had died of tuberculosis in 1747, not yet thirty years old (Martyn himself lived to be thirty-one; St John Rivers dies aged about forty). Like Martyn, Brainerd was a learned man with a frail constitution, and the two men shared 'a love for the souls of men that nothing could quench'.[28]

The latter circumstance provides a starting-point for a review of differences between Henry Martyn and St John Rivers. The most significant of them is found in Martyn's Evangelical devoutness and his awareness of the dangers of pride and ambition; like St John, Martyn was an extremely able man and could not help knowing it. John Sargent's popular *Memoir* of Martyn, which may well have been known to the Brontës, praises the 'childlike simplicity' of his faith, the 'love [that] was fervently exercised towards God and Man, at all times' and Martyn's most remarkable trait, his 'humility'.[29] In all these respects, Martyn was clearly superior to the tyrant at Morton.

A diffident and rather ineffectual preacher while still at home, Henry Martyn wrote a number of admired sermons during his years overseas and friends saw to it that they were published after his death. These sermons often discourse on Biblical passages which also feature in the Brontë novels. Several of these passages are classical set texts (for instance, 'Rejoice, O young man', etc. from Ecclesiastes 11:9, and I John 4:10 on God's love, important Biblical loci in Anne Brontë's two books). Others are less frequently referred to in devotional literature, among them Rom. 8:35–7 which Lucy Snowe remembers in her determination to accept that for her, the Kingdom of God cannot be won except 'through much tribulation'.[30] Martyn also distinguishes between a fondness for 'those ... who think with us', in which there is no merit whatever, and Christian love; Helen Burns, we remember, tries to instruct Jane Eyre along similar lines.[31] Such resemblances are probably fortuitous, though; these were issues of constant interest and many other contemporary writers dealt with them as well.

But Martyn's warnings to zealous people not to deceive themselves about the mainspring of their actions strike a note which sounds uncomfortably relevant to St John Rivers:

> [The deceitful heart] tells us ... that we have Zeal; which zeal is often no other than bitterness and ill temper. We are violent against the misconduct of others; not because they have sinned against God, but because they trouble and interfere with ourselves. We are zealous for Christ, and the spread of his Gospel; but cannot rejoice if the work be not done by ourselves and friends: nay, are often so wicked as to wish the work may not be done at all, if it cannot be done in our own way. Now if our zeal is of this nature, it is evidently pure worldliness.[32]

It is tempting to speculate that the extent to which Henry Martyn and St John Rivers differ is an authorial comment in itself; but it must not be forgotten that only a man who knew, and had surmounted, the perils of religious vanity could have written these lines. We do not know for certain that the arrogance which St John Rivers articulated at Morton would not have abated after some years of extreme exertion in India, although it is hard to believe that St John could ever have attained the humility of Brainerd and Martyn.

One thing that Charlotte Brontë's missionary does have in common with these two predecessors is the phrase with which he announces his readiness to meet Christ. As many commentators have observed, the last lines in *Jane Eyre* refer to the last-but-one verse of the Bible: 'He which testifieth these things saith, Surely I come quickly. Amen. Even so, come, Lord Jesus' (Rev. 22:20).

In a biography of Brainerd published in 1834, a book which refers to Henry Martyn's connexion with the American missionary as a well-known fact, the author describes how Brainerd repeatedly uttered the words 'Come, Lord Jesus, come quickly' when he felt death approaching.[33] On board his ship to India, pondering what lay ahead of him, Martyn wrote the following entry in his own diary:

> Sept. 15—Sunday. 'He that testifieth these things saith, behold—I come quickly—Amen—even so—come quickly, Lord Jesus!' Happy John! though shut out from society and the ordinances of grace: happy wast thou in thy solitude, when by it thou wast induced thus gladly to welcome the Lord's words, and repeat them with a prayer.[34]

Welcoming the end of earthly life in the words of St John the Divine was by no means unusual in the early nineteenth century, though, so this parallel between the two missionaries and St John in *Jane Eyre* may be coincidental.[35] Still, Rev. 22:20 was clearly a central text for Martyn; his sermon on Rev. 22:17 quotes a number of Scriptural passages, including 'Surely I come quickly!', to end with the italicised, '*Amen! even so, come Lord Jesus!*'[36]

THE CONCLUSION OF *JANE EYRE*: BALANCING THE BOOK

The bride in the Apocalypse joins the Spirit in saying 'Come' (Rev. 22:17), and the verb is often used in highly charged situations in *Jane Eyre*, as critics have noted. Sally Shuttleworth's contention that Jane's exclamation 'I am coming: wait for me!' in the mysterious-summons episode constitutes Charlotte Brontë's 'daring' and 'overtly ... sexual' rewriting of Rev. 22:20 may be mentioned as a matter of curiosity;[37] with rather more reason, Janet Gezari reminds us of Jane's and Rochester's respective exclamations, 'I wish he would come! I wish he would come!' and 'Oh! come, Jane, come!' before and after the revelation of the attempted bigamy (II.x.280 and III.i.322).[38] I think it is significant that *Jane Eyre* ends in a plea so resonant with love, both in its Biblical context and in that of the novel itself.

The shift from the happy domesticity of the Rochesters to the dying missionary has puzzled readers for generations. It has been viewed as a diversion from the main focus of the story, 'a coda ... added to salve the writer's conscience'[39] by seeming to allow that St John's noble martyrdom outshines the idyll at Ferndean.[40] Technical reasons have been considered, too. In her analysis of the ending of *Jane Eyre*, Carolyn Williams points out that '[t]he one thing an autobiographical narrator cannot do ... is to narrate her own death' and that Jane herself must, as it were, be left *in medias res* on earth.[41] This would perhaps have made for a somewhat lame winding-up. The neatest ending to the story of a life is, undeniably, a death; and as Empson said, death is 'the trigger of the literary man's biggest gun'. A splendid death makes a satisfactory conclusion, and here was one for the taking. After all, St John's demise was always his goal; he may be regarded as an embodiment of a Pauline verse with peculiarly Haworthian connotations:

'For me to live is Christ, and to die is gain' (Phil. 1:21).[42] However, such considerations, though pertinent to some degree, fall far short of solving the puzzle, and other considerations must be brought to bear on it as well.

Both Jane and St John have, as Beaty says, chosen the paths in life that were right for them.[43] Both have sought and received Divine guidance and been faithful to the claims of their God-created selves. The union of Jane and Rochester was made possible by the latter's voluntary subjugation to Divine authority, and their wedded bliss is, as Barry Qualls has pointed out, described in 'God-validated' words.[44] Theirs is not the lesser fulfilment; it is the fulfilment of God's will through the sacrament of marriage. The Rochesters' human love is in perfect harmony with Divine love and hence as close to perfection as any earthly thing can be. The interrelationship of human and Divine love is a central factor in the Brontë fiction as a whole and never more so than in *Jane Eyre*.[45]

If love is the answer, what about St John? It was argued above that love for God and Jesus is lacking in his religion as Jane conceives it at Morton, to say nothing of love for mankind. Has anything changed in that respect when the focus swings back to him as he joyfully relinquishes his hold on life?

While it is true that *Jane Eyre* does not actually describe any 'change of heart' on St John's part,[46] his own words do suggest one. Borrowed from the apostle of love whose name St John bears, they are part of a celebration of love, concluding the narrative that describes the ultimate union of Creator and creation. St John's plea expresses an eager yearning for Christ as well as that unquestioning acquiescence in God's will which is the peculiar characteristic of saved souls. The Christian, it seems, has finally got the better of the man; he is ambitious still, but his old restlessness, the 'fever in his vitals' (III.iv.361), is gone. Like Rochester, so different from him in so many ways, he has submitted to the Divine order, and now he is preparing to meet his true love, Jesus Christ.

But if St John does change so that his imminent death becomes an integral part of a love story, a story in which—to quote Beaty again—the religious and love themes merge and interact,[47] why does Jane not say so? The best answer to that question may be another query: how could she have done? She is not didactically explicit when it comes to her own spiritual growth from irreligious child to Christian woman whose faith sustains and guides her through extreme trials; and on the terms of the novel, it is difficult to see how Charlotte Brontë could have placed a convincing 'conversion' story in her heroine's mouth.[48] Framing a corresponding explanation with regard to her cousin's spiritual development on the basis of transcontinental correspondence seems an even taller order. Charlotte Brontë makes Jane pass on what she can and does know, including a quotation from one of St

John's letters. It is not unreasonable to conclude that Charlotte felt her readers must be content with that.

Many readers have not been, however, and there will probably always be a number of people who agree with Thackeray that St John is an interesting failure (though for a wide variety of reasons, including some that Thackeray would not have thought of).[49] The question of whether St John actually achieves his ambition remains open, and I believe Charlotte Brontë deliberately left it so. The ending of *Jane Eyre* is not a closure so much as a balancing of the book, which leaves the reader to contemplate two very dissimilar patterns of human endeavour under the Heaven to which both assign ultimate power. It does not seem necessary to prefer one to the other or to pronounce a verdict on either. Whatever happens to St John Rivers he does not, within the framework of *Jane Eyre*, face perdition: despite his enduring lack of humility and charity, the crucial Evangelical virtues, he is a character in a book which denies eternal punishment and experiments with the notion of the 'equality of disembodied souls' (II.vi.239). *Jane Eyre* has consistently portrayed the operations of a God who, in the reformed Rochester's words, tempers judgement with mercy (III.xii.457) and who—as, interestingly enough, both Rochester and St John affirm, quoting I Sam. 16:7—sees not as man sees (III.ix.419 and III.xi.452). The Brontë fiction as a whole reflects a reliance on Divine forgiveness which transcends the views that prevailed in the authors' time, even among eschatologically optimistic divines. Readers may judge how they like, or join Charlotte Brontë in waiving the judge's privilege.

More than anything else, the mixture of extreme qualities that is St John Rivers thus illustrates the radical enquiry into religious thought, feeling and conduct which is so characteristic of all the Brontë works. It is in evidence, for instance, when Emily Brontë stands back from articulating a definite scenario for Catherine's and Heathcliff's afterlife and when Anne Brontë refrains from even suggesting whether Helen Huntingdon's hopes for her husband's ultimate salvation are likely to be fulfilled. The Brontë spirit of religious enquiry has always affected readers—even readers not fully aware that it was a religious challenge they were responding to—in very different ways. Rooted in personal faith, unchecked by external prescriptions or considerations of propriety, and uninhibited by any urge to attain absolute answers, it will surely continue to excite and unsettle new generations as it has done for a century and a half.

Notes

1. 'Bertha and the Critics', *Nineteenth-Century Literature* 44.3 (Dec. 1989), 294.
2. Elizabeth Imlay, one of the few critics who have devoted whole chapters to St John

Rivers; see her *Charlotte Brontë and the Mysteries of Love: Myth and Allegory in Jane Eyre* (New York, London: Harvester Wheatsheaf, 1989), p. 65.

3. *BLL* ii.236–9, a letter dated 24 July 1848. A fuller, carefully edited transcript of this remarkable letter—remarkable not least because Mary Taylor found *Jane Eyre* so devoid of 'moral' and 'protest'—is provided by Joan Stevens in her edition of Taylor's letters, pp. 73–9.

4. I may have missed an observation along these lines in the vast critical literature on *Jane Eyre*, in which case I apologise.

5. *Perception and Expression*, p. 52; the St John discussion is found on pp. 42–52. See also Myer, *Charlotte Brontë*, p. 71.

6. *The Religion of the Heart*, pp. 258–9. (Unlike Judith Williams, though, Jay views St John's sainthood as a certainty.)

7. Pollard, 'The Brontës', p. 59; see also Gordon, *A Preface*, pp. 146 and 149.

8. St John can be read as a textbook case of sublimation. John Maynard recently referred to 'the cold, repressive misuse of sexual energies for their religious aims by sex-powered zealots like St. John Rivers'; see *Victorian Discourses on Sexuality and Religion* (Cambridge University Press, 1993), p. 276.

9. According to Gilbert and Gubar, St John's 'almost blatantly patriarchal name' recalls 'the disguised misogyny' of the Baptist (as evidenced in his resistance to Salome); *Madwoman*, p. 365.

10. A parallel noted by Keefe, *World of Death*, p. 111. Jane's and the Riverses' uncle Eyre's first name was John, too.

11. Thomas Arnold's sermon on 2 John 5 stresses the 'spirit of love' in which St John brought human and Divine love together. See *Sermons on the Interpretation of Scripture*, pp. 399–409. References to St John as the apostle of love abound in the writings of the period; see, for instance, Maurice's *The Kingdom of Christ*, vol. I, ch. iii, p. 134.

12. See *The Life of Henry Venn*, pp. 580–1, and Maurice, *Theological Essays*, p. 324.

13. *Perception and Expression*, pp. 42–3.

14. See Simeon's *The True Test of Religion in the Soul: or Practical Christianity Delineated, a Sermon Preached before the University of Cambridge*, 9 March 1817, and Wilberforce, *A Practical View*, p. 55. Brainerd is quoted from Josiah Pratt, *The Life of the Rev. David Brainerd* (London, 1834), p. 347. On the latter, see further pp. 215f. below.

15. Many critics have drawn attention to St John's despotism (the word is repeatedly used in *Jane Eyre*) towards Jane, and it would be superfluous to add to their discussions. See, for instance, Q. D. Leavis' introduction to the 1966 Penguin edition of the novel, now perhaps most easily available in Leavis' *Collected Essays*, vol. I, pp. 178 and 188, and Martin, *Accents of Persuasion*, pp. 85ff.

16. Branwell nourished a lasting interest in the Lucifer figure; see Robert G. Collins' edition of *The Hand of the Arch-Sinner: Two Angrian Chronicles of Branwell Brontë* (Oxford: Clarendon Press, 1993), pp. xxvi ff. St John's appearance, it might be added, tells against him in the work of an author whose true heroes are characteristically dark and unhandsome.

17. See, for instance, Bridges, *The Christian Ministry*, pp. 413–52.

18. See above, p. 264n.44 on Simeon and pastoral love.

19. *Misreading Jane Eyre*, p. 210. See also Charmian Knight, 'Reader, What Next?—The Final Chapter of *Jane Eyre*', *BST* vol. 23, part 1 (1998), 27–30, especially 29 ('The difference between Jane and St John was not of unfaith and faith, but of different interpretations of the same faith, and different vocations within it').

20. See above, p. 22.

21. Review in *Blackwood's Edinburgh Magazine* (20 (1826), 709) of Sir John Malcolm's *Political History of India* (1826).

22. See Imlay, *Charlotte Brontë*, pp. 60 and 174. As the continued discussion shows, I agree with those critics who have argued that *Jane Eyre* presents a favourable view of missionary work. For recapitulations of the post-colonial line in *Jane Eyre* criticism and a dissenting perspective, see Susan Meyer, *Imperialism at Home: Race and Victorian Women's Fiction* (Ithaca and London: Cornell University Press, 1996), pp. 60–95. See also Beaty, *Misreading Jane Eyre*, pp. 192–5.

23. See ch. 4, 'A Mission to the Heathen', in Bradley's *A Call to Seriousness*, pp. 74–93.

24. See Hopkins, *The Father of the Brontës*, pp. 12–19; Lock and Dixon, *A Man of Sorrow*, pp. 18–19, Phillips, 'Charlotte Brontë's Concepts', pp. 21–6; and Barker, *The Brontës*, pp. 10–11.

25. Richard T. France, 'Henry Martyn', in *Five Pioneer Missionaries* (Edinburgh: The Banner of Truth Trust, 1965), p. 250.

26. See, for instance, Phillips, 'Charlotte Brontë's Concepts', pp. 21–2, and Beaty, *Misreading Jane Eyre*, p. 182.

27. See Phillips, 'Charlotte Brontë's Concepts', pp. 23–6. As Tom Winnifrith points out in his edition of *The Poems of Charlotte Brontë* (Oxford: Basil Blackwell for the Shakespeare Head Press, 1984), Charlotte's poem 'The Missionary' (pp. 67–71) is 'an interesting preview of St John Rivers' (p. 363); but the speaker's references to the 'great sacrifice' of a beloved woman who '[might] not go with me' suggest Martyn and his lost love far more than St John and Miss Oliver.

28. France, 'Henry Martyn', p. 244.

29. John Sargent's *A Memoir of the Rev. Henry Martyn, B.D.* (London, 1819; this is the third edition), p. 500; see also p. 501 on Martyn's zeal being tempered with love. In his essay on the Clapham Sect (to which Patrick Brontë owed a great deal), Sir James Stephen describes how Martyn's dedication to the welfare of 'the great human family' 'partook more of the fervour of domestic affection, than of the kind and gentle warmth of a diffusive philanthropy'; see *Essays in Ecclesiastical Biography*, vol. II, p. 340. Stephen presents an outline of Martyn's life on pp. 335–42.

30. See Henry Martyn, *Twenty Sermons* (London, 1822; this is the second edition), pp. 117–39. On *Villette*, see above pp. 99f.

31. See above, p. 129.

32. Martyn, *Sermons*, p. 104.

33. Pratt, *Life of Brainerd*, pp. 345, 350 and 351. The reference to Martyn is on pp. x–xi.

34. Sargent, *Memoir*, p. 129.

35. To mention a single instance, a dying child in W. Carus Wilson's *The Children's Friend*, vol. 13, no. 150 (1836), 124–6, comments, 'with a heavenly smile', on her surviving a convulsive attack: 'I thought it had been over; come, Lord Jesus, come quickly!'

36. *Sermons*, pp. 201–2 and 205.

37. *Charlotte Brontë*, p. 179.

38. *Charlotte Brontë and Defensive Conduct: The Author and the Body at Risk* (Philadelphia: University of Pennsylvania Press, 1992), p. 87.

39. Hook, 'The Father of the Family', 102.

40. Annette Tromly feels that the ending of *Jane Eyre* expresses Jane's implicit dissatisfaction with her own 'pedestrian' life; see *The Cover of the Mask*, pp. 60–1.

41. See 'Closing the Book', p. 83. See also Knight, 'Reader, What Next?', where the final paragraphs of the book are shown to impart a sense of onward movement.

42. A favourite with Grimshaw of Haworth, the sentence appears on a teapot, a piece of funerary china which belonged to the Brontës, in the Parsonage Museum. (It should not, contrary to a widespread notion, be viewed as a summary characterisation of Aunt Branwell's religion.)

43. *Misreading Jane Eyre*, pp. 210–11.

44. *Secular Pilgrims*, p. 68.

45. See pp. 53ff. above.

46. Cf. p. 206 above.

47. See *Misreading Jane Eyre*, pp. 204 and 207.

48. True, we are given a brief, halting outline, in his own words spoken to Jane, of Rochester's 'conversion'; but it is subordinated to and in a sense carried by the mysterious-summons episode and hence less of a challenge than an account of St John's religious maturation would have been.

49. *The Letters and Private Papers of William Makepeace Thackeray*, coll. and ed. by Gordon N. Ray (Cambridge, Mass.: Harvard University Press, 1946), vol. II, p. 319, letter to William Smith Williams of 23 October 1847. (Several Brontë critics have quoted Thackeray's remark.)

JEROME BEATY

St. John's Way and the Wayward Reader

Charlotte Brontë's narrative strategy, which leads the reader as well as young Jane to be surprised by sin and only gradually to recognize the providential nature of the world, lets many of us get too closely involved with young Jane, too uncritically accepting of her worldview, enabling—virtually determining—the reading of *Jane Eyre* as a novel of rebellion and the legitimate assertion of the sovereignty of the self. The reader is immediately captivated by the spunky hero who refuses to suffer mistreatment passively and defiantly insists upon her own rights, the rights of the individual, even the small, plain, poor, and female individual—an ontological position congenial to modern norms. This "loyalty" to young Jane and her values persists, despite innumerable and explicit textual qualifications and the gradually revealed narrative structure and denouement of the novel. Such tenacity of readers' "first impressions"—the principle of "primacy"—was demonstrated in an interesting experiment. One group of readers was given two joined blocks of character descriptions of identical length but opposite meanings, another group the same two blocks but joined in reverse order. In both cases "the leading block established a perceptual set serving as a frame of reference to which the subsequent information was subordinated as much as possible." Even more surprising than the power of the first impression to "explain away" the contradictory evidence that followed was the evidence

From Jane Eyre: *An Authoritative Text, Contexts, Criticism*. © 2001 by W.W. Norton & Company, Inc.

that "the overwhelming majority of subjects did not even notice the glaring incompatibility of the information contained in the two successive segments."[1] We are well into the third and final volume and almost three-quarters of the way to the end of *Jane Eyre* before St. John Rivers appears. It is not long before we see him as Jane's suitor, Rochester's rival. Not only is he a latecomer to the fictional world, the reader having been enthralled by the powerful Rochester who seems so well suited to the rebellious Jane, but he threatens what seems to this point to be the ontology or value system of that world. He is situated most dramatically on the borderline of existing systems—roughly definable perhaps as the humanist and the religious. His position on that borderline is encapsulated in the brief description of his character by his loving sister Diana—who is so favorably presented that her words may be considered virtually "authorized":

> 'He will sacrifice all to his long-framed resolves,' she said: 'natural affection and feelings more potent still. St. John looks quiet, Jane; but he hides a fever in his vitals. You would think him gentle, yet in some things he is inexorable as death; and the worst of it is, my conscience will hardly permit me to dissuade him from his severe decision: certainly, I cannot for a moment blame him for it. It is right, noble, Christian: yet it breaks my heart.' (chapter XXX)

Secular, romantic, or post-Freudian readers, whose vision of the world of *Jane Eyre*, moreover, has been reinforced by the power of primacy, can scarcely be expected to approve the sacrifice of "natural affection"—much less the thinly veiled "feelings more potent still"—to ambition, no matter how holy. A devout reader can hardly blame a decision that, no matter how severe, is "right, noble, Christian."

Jane expresses the immediate conflict of humanistic and religious values as the conflict of the domestic and the heroic:

> The humanities and amenities of life had no attraction for him.... I saw he was of the material from which nature hews her heroes—Christian and Pagan—her lawgivers, her statesmen, her conquerors....
>
> 'This parlour is not his sphere,' I reflected; 'the Himalayan ridge or Caffre bush, even the plague-cursed Guinea Coast swamp, would suit him better. Well may he eschew the calm of domestic life; it is not his element.' (chapter XXXIV)

Strange as it may sound, Jane's values, her very nature, as here defined, are "domestic."

Having been unable to get any news about Rochester, even whether he is alive, and daily subjected to St. John's powerful presence, Jane is beginning to think that the austere life of self-denial he offers is a dreaded though glorious martyrdom: "I daily wished more to please him: but to do so, I felt daily more and more that I must disown half my nature ... force myself to the adoption of pursuits for which I had no natural vocation" (chapter XXXIV). For most twentieth-century readers, such a sacrifice would be unacceptable, perverse. But if half her nature is, in terms of a major but conflicted nineteenth-century norm, on the wrong side of the conflict between love of God and love of his creatures, the choice is not so easy.

St. John finds her worthy of being a missionary's wife, expressing his approval precisely in terms of such a norm: she is "very heroic" and with "a soul that revelled in the flame and excitement of sacrifice." Though she feels clasped in an "iron shroud" by his vision of her proper role, she is nearly persuaded that this is indeed her work and her way. It might be well to go with him to India—but, she insists, only as his sister, not his wife. This, he says, would be impractical; she must marry him, not for his pleasure, "but for my Sovereign's service." She refuses "the bridal ring," but he gives her two weeks to think it over, defining her refusal as a rejection of a life of labor not earthly love; rejection of love of God for a life of "selfish ease and barren obscurity" (chapter XXXIV).

The novel now approaches that which Jane will call her crisis and the point at which the narrative and ontological crux is defined. Jane must chose once and for all to accept or reject St. John's proposal that she marry him and accompany him to India. If she accepts, she knows it will probably mean her early death, and so will the sacrifice of choosing this life for the eternal, divine love over human love. As we read this scene, however, we must be aware of the subtlety of Brontë's handling of the first-person narration. Some passages are clearly from the perspective of the elder Jane who exists beyond the end of the immediate action and is telling the story of her earlier life. Others are from the perspective of the younger Jane, Jane-at-the-moment-of-action, passages that are sometimes signaled by quotation marks, question marks, or the present tense. Still others are "double-voiced," in which the voices of the two Janes seem merged or inseparable. This subtlety permits, even invites "misunderstanding"—that is, views that at the textual moment seem to legitimately fill gaps or project configurations of the novel and its world but turn out to be "wrong," not affirmed by later events. Moreover, the voices of the two Janes are not the only voices here: though St. John speaks in quotation marks and out of a worldview that is neither Jane's younger nor older view, his, voice and values are not ultimately or categorically denied in the novel.

On the evening Jane refused him and he had refused her refusal, St. John reads from the twenty-first chapter of Revelation, and Jane thrills as he reads what is apparently directed at her:

> 'He that overcometh shall inherit all things; and I will be his God, and he shall be my son. But,' was slowly, distinctly read, 'the fearful, the unbelieving, &c., shall have their part in the lake which burneth with fire and brimstone, which is the second death.'
>
> Henceforward I knew what fate St. John feared for me. (chapter XXXV)

Read from a worldview emphasizing the autonomous (and sensual) self, St. John is threatening Jane with damnation in order to force his will and himself upon her. Jane—both Janes—does/do not read him so. He is, after all, quoting Scripture, and she recognizes that he has a voice and a belief system of his own and has her best interest, as he understands it, at heart. He truly believes that he is saved and she, unless she accompanies him to India as his wife, is damned. Jane understands this at the moment and later, even as she narrates her story, for she gives his words in quotation marks, neither authorizing them nor denying their validity. He prays "for those whom the temptations of the world and the flesh were luring from the narrow path." We are likely to emphasize "the flesh," but "the world" and the rich man's loss of "his good things in life" emphasize the earthly and not just the earthy. Nor does either of the two Janes even hint at the possibility that he was rationalizing his physical desires. Jane with both her voices acknowledges with awe how sincerely "he felt the greatness and goodness of his purpose." His look "was not, indeed, that of a lover beholding his mistress; but it was that of a pastor recalling his wandering sheep." Just as she, on her principles, has renounced Rochester, so he, on his, has renounced Rosamond: "like him, I had now put love out of the question, and thought only of duty" (chapter XXXV).

The crisis is as much that of Jane's judgment and will as it is that of St. John's importunity. All sincere "men of talent," she says, "have their sublime moments: when they subdue and rule." At this moment "veneration" for St. John tempts her "to rush down the torrent of his will into the gulf of his existence, and there to lose my own." Does "own" refer to "existence" or "will"? If the former, it refers only to Jane's certainty that she will die if she goes to India with St. John, but if the latter, it may legitimately reinforce the cause of the rebellious, self-reliant experiencing Jane and isolate the issue as proud preservation of the self versus submergence to the "official" voice—to the patriarchy and its patriarchal God. Indeed, at this moment, St. John, for better or worse, does seem to represent the voice of religion, virtually of God: "Religion called—Angels beckoned—God commanded— ... death's gates opening, showed eternity beyond: it seemed, that for safety and bliss there, all here might be sacrificed in a second" (chapter XXXV). That life may be sacrificed for eternal bliss goes without saying for those who believe and believe that sacrifice is called for; yet it is perverse, destructive, downright evil for those for whom life ends at death. Jane is about to make the sacrifice. How close she comes, and how suspenseful the decision for the reader, can only be realized by imaginatively entertaining at least the possibility that St. John's cause is just.

Here the subtle interplay or double-voicedness may strongly influence response and interpretation. At the crucial moment the narrating Jane refers to Rochester and evokes an earlier scene and its moral register.

> I was almost as hard beset by him now as I had been once before, in a different way, by another. *I was a fool both times*. To have yielded then would have been an error of principle; to have yielded now would have been an error of judgment. *So I think at this hour, when I look back to the crisis through the quiet medium of time: I was unconscious of folly at the instant*. (chapter XXXV, emphasis added)

Jane at the moment is not recalling Rochester, and her choice is not determined, or, so far as we can tell, even influenced by her love for him. It is the narrator from the text's future ("at this hour, when I look back to the crisis") who evokes the text's past ("as I had been once before").

As the scene approaches its climax, when there is physical contact between St. John and Jane, Rochester is evoked, but in a passage of delicate and precise ambiguity: "he surrounded me with his arm, *almost* as if he loved me (I say *almost*—I knew the difference—for I had felt what it was to be loved; but, like him, I had now put love out of the question, and thought only of duty)" (chapter XXXV). How much consciousness is implied in "I knew" and in "had now put love out of the question"? Some, perhaps, but the narrator's voice seems to preempt the scene by calling attention to the fact that the very words and the punctuation of the text are the narrator's own—"*almost* ... (I say *almost* ...)." To grasp the text's full force and effectiveness here the reader must recognize that at the time of St. John's renewed and powerful proposal Jane did not consider her temptation foolish or impossible because of her love for Rochester. (Indeed, she says, "The Impossible—*i.e.*, my marriage with St. John—was fast becoming the possible.") If it is necessary for the scene's effectiveness that the reader consider St. John acceptable and his offer perhaps even desirable, why should the narrator interject the name of Rochester and juxtapose the two proposals spatially? Would not this diminish the possibility that Jane would marry St. John? For whom?

Here it might be well to recall Bakhtin's insistence on the particularly of the utterance in time and place and the productive role of the auditor/reader. Perhaps Brontë is addressing *imagined* readers who would be only too likely to forget or to prefer to forget the morally flawed Rochester for the soldier of Christ. The narrative strategy seems aimed at the kind of reader who would be shocked if Jane rejected St. John. St. John, at least, is so sure he is fulfilling a divine plan that when Jane says, "I could decide if I were but certain.... were I but convinced that it is God's will I should marry you, I could vow to marry you here and now," he assumes she has acquiesced: he exclaims that his "prayers are heard" (chapter XXXV).

The conditionality of Jane's statement is intentional, but not because of memories of Rochester. However much her own will has been overwhelmed by St. John's, she is still not sure of God's will, and it is that she wishes to ascertain and, having ascertained, to follow. She does not depart from the religious, certainly not the providentialist, tenet's, and the novel does not force her to choose between religion and life or love. It brings to the surface more clearly than ever its (and Jane's now developed) religious grounding. She appeals directly to Providence for intercession and guidance: "I sincerely, deeply, fervently longed to do what was right; and only that. 'Show me, show me the path!' I entreated of Heaven. I was excited more than I had ever been; and whether what followed was the effect of excitement, the reader shall judge" (chapter XXXV).

What follows is the merging and modification of the religious and love themes through the famous or infamous incident of Jane's hearing at this moment Rochester's voice calling "Jane, Jane, Jane!" though he is a thirty-six hour coach ride away. She believes that her prayer has been answered and she believes at this moment that her love for Rochester is now authorized by extraordinary but natural forces.

Jane has given the reader the right to interpret the nature of the call, but judgment at this point must be tentative or suspended; the reader "*shall* judge" may seem to suggest that the judgment may be immediate, but it may also hint that the reader can judge appropriately only when Jane has told the rest of her story. That the voice is only the product of her excitement is almost immediately denied. The experiencing Jane—note the quotation marks—almost immediately attributes the call to "nature":

> 'Down superstition!' I commented, as that spectre rose up black by the black yew at the gate. 'This is not thy deception, nor thy witchcraft: it is the work of nature. She was roused, and did—no miracle—but her best.' (chapter XXXV)

Nor is the case yet closed. Though the work of nature—She—the miracle of the call is also, its seems, the work or at least has the authorization of God—He—for no sooner does Jane reach her room than she falls on her knees:

> [I] prayed.... I seemed to penetrate very near a Mighty Spirit; and my soul rushed out in gratitude at His feet. I rose from the thanksgiving—took a resolve—and lay down, unscared, enlightened—eager but for daylight. (chapter XXXV)

The next morning, she entertains once more the possibility of "excitement," "a delusion," but prefers to think of it as "inspiration":

> it seemed in *me*—not in the external world. I asked, was it a mere nervous impression—a delusion? I could not conceive or believe: it was more like an inspiration. The wondrous shock of feeling had come like the earthquake which shook the foundation of Paul and Silas's prison: it had opened the doors of the soul's cell, and loosed its bands—it had wakened it out of its sleep, whence it sprang trembling, listening, aghast; then vibrated thrice a cry on my startled ear; and in my quaking heart, and through my spirit; which neither feared nor shook, but exulted as if in joy over the success of one effort it had been privileged to make, independent of the cumbrous body. (chapter XXXV)

"Inspiration," out of context, might seem to authorize the psychological and secular reading of the experience that most twentieth-century readers would doubtless prefer. But this is clearly described by Jane as an experience of the soul influenced from without: the doors of the soul's cell are opened, but the soul listens, it does not generate. Both passages contain the cautionary "seemed," and the second contains an "as if" and a question. We have not yet heard the last of the explanations or an authorized explanation.

Jane's trip back to Thornfield is full of excitement and suspense. She finds Thornfield Hall in ruins, destroyed months before by fire. She hastens to the nearby inn and suffers with the reader through the innkeeper's lengthy recapitulation of what Jane and the reader already know, the story of the mad wife and the governess.

Jane and the reader learn at last that Mrs. Rochester is dead and that Rochester, having lost a hand and an eye and having been blinded in the other in attempting to rescue his wife, is living at Ferndean. The lost hand and eye point to the passage in Matthew 5.27–32 that deals with adultery, advising those who are tempted to sin to pluck out their right eye and cut off their right hand rather than succumb. The Matthew passage has been alluded to earlier in *Jane Eyre*, more than once, most recently in an emphatic position at the very beginning of chapter XXVII, when Jane's inner voice tells her to flee Thornfield after the revelation of Bertha's existence.

As soon as she learns his whereabouts, Jane is off to seek Rochester, and the chapter ends. The scene that many readers have long been waiting for, the reunion of Rochester and Jane, now quickly follows. Jane is at her sauciest, and most tender, teasing him with suspense and jealousy. At this point once more the love and religion themes interact and are at last harmonized. Rochester tells her of his own conversion: "Jane! you think me, I daresay, an irreligious dog: but my heart swells with gratitude to the beneficent God of this earth just now" (chapter XXXVII). He admits the justice of her having been snatched away from him and even of the lowering of his pride in his strength. "Of late, Jane—only—only of late—I began to see and acknowledge the hand of God in my doom. I began to experience remorse, repentance; the wish for reconcilement to my Maker. I began sometimes to pray" (chapter XXXVII). His path has been in its way similar to that which Jane has trod, from rebellion to humility, from self-reliance to acknowledgment of Providence. Jane has gone through only metaphoric flood, Rochester through real and metaphoric fire. He then tells her that four nights ago, on Monday, near midnight, having long felt that Jane must be dead, he prayed that if it were God's will, he might die.

> 'I asked of God, at once in anguish and humility, if I had not been long enough desolate, afflicted, tormented; and might not soon taste bliss and peace once more. That I merited all I endured, I acknowledged—that I could scarcely endure more I pleaded; and the Alpha and Omega of my heart's wishes broke involuntarily from my lips, in the words—"Jane! Jane! Jane!"' (chapter XXXVII)

She cross-examines him—did he speak aloud? the very words? Monday night near midnight? Yes. Yes. Yes. And he says he heard her reply, which he repeats. "Reader, it was Monday night—near midnight—that I too had received the mysterious summons: those were the very words by which I had replied to it." Jane is overwhelmed by the implication, for what this means is that the telepathy was not the work of nature, not intuition, if that implies only a secular inner voice, but it was the work of Providence, of Divine Will:

> The coincidence struck me as too awful and inexplicable to be communicated or discussed. If I told anything, my tale would be such as must necessarily make a profound impression on the mind of my hearer: and that mind, yet from its sufferings too prone to gloom, needed not the deeper shade of the supernatural. I kept these things, then, and pondered them in my heart. (chapter XXXVII)

This is the final confirmation of the ontological world of *Jane Eyre*, a world governed by Providence. Not Fate if Fate implies predestination, but the intercession of God in warning and guiding the sinner, giving him or her every chance to follow the straight and narrow path, but giving choice, free will, whether to follow or not. Those recognizing and accepting this providential reading, now trace the theme backward, through Jane's plea to God when besieged by St. John to "skew me the path," to her plea on the moors for Providence to "aid—direct me," to the chestnut tree that first twists and is then shattered on the night of Rochester's secretly illicit proposal, and between and beyond on the way back to the very beginning. For such readers, *Jane Eyre* has finally taken its full shape.

Rochester now knows that it was not a mere vision and utters a prayer of thanksgiving for Jane's return and an entreaty that he be given "the strength to lead henceforth a purer life." It is only now, when human love and divine are harmonized that Jane and Rochester can enter the wood and wend their way "homeward"—the last crucial word of the body of the autobiographical narrative that began with the protagonist exiled from family and hearth. Only then that we can turn to the "Conclusion," which brings the narrative up to the reading present and begins with those plain but memorable words, "Reader, I married him" (chapter XXXVIII).

The conclusion is in many ways typical of Victorian final chapters that bring the events of the narrative up to the time of the narration, if not to the first-readers' present. There is a brief description of the wedding day and an account of how Jane spread the news to those we know, including but not ending with St. John Rivers. Then there is a summary of the ten years since—their happiness, Rochester's recovery of his sight, their firstborn (a boy, of course)—and then a surprising return to Rivers.

The last three paragraphs of the novel are devoted to St. John Rivers. He knows his death is imminent, he writes from the East. "My Master ... has forewarned me. Daily he announces more distinctly,—'Surely I come quickly!' and hourly I more eagerly respond,—'Amen; even so come, Lord Jesus!'" (chapter XXXVIII). These are the last words of the novel, somewhat reminiscent of the call of Jane's "Master" and her response, but much more directly an echo of the penultimate line of the final book of the New Testament, the Revelation of St. John the Divine.

Why, in the autobiography of Jane Eyre, should St. John have the emphatic, sanctioned, if not sanctified, closing words that seem to echo, even encapsulate, her own narrative closure?

That Providence leads Jane, when she asks for guidance, back to Rochester, away from St. John, does not meant that St. John's way is wrong or anti-life, as many modern readers would have it, but only that his way is not Jane's way. His path to salvation lies through self-denial, self-sacrifice, martyrdom. His is the life of *agape*. Jane's way to salvation—as the leadings and her experience and Rochester's indicate—lies through everyday, domestic life, the life of *eros* (Eyre-os?). St. John's way is wrong—for Jane; Jane's way, which for him would mean marriage to Rosamond Oliver, would be wrong for him.

To fully understand the religious ontology of *Jane Eyre*, it is necessary to see the two as different ways for different kinds of individuals, but each way as equally viable for the appropriate pilgrim. It is difficult, however, in a first-person novel to make the Other equal. The mode is almost by definition ego centered. But the function of the fictional autobiography in the mid-nineteenth century, in the move between Romantic egoism and Victorian "duty" or socialization, is to exorcise that Romantic ego or transcend—not escape or ignore—egoism. Just as Jane must see that she is not in total control of her life (and Rochester that he is not in control of his) but that the control of all is God's, so she as narrator, or Charlotte Brontë, must insist that there has to be more than just Jane's personal salvation at stake: there must be room for the Other. In a first-person narrative it is impossible to give St. John equal time or space, but he is given pride of place, the final words of the novel, a voice that powerfully echoes both Jane's at the climactic moment of her life and the language of scriptural closure, thus validating his "way," though it is Other. Though she is not "wrong," neither is Jane's way the only right way. Her way and her life story, her narrating "I," are decentered, not just to make room for St. John but to reveal the real center, which, in the world of Brontë's novel, is always and everywhere God.

What I have attempted here is a reading of *Jane Eyre* as a member of what Peter J. Rabinowitz calls "the authorial audience," readers who initially ask "of a literary text ... What is the author saying?" He cautions that

> In arguing, however, for the importance of reading as authorial audience, I am not suggesting that it is either the final reading or the most important.
>
> Were I teaching ... Brontë, I would be disappointed in a student who could produce an authorial reading but who could not ... move beyond that reading to look at the work critically from some perspective other than the one called for by the author. But while the authorial reading without further critique is often incomplete, so is a critical reading without an understanding of the authorial audience as its base.[2]

I have read Jane Eyre as a member of the authorial audience, then, because such a reading is a necessary first step in coming to terms with its text, because what seems to me a satisfactory authorial audience reading is not readily available, and because most recent critical discussion of *Jane Eyre* has "gone beyond the text," interpreting before acknowledging or recognizing the "literal meaning."

The "critical reading" of *Jane Eyre*, as I suggested at the beginning of this essay, largely derives from the power of primacy and the powerfully attractive presentation of tough-minded, rebellious, independent young Jane. What makes her values to readers of today—our "community of interpretation"—more compelling is that they are closer to our norms and values. These factors have too often allowed us to ignore the literal, Providential meaning of the text, its strategies, and details.

But how can such a reading, based on values that are modified or denied by the final shape of the text, be justified by merely saying that a critical reading or interpretation requires some perspective other than the one called for by the author? The attractiveness of young Jane's values and their congeniality for modern readers—and the fact that in Brontë's own time there were conflicting norms, roughly between humanist and religious values, in Charlotte Brontë's own culture—may explain why so many readers go beyond the text before reading it attentively as a member of the authorial audience. But that does not mean that their interpretations are "wrong," subjectively imposed readings supporting and supported by prior values, and that the likely more literal meaning of an authorial reading is "right," because it is more "objective" or disinterested.

How can we read *Jane Eyre* as a member of the authorial audience and *justify* a reading that goes beyond? One way may be to pay closer attention to the autobiographical form of the novel. The mature Jane; a happily married mother restored, or even elevated into gentility, is writing the story of her life as it now seems to have unfolded and revealed its meaning. It seems legitimate to find her interpretation unconvincing—a self-justifying, after-the-fact version—and to entertain the possibility of her life story's having a different meaning. Such a reading does not imply that she is falsifying the events, but only recollecting them from her new vantage point—selecting the events that fit her new vision, reimagining her earlier thoughts and feelings, and shaping them to the outcome. Memory, as we now know, is not the calling up of an accurate computer-like file of the past, but a recreation. We can read and experience the novel from the beginning as a story of that young Jane who would resist hell by not dying, would not turn the other cheek and let the unjust rule. We can read it, then, fully acknowledging the literal meaning imposed upon her life story but in a dialogue with the values of young Jane, values that had they been retained would tell the life story and its meaning rather differently.

The concept and analysis of novels as open-ended dialogues between the narrator (first- or third-person) and the characters is identified with the work of the Russian philosopher and critic Mikhail Bakhtin. Central to the concept is the understanding that the narrator or narrator/author is not "right" and the characters "wrong," but that each speaks from a different worldview and that the differences are not compromised or reconciled. The work is not thereby fragmented, because unity arises from its representation of what Bakhtin calls an "event," a cultural moment with its conflicting norms, issues, and values. The dialogue and values do not synthesize; there can be no totally convincing ontological closure. If the views of characters that challenge the narrator are merely represented as "wrong" and the narrator as "right," the novel is "monologic"—limited to the narrator's or author's view of its literal meaning—not "dialogic."

But isn't it precisely the case in *Jane Eyre* that young Jane is wrong and the mature narrator right? If so, the novel is monologic and has to be read for its literal meaning alone. Bakhtin admits that even in Dostoevsky—his paragon of dialogism—there is pressure for closure, resolution:

> In Dostoevsky's novels a unique conflict exists between the internal open-endedness of the characters and dialogue, and the *external* (in most cases compositional and thematic) *completedness* of every individual novel.... [A]lmost all of Dostoevsky's novels have a *conventional literary, conventional monologic* ending (especially characteristic in this respect is *Crime and Punishment*).[3]

The surface, subject matter, and texture of *Crime and Punishment* and *Jane Eyre* would seem to have little in common. But Dostoevsky's novel, like Brontë's, ultimately reveals its providential world—though revelation lies chiefly in its epilogue—thus Bakhtin's suspicion of endings. If the culture and the moment in which Dostoevsky's novel is embedded are not identical to those of *Jane Eyre*, there is a general Western late-nineteenth-century culture, and there are many British novels of the period that struggle with the problem of closure in a culture of conflicting and shifting social, ontological, epistemological, and aesthetic norms. The two endings of *Great Expectations* is a sign of such struggle, and it is more directly stated in the footnote Hardy inserted in a later edition of *Return of the Native*, inviting readers who wanted the ending to be otherwise to reject the conventional ending in favor of one more open-ended and more rigorously aesthetic.

To see *Jane Eyre* externally—as a dialogue between the conflicting, open-ended worldviews of the younger and older Jane, representing a moment in the culture—seems an appropriate extrapolation of the *internal* reading of the literal text as an unresolved dialogue between the values of both Janes and those of St. John's way.

NOTES

1. Meir Sternberg, *Expositional Modes and Temporal Order in Fiction* (Baltimore: The Johns Hopkins University Press, 1978) 94.

2. *Before Reading* (Ithaca: Cornell University Press, 1987) 30–32.

3. *Problems of Dostoevsky's Poetics* (Minneapolis: University of Minnesota Press, 1954) 39–90.

HEATHER GLEN

Triumph and Jeopardy: *The Shape of* Jane Eyre

Charlotte Brontë's account of what her first novel was not could serve as a description of her second. Those 'sudden turns' denied to Crimsworth—unearned wealth, a transformative marriage, excessive happiness—are central to Jane Eyre's story. This is no chilly narrative of self-help, but a much more compelling tale of the 'wild wonderful and thrilling', the 'strange, startling and harrowing';[1] of starvation and destitution, and the glamour of aristocratic life. The awkward abrasiveness of that earlier novel is here replaced by a passionate directness, 'more imaginative and poetical', 'more consonant with ... sentiments more tender—elevated—unworldly' (*P*1–2) than the cool, unromantic irony with which Edward Crimsworth was seen.

Indeed, *Jane Eyre* seems hardly to question its narrator's point of view. There is nothing here like that deliberate refusal of intimacy with the reader with which *The Professor* opens, nothing like Crimsworth's constant denial of feelings evoked in the prose. As generations of readers have attested, identification with Jane is difficult to resist not least because she first appears not as an unattractively defensive adult, but as a vulnerable, mistreated child. 'You are a dependant, mama says; you have no money; your father left you none; you ought to beg, and not to live here with gentlemen's children like us,' John Reed tells Jane (11). 'You are under obligations to Mrs Reed: she keeps you,' warns Bessie. 'If she were to turn you off, you would have to go

From *Charlotte Brontë: The Imagination in History*. © 2002 by Heather Glen.

to the poor-house' (13). The England depicted here is that of the New Poor Law, in which the cold calculations of political economy have replaced the traditional conception of 'charity' as a God-given responsibility to help the less fortunate; and the 'poorhouse' is a place of deterrence, not a refuge for those in need.[2] 'Charity', here, is something chilling and mystifying, less to be welcomed than feared. 'It is partly a charity-school,' says Helen Burns, seeking to explain Lowood institution to the bewildered child who has just begun to experience its rigours (50); 'cold charity must be entreated before I could get a lodging', Jane agonizes, on her flight from Thornfield (323); when her parents die, it is 'Charity ... cold as [a] snowdrift' that receives the infant Jane (379). Orphans, here, are abused and starved, and the destitute treated with hostile suspicion; those without power or position seen as hardly human at all. A 'rat', John Reed calls his cousin (11); 'like a mad cat', says Bessie (12); ten years later her aunt recalls the fear the child's outburst inspired in her—'as if an animal that I had struck or pushed had looked up at me with human eyes and cursed me in a man's voice' (239). A governess is a mere 'creature'; able to 'bear anything'—thus, even the amiable daughters of the Eshton family (178). And the workings of the larger society seem merely the large-scale expression of such dehumanizing habits of thought. 'Brought face to face with Necessity', Jane sums up its measure of human value in a telling series of appositions: 'I stood in the position of one without a resource: without a friend; without a coin' (326). The world through which she journeys, alone and destitute, is one in which there can be no reliance on others; in which want is met with suspicion and it is humiliating to ask for aid. 'I blamed none of those who repulsed me,' she says. 'I felt it was what was to be expected' (328). As she lies perishing of 'want and cold' (330)—within sound of a church-bell, at the door of a parsonage, in a 'civilized' Christian country—her plight becomes the index of a whole society's failure to sustain the values of community.

It appears that in this, her second novel, Charlotte Brontë is deliberately choosing to emphasize the dark underside of that gospel of self-sufficiency which Crimsworth sought to celebrate in his tale of successful self-help. Here, early nineteenth-century English society is seen not from the point of view of one of its makers and shapers, but from that of one whose claims on human existence it would deny. Yet from a twenty-first century perspective, it is hard to see in Jane's narrative the straightforward 'moral Jacobinism' that one contemporary found. For this heroine's account of her sufferings is shaped by her society's assumptions, even as her experiences might seem to question them. Thus, as she wanders starving on the moor, one voice within her insists on her right—indeed, her duty—to preserve life: 'But I was a human being, and had a human being's wants: I must not linger where there was nothing to supply them ... Life ... was yet in my possession, with all its requirements, and pains, and responsibilities. The burden must be carried; the want provided for; the suffering endured; the responsibility fulfilled' (324–5). But this voice is countered by another, with a different definition of 'right': one that judges human interaction by the standards of an instrumental calculation: 'I wandered away: always repelled by the consciousness of having no claim to ask—no right to expect interest in my isolated lot ... As to the woman who would not take my handkerchief in exchange for her bread, why, she was right, if the offer appeared to her sinister, or the exchange unprofitable' (327, 329). That sense of 'dependence' as shame that was instilled in the child in the opening pages is echoed here, as the narrating Jane unquestioningly equates need with debasement. Her frantic efforts to obtain work and food are to her a 'moral degradation'; to 'ask relief for want of which I was sinking' is, to her, to be 'brought low' (327–8). 'I felt it would be degrading', she says, 'to faint with hunger on the causeway of a hamlet' (325): privation, it seems, must be hidden from others' gaze. If this is psychologically realistic, it is from the perspective of hindsight hardly the voice of that revolutionary anger which some contemporaries found in the novel—'the tone of the mind and thought which has overthrown authority and violated every code human and divine abroad, and fostered Chartism and rebellion at home' (*CH* 109–10).

Of course, in presenting the story of a woman's struggle for independence, Charlotte Brontë was offering a much more overt challenge to early Victorian expectations than she had in *The Professors* masculine tale of self-help. Sixty years after the publication of *Jane Eyre*, Marianne Farningham, author of a best-selling book of advice for girls, was to recall of her girlhood in the 1840s:

> My father gave us two monthly magazines published by the Sunday School Union, the 'Teacher's Offering' and the 'Child's Companion'. In one of these was a series of descriptive articles on men who had been poor boys, and risen to be rich and great. Every month I hoped to find the story of some poor ignorant girl, who, beginning life as handicapped as I, had yet been able by her own efforts and the blessing of God upon them to live a life of usefulness, if not of greatness. But I believe there was not a woman in the entire series.[3]

The view that woman was not formed for independence was propounded again and again in early nineteenth-century England, not so much as an economic doctrine for it was acknowledged that in unfortunate circumstances even the middle-class woman might be forced to earn her own living), but as a moral, religious, or psychological truth. 'All independence is unfeminine: the more dependent that sex becomes, the more will it be cherished,' declares the anonymous author of *Woman as She Is and As She Should Be* (1835);[4] 'If the Bible did not say that she was created for man, and that the wife ought to be in subjection to her husband, her nature would testify no less plainly that she yearned to be dependent on, and, by consequence, subject to, the other sex,' opines William Landels, a quarter of a century later, in *Woman's Sphere and Work Considered in the Light of Scriptures* (1859).[5] Such views found a different, but perhaps even more compelling, inflection in the language of Byronic romantic love:

> ... she was one
> Made but to love, to feel that she was his
> Who was her chosen: what was said or done
> Elsewhere was nothing
>
> (*Don Juan*, Canto II, 202)

And they were, as we have seen, writ large in the marriage laws, which made of the wife a *femme coverte*, whose legal identity was 'covered' by that of her husband.

Small wonder, then, that Jane's insistence that 'I care for myself' was deplored by some early reviewers; or that twentieth-century feminist critics hailed her as a feminist heroine. Yet in many ways, it is as difficult to see her thus as it is to see her as a 'moral Jacobin'. When she returns to Rochester as an 'independent woman' it is not as one of the anomalous, self-supporting kind. She seems anxious, indeed, to define herself as more proper than other women: her tale is populated by warning images of those who have lacked self-control—the maniac Bertha, the demimondaine Celine (from likeness to whom the 'lively' Adèle must be carefully trained away), the 'showy' and 'striking' Blanche Ingram, all rivals for Rochester's love. The woman who as a child of 10 gave her 'furious feelings uncontrolled play' (37), and who says of herself at 18 that 'the restlessness was in my nature' (109), becomes a disciplinarian—instructing the pupils in her school 'in doing their work well; in keeping their persons neat; in learning their tasks regularly; in acquiring quiet and orderly manners' (366), supervising the education that makes Adèle an 'obliging companion: docile, good-tempered, and well-principled' and corrects her 'French defects' (450). Despite her impassioned paean on behalf of 'women'—'they need exercise for their faculties, and a field for their efforts as much as their brothers do' (109)—she is only too happy to end her days in quiet domestic seclusion, far from that world whose rigours her story has exposed. Most problematically of all, this 'independent' heroine is peculiarly susceptible to the attractions of masculine power. In love with her employer, she finds his face and features 'full of an interest, an influence that quite mastered me,—that took my feelings from my own power and fettered them in his' (174–5). As her handsome, 'heroic' cousin urges her to go to India, she feels 'his influence in my marrow—his hold on my limbs', and contemplates 'the possibility of conceiving an inevitable, strange, torturing kind of love for him' (406, 416). And on suddenly hearing a 'mysterious summons' from him whom she calls her 'Master', she abandons 'free and honest' self-sufficiency for the promptings of romantic love (359). As twentieth-century critics—less concerned with propriety than with ideological correctness—have not been slow to point out, the contradictions that emerge in her story—between her rhetoric of equality and her acceptance of social distinction, between her romantic desire for self-fulfilment and her deference to 'laws and principles ... preconceived opinions, foregone determinations' (317)—are, in the end, smoothed over. Her problems are resolved by a series of fairy-tale coincidences—a fortunate legacy, a luckily discovered family, a convenient death. *Jane Eyre* came to be seen by critics of the twentieth century as a novel in which the ideological assumptions and social arrangements of early nineteenth-century England are ultimately not questioned, but endorsed.

Yet *Jane Eyre* has never been *felt* to be a conformist work. And analyses such as these—focusing as they do on that central character Jane, her choices, her attitudes, her development—seem hardly to capture what is most distinctive in the novel: the prose within which what the reader constructs as 'character' is created; and within which, as we have begun to see, the coherent, unified selfhood presupposed by the novel's subtitle is interrogated in unexpected ways. For that which can be traced at a microlevel is writ large in the 'melodrama and improbability',[6] the Gothic and fairy-tale suggestions that run through Jane's narrative. This is a novel that seems quite deliberately to flout the 'realist illusion' which—as one of the finest of its critics has suggested—it also consummately creates.[7] For it is one within which both 'dependence' and 'independence' appear in configurations more violent, more extreme, more disquieting, than a realist reading can contain.

Unlike Crimsworth's, Jane's story begins in childhood. Yet if this might seem to signal a new kind of emphasis on psychological development, the expectation is not exactly fulfilled. There is nothing in *Jane Eyre* like that sense of a childish consciousness coming into focus with which *Great Expectations* begins:

> My first vivid and broad impression of the identity of things seems tome to have been gained on a memorable raw afternoon towards evening. At such a time I found out for certain, that this bleak place overgrown with nettles was the churchyard ... and that the low leaden line beyond, was the river; and that the distant savage lair from which the wind was rushing, was the sea; and that the small bundle of shivers growing afraid of it all and beginning to cry, was Pip.

Unlike this uncertain 'bundle of shivers', whose development into a moral agent the novel goes on to trace, Jane is there from the beginning, distinct and defiant, not gradually gaining a sense of herself and her world but insisting on her own point of view. To that first crushing denial she opposes her own negative energy: 'I was glad of it: I never liked long walks'. She is, indeed, an oddly undetermined entity. If others are prominent in her narrative, she herself does not appear shaped by her relations with them. In this, *Jane Eyre* stands in striking contrast not merely to such later Victorian novels of childhood as *David Copperfield* and *The Mill on the Floss* but also to that with which its author was most familiar, her sister Emily's *Wuthering Heights*. That sense, expressed by Catherine Earnshaw, that the self is fundamentally defined by the earliest childhood ties ('My great miseries in this world have been Heathcliff's miseries, and I watched and felt each from the beginning ... If all else perished, and *he* remained, I should still continue to be') is strikingly absent here. So also is that Wordsworthian concern with the conflict between loyalty to the personal past and aspiration beyond it which Dickens and George Eliot were to explore in their later novels. Jane's trajectory points all one way. There is little in her childhood that demands her fidelity. The Reeds are not her family, as the Tullivers are Maggie Tulliver's or the Dorrits are Amy Dorrit's: she is not held to them by the difficult bonds of love. Rather, she insists on her difference even from those to whom she is closest as a child. Both Helen Burns and Miss Temple definitively disappear from her narrative: their influence passes with them, and self reasserts itself unchanged. Likewise—indeed, more extremely—she is independent of her adversaries: if she is confronted by a number of hostile descriptions of herself—a 'dependant', 'less than a servant', 'an underhand little thing', 'not quite the character and disposition I could wish',—such characterizations are bafflingly alien, to be rejected, rather than assimilated, as her narrative proceeds. 'All said I was wicked and perhaps I might be so', she thinks to herself in the red-room; but her development consists less in negotiating any very deeply internalized awareness of others' views than in gaining the power to assert her own perspective in opposition to theirs.

Here, as in *The Professor*, relations with others are figured as sites of antagonism. The love between Jane and Rochester is portrayed less as a growing concord than as a continual struggle for dominance. In their early days together, she 'delignts' in sparring with him. 'I knew the pleasure of vexing and soothing him by turns ... Beyond the verge of provocation I never ventured; on the extreme brink I liked well to try my skill' (158). 'Soft scene, daring demonstration, I would not have; and I stood in peril of both,' she says of her affianced lover; 'a weapon of defence must be prepared.' And she holds him at a distance with the 'needle of repartee' (273). 'I felt an inward power; a sense of influence, which supported me,' she tells of her ultimate resistance. 'The crisis was perilous; but not without its charm' (302). Such exchanges as these are pleasurable, even at moments of extremity.[8] As Rochester's speeches make clear, a dynamic of conquest and submission is inscribed in the commonplace clichés of Byronic romantic love: 'You please me, and you master me—you seem to submit, and I like the sense of pliancy you impart ... I am influenced—conquered; and the influence is sweeter than I can express; and the conquest I undergo has a witchery beyond any triumph I can win' (260–1). Yet in *Jane Eyre* such clichés as these are emphasized in a way that led Mrs Oliphant to complain in 1855 that the novel portrayed romantic love as 'a battle ... deadly and uncompromising, where the combatants, so far from being guided by the old punctilios of the duello, make no secret of their ferocity, but throw sly javelins at each other, instead of shaking hands before they begin'.[9]

Here, as in *The Professor*, the self is most fully itself in so far as it is impervious to others'—even beloved others'—influence. But here the sense is less of guarded self-defensiveness than of a more heroic endeavour. 'My mind had put off all it had borrowed of Miss Temple', says Jane, of her beloved teacher's departure, 'and ... now I was left in my natural element; and beginning to feel the stirring of old emotions' (84). The idiom is not that of 'self-help'—an individualistic determination 'to do more, earn more, be more, possess more' (*P* 161)—but of romantic self-assertion; of a self more essential, more 'natural', more gloriously unsubmissive, than can be accommodated within the social world. And throughout the novel, this idiom merges with and is reinforced by another (also, it seems, unironized): an idiom of spiritual struggle in which Jane, like Bunyan's Christian, struggles to preserve herself in face of temptation and threat. Here the echoes of *Pilgrim's Progress* are more pervasive and less sardonic than they are in *The Professor*. Jane's resistance to Rochester is portrayed in biblical terms, as a 'soul'-securing victory: 'physically, I felt, at the moment, powerless as stubble exposed to the draught and glow of a furnace—mentally, I still possessed my soul, and with it the certainty of ultimate safety' (317).[10] 'Conqueror I might be of the house', he says of her imagined surrender; 'but the inmate would escape to heaven before I could call myself possessor of its day dwelling-place' (318). There is nothing here like *The Professor's* peculiar exposure of the contradictions inherent in its narrator's stance: romantic and religious suggestions merge to underwrite rather than question Jane's stubborn assertion of self. For if Crimsworth's insistence on his own 'independence' is exposed in *The Professor* as a process of self-division, Jane's is seen as a struggle, in face of assault and temptation, to preserve an apparently unambiguously valued integrity. And if Crimsworth's narrative bespeaks the contorted deadlock of impulse denied, the inward-turned energy of 'self-control', Jane's is framed in a language of expressiveness, liberty, transcendence: a language not of repression, but of power.

Like Crimsworth's, Jane's drive towards 'independence' is inscribed most intimately in her narrative: everything in her world is seen from her controlling point of view. But where that earlier narrator was portrayed, ironically, as a self-defensive spy, there seems to be no such questioning of Jane's perspective in *Jane Eyre*. It is true that those who threaten Jane most are distanced throughout her narrative by a cool, analytic observation. 'I knew he would soon strike,' she says of the bully John Reed, 'and while dreading the blow, I mused on the disgusting and ugly appearance of him who would presently deal it' (10). 'His face riveted the eye', she confesses of St John Rivers; but compulsion becomes a categorizing power as she proceeds to anatomize his appearance: 'It was like a Greek face, very pure in outline; quite a straight, classic nose; quite an Athenian mouth and chin' (345). Left alone, as a child, with the forbidding Mrs Reed, she occupies herself in 'watching her ... I examined her figure; I perused her features' (35). (In a review that connected this sharpness of observation with deplorable 'want of feeling', the *Christian Remembrancer* complained that Jane's aunt's 'unrepentant' deathbed was 'described with as deliberate a minuteness and as severe a tranquillity as a naturalist might display in recording the mortal orgasms of a jelly-fish').[11] But if this objectifying of others is reminiscent of Crimsworth, the world through which Jane moves is more passionate and more threatening than that place of mutual surveillance in which he defends himself. At Lowood, accused of being a liar, she feels the eyes of the school 'directed like burning-glasses against my scorched skin' (66). 'The fiery eye glared upon me' is her worst, fragmented memory of the crazed Bertha's murder attempt (284). 'He searched my face with eyes that I saw were dark, irate and piercing,' she tells of her first evening at Thornfield with Rochester (121); 'he seemed to devour me with his flaming glance', of the moment in which she flees from him (317). If her vision, like Crimsworth's, is a weapon, it is wielded in a fierier, snore heroic struggle than his.

And that 'vision' is not questioned or ironized, but figured throughout in images of romanticism, creativity, transcendence. She who as a child took care that her book 'should be one stored with pictures' (7), who longed to examine the design on a pretty plate (20), who even in hunger notes first 'how pretty... the china cups and bright teapot look' (72), sees her world with an artist's eye: again and again in her narrative, scenes, faces, rooms appear in pictorial terms. Thus, she describes the 'rude noise' of Rochester's horse approaching and disturbing the evening peace, 'as, in a picture, the solid mass of a crag, or the rough boles of a great oak, drawn in dark and strong on the foreground, efface the aërial distance of azure hill, sunny horizon and blended clouds, where tint melts into tint' (111–12): his face, first seen, is 'like a new picture introduced to the gallery of memory; and ... dissimilar to all the others hanging there' (115). The child who on her first evening at Lowood 'puzzl[es] to make out the subject of a picture on the wall' (43), who feasts in her dormitory bed 'on the spectacle of ideal drawings' (74), grows into a woman accomplished in drawing and painting. And this sense of the narrator as artist carries with it suggestions of her superior, visionary power—a power that seems, magically, to penetrate to the essence of things and, at crucial points in the novel, to point prophetically forward. The fairy-tale horror with which her childish gaze invests Brocklehurst—'What a face he had, now that it was almost on a level with mine! what a great nose! and what a mouth! and what large, prominent teeth!' (32)—is not, like Pip's first, appalled vision of Magwitch, replaced by the clearer vision of maturity: it is proved true by subsequent events, and echoed as Jane's story unfolds. 'What a hot and strong grasp he had!' she says, as she recalls Rochester's demeanour at the altar on their bigamous wedding day, 'and how like quarried marble was his pale, firm, massive front at this moment! How his eyes shone, still watchful, and yet wild beneath!' (289). Hers is a vision quite different from Crimsworth's—revelatory, transformative, creative, surrounded by suggestions of prophecy and preternatural power. It is closer to that of the Genii than to the perspective of the creatures of Glass Town.

For there is nothing like it in the novel. The logic of Crimsworth's watchfulness is objectified in the unresting mutual surveillance, the constant suspicion and antagonism, of the world that he confronts. But Jane's vision is not thus mirrored; and Jane's story—framed in the language of heroic struggle, of romantic love, of creative freedom—does not seem to offer this kind of implicit judgement on its narrator's existential stance. Her eye remains pre-eminent. Her viewpoint is confirmed, even celebrated. Hers is an extreme, absolutist version of that which is to some extent implicit in all first-person narrative: the power of the teller to shape the fictional world. In *The Professor* the narrator's announced 'independence' was fictionally undermined. But there is no such narrative irony in *Jane Eyre*. The story that unfolds from Jane's perspective is one in which her view of her world is unequivocally confirmed, and she assumes a position of unassailable power. Those others who have threatened her are one by one themselves confounded. Investigation into the affairs of Lowood produces 'a result mortifying to Mr Brocklehurst' (83); John Reed's is a 'shocking' death, and his mother's a desolate one. The Reed sisters are disposed of, the one to a loveless marriage with a 'worn-out man of fashion', the other to be 'walled up alive in a French convent' (242); Bertha Rochester perishes; the 'glorious sun' of St John Rivers 'hastens to its setting' as the novel ends. Less violent offenders are chastened. Little Adèle, 'who had been spoiled and indulged, and therefore was sometimes wayward', is made tractable to Jane's influence (108, 450); her rival, Blanche Ingram, is categorically dismissed by the man she has sought to entrap. Rochester is blinded, injured, and domesticated: no longer the figure with the 'flaming glance' (317) who offered 'glimpses' of a wider world to an 'honoured' and 'gratified' Jane (146), but dependent on her both for 'vision' and for his 'right hand' (451). Jane's friends, on the other hand, prosper. The Rivers sisters share her inheritance; Miss Temple marries 'an excellent man, almost worthy of such a wife'; even Helen Burns's grave is now marked by 'a grey marble tablet ... inscribed with her name, and the word "Resurgam"' (82). The logic is that of fairy tale, in which moral complexity is replaced by an absolute opposition between the deserving who succeed and the bad who get their just deserts. And of this tale Jane is the triumphant heroine—the Cinderella who surpasses her ugly sisters and stepmother, and receives unlooked-for fairy gifts; the Bluebeard's wife who survives to tell her story; the changeling who is recognized by her kinsfolk; the Beauty who finally tames the Beast. By the end, she is paramount: those who have so Light to wrong her are punished, her decisions are vindicated and her desires fulfilled. Hers is a trajectory more violent, more extreme than that of the conventional *Bildungsroman*, in which subjective desires are countered and tempered by the world into which the protagonist goes.

Yet it is no less questioned than Crimsworth's, though in an entirely different way. For if Jane's uncontested narrating voice, rewarding her friends and punishing her enemies, oddly recalls the great Genii of Glass Town, much that is most distinctive in *Jane Eyre* evokes also the quite different viewpoint of their creatures. From the opening chapter, where the terrorized child fantasizes about the 'death-white realms' depicted in the book on her lap, to the closing paragraphs, in which 'Jane Eyre' has become Jane Rochester, this tale of egocentric triumph is counterpointed by another story, in which the protagonist is not all-powerful, but precarious, powerless, threatened: one that speaks not of self-confirming triumph, but of uncertainty and impotence. It is a story that begins in very first sentence of the novel, with its uncompromising negative—'There was *no possibility* of taking a walk that day'. This is quite unlike the negatives with which Crimsworth opens his tale. For that which is here configured is not simply or primarily an oppositional stance, but the intransigence of a world beyond the narrator's control. Jane's fast direct statement of feeling—'I was glad of it: I never liked long walks'—is less assertive than reactive: it is succeeded by a series of clauses in which her impotence is stressed: '*dreadful to me* was the coming home in the raw twilight, with *nipped* fingers and toes, and a heart *saddened* by the chidings of Bessie, the nurse, and *humbled* by the consciousness of my physical inferiority to Eliza, John, and Georgiana Reed' (my italics). Where, at the opening of *The Professor*, others' words were reported by a controlling narrative voice, here they loom larger, unmediated, imperfectly understood. Others, in these opening pages, speak not so much *to* Jane as *of* her:

> 'She never did so before,' at last said Bessie, turning to the Abigail.
>
> 'But it was always in her,' was the reply. 'I've told Missis often my opinion about the child, and Missis agreed with me. She's an underhand little thing: I never saw a girl of her age with so much cover.' (12)

> 'Mr Brocklehurst, I believe I intimated in the letter which I wrote to you three weeks ago, that this little girl has not quite the character and disposition I could wish.' (33)

To such characterizations, it seems, there can be no reply, any more than there could be a reply to the murmuring voices of 'Strange Events'. Indeed, it is in words that echo Lord Charles Wellesley's that the narrator describes her habitual childish awareness of this weight of others' speech: 'I had nothing to say to these words: they were not new to me: my very first recollections of existence included hints of the same kind. This reproach of my dependence had become a vague sing-song in my ear; very painful and crushing, but only half intelligible' (13). Others are not here rejected, as they are in *The Professor*, in a movement of antagonism. They are 'painfully' and 'crushingly' unanswerable: for the order of being they occupy is—like that of the mighty other whom Lord Charles Wellesley sees—more effective, more definitive than that of the helpless protagonist.

The hostile others who inhabit Jane's world are far more substantial than she. The physical and moral violence of John Reed and of Mr

Brocklehurst is made worse by their grotesque solidity. John Reed is 'large and stout for his age', with 'thick lineaments in a spacious visage, heavy limbs and large extremities': he 'gorge[s] himself habitually at table' (9). Mr Brocklehurst has the surrealistic rigidity of 'a black pillar! ... standing erect on the rug'; his 'grim face' is 'like a carved mask, placed over the shaft byway of capital' (31). St John Rivers, ascetic as he is, has a different, but comparable solidity: his face is 'like chiselled marble' (377): at the fireside he appears like 'a cold cumbrous column, gloomy and out of place' (393). John Reed's sisters grow up into women much larger than Jane: 'Miss Reed is the head and shoulders taller than you are; and Miss Georgiana would make two of you in breadth,' Bessie tells her (90). Mrs Reed has a 'stony eye—opaque to tenderness, indissoluble to tears' (231). Bertha Rochester is 'a big woman ... and corpulent besides', her 'lurid visage' and 'bloated features' make her like a 'clothed hyena' (293). Rochester has a 'square, massive brow ... strong features, firm, grim mouth,—all energy, decision, will' (174).

And if such presences seem larger, more unyielding, more grossly material than life, they have also a preternatural potency. The world through which Jane moves is one of fairy-tale malevolence: a place of spells, of curses, of charms. 'What a face he had, now that it was almost on a level with mine! what a great nose! and what a mouth! and what large, prominent, teeth!' exclaims Jane of Mr Brocklehurst (32). What a pigmy intellect she had, and what giant propensities!'says her husband of Bertha Rochester. 'How fearful were the curses those propensities entailed on me!' (306). At Gateshead, a 'switch' lurks in a corner, 'waiting to leap out imp-like and lace my quivering palm or shrinking neck' (230); at Thornfield a raving lunatic is 'prompted by her familiar to burn people in their beds at night, to stab them, to bite their flesh from their bones' (301); in face of St John's importunings, Jane feels 'as if an awful charm was framing round and gathering over me: I trembled to hear some fatal word spoken which would at once declare and rivet the spell' (402). 'Like a giant', her cousin appears, on the final page of the novel, 'hew[ing] down the prejudices' that 'encumber' 'his race' (452).

Jane, however, is evanescent: as she puts it, 'like nobody there' (15).[12] 'A strange little figure... like one of the tiny phantoms ... Bessie's evening stories represented,' she appears to herself in the red-room mirror (14); to Rochester, years later, she is a 'mocking changeling' (438), 'a strange ... almost unearthly thing' (255), like one who comes 'from the abode of people who are dead' (245). 'I hardly know what thoughts I have in my head,' she says to him on their wedding eve. 'Everything in life seems unreal' (279). If the fairy-tale portents, prefigurative metaphors, and premonitory dreams that punctuate her story seem to underwrite her progression to triumph, they also question and qualify that narrative of effective self-making implied by its 'autobiographical' form. For even at decisive moments, she is figured less as shaping her own destiny than as propelled by mysterious powers—by the 'fairy' gift of a suggestion (86), by a strange 'human form... in the azure' (319), by a supernatural call that makes the 'flesh quiver on the bones' (419). Indeed, this sense of self as passive object, rather than as active subject, runs in a different way through her most private self-communings. For the Jane who insists so urgently on her right to self-determination is repeatedly portrayed as the helpless, imperilled object of forces beyond her control; at the mercy not merely of more powerful others, but of a whole constellation of emotions that threaten and assail her from within. Her feelings are represented less as impulses emanating from herself than as entities with lives of their own. 'A hand of fiery iron grasped my vitals,' she says, of her resistance to Rochester. 'My very Conscience and Reason turned traitors against me, and charged me with crime ... They spoke almost as loud as Feeling: and that clamoured wildly. "Oh, comply!" it said' (315, 317). Like the external world through which she moves, this inner landscape has the malevolence of fairy tale. 'Something of vengeance I had tasted for the first time; as aromatic wine it seemed on swallowing, warm and racy: its after-flavour, metallic and corroding, gave me a sensation as if I had been poisoned' (38). 'Oh, that fear of his self-abandonment ... how it goaded me! It was a barbed arrow-head in my breast: it tore me when I tried to extract it; it sickened me when Remembrance thrust it further in' (321); 'My iron shroud contracted round me: persuasion advanced with slow sure step' (404).[13]

The others who populate Jane's narrative are not merely more solid, more effective, than she: they are actively persecutory. Each of those on whom she is dependent threatens her very existence; not metaphorically, but literally. Mrs Reed, like a fairy-tale evil stepmother, has her taken away and locked up, giving her 'nerves' such a 'shock' that even the phlegmatic Bessie is afraid that 'she might die' (19–20). 'What did they do with her at Lowood?' Jane's aunt wonders on her deathbed. 'The fever broke out there, and many of the pupils died. She, however, did not die: but I said she did—I wish she had died!' (232). 'I must keep in good health, and not die,' Jane tells Mr Brocklehurst; but 'How can you keep in good health?' he asks, unanswerably, in reply (32). His 'institution' is a place of death, in which she is starved and frozen, and threatened with hell-fire. The 'master' into whose employment she goes likewise jeopardizes her life. His house is a 'Bluebeard's castle' where a 'Vampyre'-like figure tries to kill her; his attempts to persuade her to stay with him turn her 'stone-cold with ominous terror' (316); and the flight to which he drives her is figured as a dreadful death: 'He who is taken out to pass through a fair scene to the scaffold, thinks not of the flowers that smile on his road, but of the block and axe-edge; of the disseverment of bone and vein; of the grave gaping at the end' (321). Reduced, by that flight, to destitution, she almost dies of 'want and cold' (330). Her rescuer, St John Rivers—Jane's only living male relative, and hence her natural protector—proves, as his sister warns, 'inexorable as death' (356). His proposal of marriage appears as a threat to her very life: 'I felt how—if I were his wife—this good man, pure as the deep sunless source, could soon kill me, without drawing from my veins a single drop of blood, or receiving on his own crystal conscience the faintest stain of crime' (411). More prosaically, Jane reflects on his desire to conscript her as a missionary: 'if I go to India, I go to premature death' (404).

Above all, perhaps, Jane's account of her love for Rochester is informed throughout by a sense of her own precariousness and of this other's potency. Her 'master' is her employer; she is 'his paid subordinate' (134). He is accustomed to possess and control (124); she is effective, if at all, only in a contracted sphere. He has travelled throughout Europe, 'provided with plenty of money, and the passport of an old name' (311); she gazes yearningly outwards towards the wider world. Like a Genie, he offers to transform her life—'I shall waft you away at once to town ... I shall bear my treasure to regions nearer the sun' (259)—and to load her with fairy gifts. 'I will myself put the diamond chain around your neck, and the circlet on your forehead ... and I will clasp the bracelets on these fine wrists, and load these fairy-like fingers with rings' (259). Such promises, to Jane, pose a threat to her very being: 'And then you won't know me, sir; and I shall not be your Jane Eyre any longer, but an ape in a harlequin's jacket,—a jay in borrowed plumes' (259). From the clichés of his love-song—'My love has sworn, with sealing kiss, I With me to live—to die'—she extracts, half-humorously, a serious meaning, 'I should ... not be hurried away in a suttee' (273). And as he responds to her greeting—'It is Jane Eyre, sir'—with 'Soon to be Jane Rochester', she feels 'something stronger than was consistent with joy—something that smote and stunned: it was, I think, almost fear' (258). In an access of triumphant possessiveness, Rochester repeats her future, altered name. But Jane's response—'It can never be, sir: it does not sound likely'—hints at a darker feeling. 'It can never be': for to conceive of the subject 'Jane Eyre', becoming that other-defined object, 'Jane Rochester', is as impossible as imagining her own death, her replacement by another—'not I, but one Jane Rochester'—one who will displace her as surely as 'garments said to be hers had already displaced my black stuff gown and Lowood bonnet' (275).

A heroic 'determined revolt' (400) against the violence of such monstrous figures as a Mrs Reed or a Mr Brocklehurst is comparatively easy.

Those to whom Jane is drawn pose a far more insidious threat. As she gazes unobserved at Rochester, she feels 'a precious yet poignant pleasure; pure gold, with a steely point of agony: a pleasure like what the thirst-perishing man might feel who knows the well to which he has crept is poisoned, yet stoops and drinks divine draughts nevertheless' (174); on the eve of her wedding, she tells him, 'I cannot see my prospects clearly to-night ... Everything in life seems unreal' (279). 'I was tempted', she says of St John Rivers, 'to cease struggling with him—to rush down the torrent of his will into the gulf of his existence, and there lose my own' (418). Again and again in her narrative the image reappears of a potent, compelling other engulfing independent self. Thus, she finds Rochester's features 'full of an interest, an influence that quite mastered me,—that took my feelings from my own power and fettered them in his' (175); thus, on the morning of the abortive wedding, 'my heart was with my eyes; and both seemed migrated into Mr Rochester's frame' (287). Thus, St John Rivers' 'influence' takes over and shapes her own purposes—'My work, which had appeared so vague, so hopelessly diffuse, condensed itself as he proceeded; and assumed a definite form under his shaping hand' (404). Thus, Rochester, even in absence, is able to dominate and control:

> His idea was still with me; because it was not a vapour sunshine could disperse; nor a sand-traced effigy storms could wash away: it was a name graven on a tablet, fated to last as long as the marble it inscribed. The craving to know what had become of him followed me everywhere: when I was at Morton, I re-entered my cottage every evening to think of that; and now at Moor House, I sought my bedroom each night to brood over it. (399)

Here, as when she was a child at Lowood, Jane is less agent than sufferer, 'nipped' by 'cold without' and gnawed 'by hunger within'—though here the cold is not literal cold, but the icy passion of St John Rivers, and the hunger not literal hunger, but a 'craving' to know what has happened to her beloved. At this stage in her narrative, she has arrived at a much surer identity than that bewildered charity-child. An heiress, and now herself a 'benefactress' she is living amongst kinsfolk. '*I* care for myself' she has insisted to the man she loves (317). Yet like that literal 'stone-tablet', the mere 'idea' of this other seems more persisting, more unquestionable, more potent than the ineffectual, helplessly driven self.

That sense of egocentric omnipotence which is in one way inscribed in *Jane Eyre* is, then, counterpointed throughout by a sense of absolute jeopardy: one that culminates, indeed, in the disappearance of 'Jane Eyre'.

For as the novel draws to a close, and the narrator becomes 'not I, but one Jane Rochester', that embattled, precarious 'I' is transmuted into a 'we':

> I am my husband's life as fully as he is mine. No woman was ever nearer her mate than I am: ever more absolutely bone of his bone, and flesh of his flesh. I know no weariness of my Edward's society: he knows none of mine, anymore than we each do of the pulsation of the heart that beats in our separate bosoms; consequently, we are ever together. (450)

And Jane's description resonates not merely with the biblical account of the creation of Eve as Adam's helpmeet,[14] but also with Milton's far darker portrayal of Adam's appalled confrontation of their inescapably conjoined doom:

> flesh of flesh
> Bone of my bone thou art, and from thy state
> Mine never shall be parted, bliss or woe.
> (*Paradise Lost*, 9.914–16)

This is a curious ending to that story of a singular self, desperately 'tenacious of life' (121) which is inscribed in the novel's imagery of basic biological need. The sparring opposition between Jane and Rochester here gives way to the image of a union in which each of those striving egos disappears: 'We talk, I believe, all day long: to talk to each other is but a more animated and an audible thinking. All my confidence is bestowed on him; all his confidence is devoted to me: we are precisely suited in character; perfect concord is the result' (451). And the absence of the desperate struggle that has animated Jane's story contributes at least as much to the feeling of an energy gone from these passages as does the more overt fact of Rochester's blind and crippled state. Like that informing imagery of two becoming one flesh, this insistence on a unity that denies division ('all ... all ... precisely ... perfect') works oddly against the narrator's protestations of happiness. The intimation that 'Jane Eyre' has gone is reinforced by the hints of death that play through the novel's descriptions of what becomes her final home. Ferndean is a 'desolate spot', with 'dark and green ... decaying walls', which has long been unlettable because of its 'ineligible and insalubrious site'. 'Can there be life here?' asks Jane (430). Her expansive reaching out for 'all of incident, life, fire, feeling, that I desired and had not' has contracted to a single object 'loving him, being loved by him' (367); her longing for a 'power of vision' that might 'overpass' bounding 'limits' has ended in viewless retirement, deep in a 'gloomy wood' with 'no opening anywhere' (430).

Throughout the novel, then—not merely at those points at which its heroine almost perishes (from 'a species of fit' at Gateshead, from typhus at Lowood school, at the hand of the mad Bertha, from starvation on the moor, by choosing to go to India) but even in her account other love for Rochester—runs the constant suggestion that the narrating 'I' is in imminent danger of extinction. Even in the final pages this sense remains, complicating and questioning that story of desire fulfilled which Jane's 'independent' return to the dependent Rochester in one way seems to be. It is a sense that is underwritten by the novel's closing paragraphs, where that 'we' who live in satisfied retirement (broken only by letters and visits and consultations with oculists) give way to an as yet unsatisfied 'I', who labours undaunted in a wider world, urged onward in his 'high ambition' by all that self-assertive energy which has vanished from its heroine's tale; one whose assured invocation of the supreme authority of Scripture emphasizes that hers is a choice of finite, earthly 'blessedness'. 'No fear of death,' says Jane, 'will darken St John's last hour'; and the insistent third person of the sentence that follows—'*his* mind will be unclouded; *his* heart will be undaunted; *his* hope will be sure; *his* faith steadfast' (452, my italics)—suggests that there maybe no such confidence for her.

This final, troubling image of one other than the narrator seems less to turn away from the questions raised in her story than to focus the contradictions that conformations emphasize. That longing to break the bounds of a confined existence which propelled Jane away from Lowood, which unsettled her at Thornfield, is echoed here in St John Rivers's hunger for immortality; that impulse towards subjugation of the other which surrealistically shapes her narrative has its counterpart here in his imperializing zeal. That sense of self as annihilable and of other as all-powerful which quite differently haunts her story is paralleled here by his evangelical self-surrender: his final call to his yearned-for 'master' resonates with hers. Like the intimations of violence that disrupt Crimsworth's closing descriptions of domestic bliss, this strange, suggestive portrait appears less as an irrelevant coda to an already finished narrative than as an emphatic, final image of that peculiar double logic that is inscribed in it throughout.

It is a doubleness very different from *The Professor*'s two-dimensional irony. *Jane Eyre* tells not a single, fictionally undermined story, but two opposing and incommensurate ones. The self at the centre of each appears in a radically different way: in one, as magically omnipotent, triumphing absolutely; in the other, as insubstantial, the constantly jeopardized object of forces beyond its control. And as the suspense that attends even repeated rereadings suggests, these conflicting stories can hardly be reconciled by reading the novel as an account of the 'resolution' arrived at by the developing character Jane. Those opposing configurations of triumphant omnipotence and imminent annihilation which animate her narrative remain to the end unresolved: indeed, they are brought together and imaged in the potent yet death-bound figure both of romantic self-assertion and of evangelical self-immolation who has the novel's final word. And in this these final paragraphs of *Jane Eyre* point not away from but towards the mid-nineteenth-century world.

NOTES

1. 'The feeling was not like an electric shock; but it was quite as sharp, as strange, as startling', says Jane of the moment when she hears Rochester's call (419).

2. The debates surrounding the introduction of the New Poor Law were familiar to Charlotte Brontë, both through *Blackwood's Magazine*, which had in the 1820s and 1830s championed the old Poor Laws; and more immediately through her father, who had in the late 1830s played an active part in local opposition to the Poor Law Amendment Act of 1834. (Barker, 265–9).

3. Marianne Farningham, *A Working Woman's Life: An Autobiography* (London: James Clarke, 1907), 14.

4. Anon., *Woman: As She Is and As She Should Be* (2 vols.; London: James Cochrane & Co., 1835), ii, 37.

5. William Landels, *Woman's Sphere and Work Considered in the Light of Scriptures* (London: James Nisbet, 1859), 27.

6. [G.H. Lewes], review of *Jane Eyre, Fraser's Magazine* 36, December 1847 (*CH* 85).

7. Sally Shuttleworth, *Charlotte Brontë and Victorian Psychology* (Cambridge: Cambridge University Press, 1996), 1–3.

8. On the 'erotics of power' in such scenes, see Shuttleworth, *Charlotte Brontë and Victorian Psychology*, 170–3.

9. *CH* 312–13.

10. The reference is to Isaiah 5:24.

11. *Christian Remembrancer*, 15 (1848), 399.

12. For a suggestive discussion of this 'remoteness of that very "I" which dominates the novel' see Karen Chase, *Eros and Psyche: The Representation of Personality in Charlotte Brontë, Charles Dickens, George Eliot* (London: Methuen, 1984), 70–9.

13. The 'iron shroud' is the subject of a *Blackwood's* tale of terror with which Brontë had probably been familiar since childhood—William Mudford's 'The Iron Shroud' published in August 1830, in which a prison cell contracts and crushes its occupant to death. (See J. M. S. Tompkins, 'Jane Eyre's "Iron Shroud"', *Modern Language Review*, 22 (1927), 195–7).

14. Genesis 2:23.

WARREN EDMINSTER

Fairies and Feminism: Recurrent Patterns in Chaucer's "The Wife of Bath's Tale" and Brontë's Jane Eyre

> I have received it and told it anew.... I stand in the chain of narrators, a link between links; I tell once again the old stories, and if they sound new, it is because the new already lay dormant in them when they were told for the first time.
>
> Martin Buber, preface to *Die Legende des Baal Schem*, 1908
> (Trans. Maurice Friedman)

Literature is in one sense evolutionary, a series of voices co-opting and adapting what has been said and in turn being co-opted and adapted by those voices which follow. In our enthusiasm to study individual authors, we often forget the central influence that the tradition of literary development has had on their work—Dante's tendency to incorporate and use Virgil, for example, just as Virgil adapted the works of Homer. Victorian co-opting of medieval culture perfectly exemplifies this type of adaptive creativity. From the literature of Scott and Tennyson through the aesthetic philosophies of Carlyle, Ruskin, and Morris, Victorian medievalism held up an ideal, mythical medieval world as a contrast to the soulless, rational industrialism of the nineteenth century.[1] In Charlotte Brontë's *Jane Eyre*, Jane engages in just such an idealization of the past, lamenting the passing of fairies and elves from the world. In fact, the passing of the fairies becomes symbolic of the flaws and corruption of Jane's world, and Jane is herself repeatedly identified

From *The Victorian Newsletter* no. 104 (Fall 2003). © 2003 by *The Victorian Newsletter*.

as a fairy, out of place in the cold, rational, patriarchal society of Victorian England. Jane's lament is not novel, however; it echoes a similar lament for the passing of fairies and elves in Geoffrey Chaucer's "The Wife of Bath's Tale." Yet the echo is far from a passing resemblance. Both narratives treat women struggling to gain control and independence in a masculine world, and both use fairies and fairy magic as symbolic representations of that struggle. The number of close structural and thematic parallels is intriguing. They suggest the possibility that Brontë consciously adapts the symbolic structure of Chaucer's rape tale, perhaps the clearest literary expression of the female perspective up to that time, to her own examination of gender oppression and conflict within Victorian society. If, on the other hand, the parallels are not the result of conscious adaptation, we are left with an equally intriguing possibility—that these two authors, separated by time, cultural development, and sexual difference, nonetheless employ the same narrative components to reach the same narrative conclusions about the boundaries of gender and power in Western culture.

Not that Chaucer was in any way foreign to the Victorians. In the late eighteenth century, several scholars finally mastered and explained his metrical manner, which had been previously disparaged as "quaint" and "rough." Tyrwhitt brought out a reasonably correct text of the *Canterbury Tales* in 1775, and John Bell immediately pirated and popularized it in his 1782 *The Poets of Great Britain* (Brewer 37). Readers quickly rediscovered the original Chaucer and devoured his works as they had not for 400 years. Many nineteenth-century writers were heavily influenced by Chaucer. Blake, Scott, Lamb, Southey, the Wordsworths, Coleridge, Landor, Shelley, Hazlitt, Ruskin, and Hunt, among others, all read Chaucer and spoke glowingly of his work; Byron disliked him, but the number of times he mentioned Chaucer shows at least that he read him (Spurgeon lxii–lxv). Scholarly criticism of Chaucer also exploded. Writing in 1908, Caroline Spurgeon, author of the landmark *Five Hundred Years of Chaucer Criticism and Allusion*, notes that "It would be impossible here to mention all the Chaucer scholars of the Nineteenth Century, for the study of our first great poet has been taken up with enthusiasm, not only in England, but also in Germany and America" (cxxiii). Chaucer was everywhere and on everyone's mind.

Given the broad circulation of so many of Chaucer's texts, and given their popularity at the time, Charlotte Brontë most likely read Chaucer somewhere. If he didn't grace her father's library, she might have seen him at the Heaton's library at Ponden House, to which Gerin says the Brontë sisters "had early access"; or she might have found him in the "subscription volumes from the Keighley Mechanics' Institute Library" or in the library at Roehead (24). Brontë never mentions Chaucer by name in her famous letter to Ellen

Nussey, but the Nussey letter is clearly prescriptive of what a young woman should read rather than descriptive of what she herself read.[2] At any rate, Brontë does mention Pope, many editions of whom included Pope's "modernization" of Chaucer's "The Wife of Bath's Tale."[3] It is thus likely that she read the tale somewhere in some version.

The importance of "The Wife of Bath's Tale" to a woman concerned with the treatment of women is clear. Chaucer's Wife was a common type in medieval literature, but the clarity of her argument and the skill of her storytelling were unique in English literature.[4] In fact, until the period in which Brontë herself wrote, "The Wife of Bath's Tale" stood out as one of the most convincing literary apologies for the idea of feminine equality and independence. The fact that it was written by a man who was actually accused of "raptus" makes it a suspect document to modern feminists, but this controversy was absent from nineteenth-century discussion of Chaucer and wouldn't have influenced nineteenth-century views.[5] At any rate, the tale itself provided one of the few existing examples of how fiction could be used to express a feminine worldview, something with which Brontë certainly seems fascinated. In writing *Jane Eyre*, arguably the first of the great feminist novels, and certainly a novel whose primary theme is gender equity and justice, Brontë would have found few models more appropriate to her topic than "The Wife of Bath's Tale."

Readers will recall that the Wife of Bath first gives a long prologue dealing with power politics between men and women in marital relationships, especially her own experiences in such matters. With each of her five husbands, the wife tells us, she had to win dominance before there could be happiness in the marriage. The tale then begins with a speech bemoaning the departure of fairydom:

> In th'olde dayes of the Kyng Arthour,
> Of which that Britons speken greet honour,
> Al was this land fulfild of fayerye.
> The elf-queene, with hir joly compaignye,
> Daunced ful ofte in many a grene mede.
> This was the olde opinion, as I rede;
> I speke of manye hundred yeres ago.
> But now kan no man se none elves mo. (ll. 857–64)

Jane Eyre begins with a similar sentiment; even as Jane wonders about her surroundings and begins making her first references to her changeling-like orphanhood, she muses about the attractive but unbelievable world of fairies:

> for as to the elves, having sought them in vain among foxglove leaves and bells, under mushrooms and beneath the ground-ivy mantling old wall-nooks, I had at length made up my mind to the sad truth, that they were all gone out of England to sonic savage country where the woods were wilder and thicker, and the population more scant. (17)

Later, when Rochester teasingly accuses her of being an elf, she repeats her conclusion that fairies have left England:

> "The men in green all forsook England a hundred years ago," said I, speaking as seriously as he had done. "And not even in Hay Lane, or in the fields about it, could you find a trace of them. I don't think either summer or harvest, or winter moon, will ever shine on their revels more." (107)[6]

These laments are not simple, random expressions of nostalgia in either story. In both *Jane Eyre* and "The Wife of Bath's Tale," the loss of the faery world is symbolic of a much larger problem, and the problems themselves are strikingly similar. In "The Wife of Bath's Tale," the central dynamic of the story, masculine oppression of women, is directly related to the cause of the fairies' departure. The current fairy shortage, as the Wife tells us, is caused by the prayers of thronging numbers of clerics and friars, "thikke as motes in the sonne-beem" (l. 868). The intrusion of the friars, or "lymytours," in "every lond and streem" (l. 867), in the "halles, chambres, kitchenes, boures, / Citees, burghes, castels, hye toures, / Thropes, bemes, shipnes, dayeryes" (ll. 869–71), and in other places where "wont to walken was an elf" (l. 873) has made fairy magic scarce.

The replacement of fairy magic with the religious practice of friars ("lymytours") has caused a distinct change in the expectations of women, a change, as the wife sarcastically points out, not completely beneficial:

> Wommen may go now saufly up and doun.
> In every bush or under every tree
> There is noon oother incubus but he,
> And he ne wol doon hem but dishonour. (ll. 878–81)

In other words, women are now "safe" from the enchantment of fairies; all they need worry about is the mild "dishonour," namely sexual dishonor, which lymytours will do to them if they catch them alone in the forest.[7] This early hint of rape foreshadows the upcoming crime by the knight; it also confirms an already established relationship between religious practice and male oppression. The ambassadors of the Church may sexually dishonor women, but, as the Wife's prologue has shown, the Church as a whole dishonors women spiritually, socially, and morally. The Wife's fifth husband, a clerk educated by the Church, is a raving misogynist. He brings to their marriage a text compiled and copied within the Church. From this text, the clerk reads to the Wife stories about weak, unfaithful, and generally dishonorable women. These stories support and justify the clerk's oppression of the Wife and finally lead to the domestic violence between them. The Church is also exclusionary towards women. The Wife recognizes this in the prologue when she asserts that the books are slanted against women because only men write them. She says,

> By God! if wommen hadde writen stories,
> As clerkes han withinne hir oratories,
> They wolde han writen of men moore wikkednesse
> Than al the mark of Adam may redresse. (ll. 693–96)

In the Wife's view, therefore, religion is a tool used by men to rationalize their oppression of women. The clerk may behave monstrously towards his wife as long as he has the religious stories in his book to justify his actions.

While religious practice is symbolic of male oppression, the world of faery is symbolic of the feminine. There is ample evidence of this gender split even in the introduction to the tale. Religion here is represented by the masculine "lymytour," who is called by the masculine pronouns "himself," "his," "his," "he," "his" and "he" in only seven lines. Fairy magic, on the other hand, is represented by the feminine elf queen and "hir joly compaignye" (l. 860). Moreover, the effect of the friars' religious invasion is specifically upon fairies and women; the fairies are banished, and the women are molested by holy men claiming to protect them from fairy enchantment. This enchantment, as we see in the story, actually benefits women and undermines the male power system. The tale thus establishes a clear dichotomy; masculine forms, which are represented by religion, are ranged against feminine forms, which are associated with faery. In the Wife's world, fairy magic and feminine expression have both been banished by the rationalization and limitation of a patriarchal religious value system. The Wife of Bath's choice to set her narrative back in the legendary times of fairy magic is an attempt to create an idealistic world where feminine expression and independence exist and can be brought to bear on the types of male oppression which are symbolized by the knight's rape.

Jane Eyre explores a similar lack of feminine expression and independence in a patriarchal world. From the beginning of the novel, women display a pitiful inability to maintain space or autonomy against male intrusion or control. John's brutal invasion of Jane's window nook, for example, which sets the tone for the entire novel, is at least symbolically similar to the forced invasiveness of the physical rape in the Wife's tale. Like women in the Wife's world, women in *Jane Eyre* have no personal space which is not subject to male intrusion and control.

Yet as in "The Wife of Bath's Tale," male oppression isn't merely random meanness; it is enabled by a specific value system and thought process. Men justify their oppression of women through rationality and morality. For example, the Reverend Brocklehurst's holier-than-thou damnation of long-haired girls at Lowood is a mixture of twisted rationalization and religion which is curiously reminiscent of the clerk's use of religious stories. Both use a patriarchal value system to rationalize and justify oppressive and violent actions against women. Similarly, just as molesting friars can hypocritically congratulate themselves for saving women from the threat of fairy enchantment in "The Wife of Bath's Tale," Brocklehurst self-righteously saves the girls at Lowood from the self-indulgent sins of vanity and comfort by ordering that all their hair be cut off.

Similarly, just as the religious practice of friars has driven off fairies and elves, so too have the practical values of a patriarchal intellectual and moral system banished the possibility of fairy magic in *Jane Eyre*. Robert Martin notices this trend in the novel when he says that "In the world of the Patriarchy, the older system of knowledge and religion [i.e. the feminine world of faery] must go underground, as Christianity prevails and suppresses nature" (86). To the Brocklehursts and St. Johns of Jane's world, there is no room for the imaginative, romantic, or impractical. Helene Moglen notes that (much like the Wife's fifth husband) Brocklehurst "cloaks his greed, selfishness, and vanity in the hypocritical vestments of religious principles" (113). Brocklehurst sees no value in little girls feeling pretty or feminine; all such needs are unmeasurable, and he has rationally-determined proportions for all physical needs. Variety in the food at the school is not necessary for sustenance: burnt food will meet the girls' physical needs, so no deviation from the budget is necessary. By the same reasoning, St. John concludes that love is not as important to a marriage as is a practical helpmeet. Love is intangible and, therefore, irrelevant. He commands Jane to become his wife in mission work to serve himself and others even though he admits he does not love her. This value system of rigid, patriarchal morality and practicality repeatedly denies the existence of important intangibles such as beauty, love, imagination, and, of course, fairy magic.

Not that fiction can't exist in Jane's world. Jane is able to conceive of even such outlandish stuff as *Gulliver's Travels* because it explains its fiction in terms which relate to the factual, scientific practicality of the male intellectual system. Even though Lilliputians and Brobdinagians are outrageously fantastic, they are related with sufficient mathematical measurements and scientific calculations to make them seem believable. Jane considers *Gulliver's Travels* to be "a narrative of facts," and as a factual narrative, it becomes "eerie and dreary" to her (17). Fairy tales, on the other hand, reject such pseudo-scientific pretensions. They speak of "once upon a time" and of spells and wonders which defy a rational worldview. Consequently, they are unbelievable within and banished from the patriarchal world in which Jane finds herself.

Thus, as in "The Wife of Bath's Tale," the loss of fairy magic parallels and is symbolic of the loss of feminine expression and independence which is so central to the dilemma in *Jane Eyre*. And as Jane begins to cope with and overcome this dilemma, fairy magic returns in her own person. In identifying Jane Eyre with the fairy world, Brontë too evokes an idealistic, extra-masculine and extra-rational world where female expression and independence can be used to address the problem of male oppression. Martin argues,

> The appeal of the world of faery for Charlotte Brontë was the appeal of a poetic system which still believed in magic and which was still centered around the role of women. In the nineteenth century it was only in the fairy tale that Charlotte Brontë was likely to find traces of a non-patriarchal world. The divided world of her fiction has yet one more division, that between women's world of fairy tale, and the men's world of Christianity. (94)

Like Chaucer's Wife of Bath, Brontë uses this division to undermine patriarchal Wisdom and establish a new set of feminine values.

The similarities in the tales go beyond general thematic and symbolic parallels, however. In the story of the relationship between Jane and the dominant male character, Edward Rochester, *Jane Eyre* develops many of the same specific plot elements that are found in "The Wife of Bath's Tale." For example, in the Wife's tale, male oppression is represented by the clearest example of such oppression, physical rape. The knight rapes a young virgin "by verray force," (l. 888) but the Wife phrases the deed in such a way as to imply far more than a physical crime. When she says, "he rafte hir maydenhed," (l. 888) she insinuates that the knight's actions, in addition to depriving the virgin (or maid) of her hymen, also deprive the "mayde" (or woman) of her self-identity, the very essence of what makes her what she is.

The "clamour" caused by the knight's action attracts the attention of King Arthur, who condemns the young knight to die, a patriarchal punishment by which the knight—and by extension men in general—will learn nothing. The knight is given a chance to escape his doom by the queen and her ladies, however, who agree to pardon him if he can, within "twelf-month and a day," (l. 909) tell the court "What thyng it is that wommen moost desiren" (l. 905). Despite months of searching for a solution among women everywhere, the knight can find no acceptable answer, and he turns homeward towards his doom. Thus, the Wife presents us with a man guilty of a male crime against a woman, seeking to release himself from the damnation of that crime, who has exhausted all of his own resources and turned towards home without hope of salvation. At this point, he runs smack into the direct agent of fairy magic (and the central dispenser of female justice), the elf queen herself.

Male oppression takes many forms in *Jane Eyre*, but the central male character, Edward Rochester, parallels the knight in the Wife's tale in a number of ways. As John Maynard notes, Rochester "is simply male, the phallic force" (112) that stands out most clearly in the novel. Rochester pursues his own fulfillment without regard for the consequences to women. Like the knight, he is guilty of selfishly using and then discarding a woman. By marrying Bertha without love to insure his wealth, and by carrying her away from her native land to keep her locked in an attic, Rochester has deprived her of her very identity and worth. Within an easily-outraged Victorian value system, these actions come about as close to rape as Brontë is able to come. Bertha's madness is Rochester's doom; for his selfish actions, he is now condemned to eternal union with a crazed wife, in his eyes a death in itself. Like the knight, he has searched for an escape from this doom among women across the European continent, but he has found only "a useless, roving, lonely life—corroded with disappointment" (275). Again like the knight, having exhausted all of his own resources trying to remove the curse on his head, Rochester turns homeward without hope, actually thinking of taking his own life, another solution by which he will learn nothing. Like the knight, Rochester at this point runs right into the joint symbol of female expression and fairy magic in the story, *Jane Eyre*.

In "The Wife of Bath's Tale," we know the woman who meets the knight is the elf-queen because she matches the description given at the beginning of the tale: "The elf-queene, with hir joly compaignye, / Daunced ful oft in many a grene mede" (ll. 860–61). As the knight rides back towards the court, the Wife tells us,

> And in his wey it happed hym to ryde,
> In al this care, under a forest syde,

> Wher as he saugh upon a daunce go
> Of ladyes foure and twenty, and yet mo. (ll. 989–92)

When the knight approaches the dance, the ladies disappear, and only an old hag is left in their place. When the knight tells her his quest, the disguised elf queen assures him that she can answer the question and save him from his doom, but he must first agree to grant her whatever she asks whenever she asks it. The knight agrees, and they travel together to court. The knight gives the hag's answer, that women most desire "sovereyntee / As wel over hir housbond as hir love, / And for to been in maistrie" (ll. 1038–40). The queen and her ladies agree and release the knight from his doom.

The knight believes he has escaped without significant consequence to himself, but, as we see, the elf queen ultimately binds him within an appropriate punishment and brings him to a reluctant awareness of the importance of respecting women. Before the knight can leave, the hag leaps up and demands that the knight give himself to her in wedlock. The knight is shocked; here is a fate as bad as the one he has just escaped. The hag is hideous and old, the antithesis of the pretty young "maydes" he so impulsively desires. More importantly, however, the marriage represents a loss of choice or self-determination for the knight. He begs the hag to take all of his goods but to "fat my body go" (l. 1061). He is horrified by the proposed disgrace of being married to such a disgusting and ignoble creature: "'Allas! that any of my nacioun / Sholde evere so foule disparaged be'" (l. 1069). The hag/elf queen refuses to relent, however. The marriage, and his resulting loss of choice, is her condition for his release from his own self-imposed doom. He must submit to her request, regardless, as the Wife tells us, of what he wishes: "... the ende is this, that he / Constreyned was, he nedes moste hir wedde" (ll. 1070–71).

The knight's submission is further emphasized by the final resolution of the story. On their wedding night, as the knight woefully bemoans his fate, the old hag points out that at least he need never fear being cuckolded, whereas if she was young and beautiful, he could never be sure of her faithfulness. She then allows him the choice of having her beautiful and unfaithful, or foul and faithful. After thinking it over, the knight submits to her "maistrie" and asks her to choose for him: "'My lady and my love, and wyf so deere, / I put me in youre wise governance; / Cheseth youreself'" (ll. 1230–32). She then asks him if he has thus given her mastery over him, and he answers, "'Ye, certes, wyf'" (l. 1238). For this control, the elf queen gives him both: she becomes beautiful and pledges her faithfulness to him.[8] Through his submission to her mastery, and by learning to respect the wishes of women, the knight has finally achieved that which he always sought. Thus, the Wife uses fairy magic to address male crime. The man who is condemned by his crime is offered a chance of escape. Initially, he sees the old woman as a means of delivering himself from his doom without any major change to or impact upon himself. He soon finds out, however, that he can escape the consequences of his crime only by giving up his choice, independence, and "maistrie" to the representative of women, the elf queen. In his submission, he becomes a candidate for redemption and is hence allowed the best of all possible outcomes.[9]

Jane Eyre follows a similar development. The story contains multiple references to fairies, and Jane is clearly a fairy figure from the beginning of the novel. She is physically small and ethereal. She is attracted to birds and nature, and she feels oppressed by the walls and locks of Gateshead. She feels out of place among her adopted family, much as a changeling might feel out of place in a human family, and the Reeds feel the same way about her. Jane says,

> I was a discord in Gateshead Hall: I was like nobody there; I had nothing in harmony with Mrs. Reed or her children, or her chosen vassalage. If they did not love me, in fact, as little did I love them. They were not bound to regard with affection a thing that could not sympathize with one amongst them: a heterogeneous thing, opposed to them in temperament, in capacity, in propensities. (12)

Not until the encounter with Rochester, however, do Jane's elfish qualities become obvious. The circumstances parallel those in the Wife's tale. Jane is alone in the countryside for the first time in the story. Meanwhile, returning from his fruitless search for release among European women, Rochester is riding to his doom on a horse, sounding much like a knight himself. Jane describes his approach as "a positive tramp, tramp; a metallic clatter" (98). Suddenly the faery world bursts into the novel. Jane is reminded of fairy tales: "As this horse approached, and as I watched for it to appear through the dusk, I remembered certain of Bessie's tales, wherein figured a North-of-England spirit, called a 'Gytrash,' which, in the form of a horse, mule, or large dog, haunted solitary ways, and sometimes came upon belated travelers" (98).

Ironically, Jane herself performs the "Gytrash" role. As Rochester rides past, his horse slips and throws him, apparently because of a sheet of ice, but coincidentally nearby the fairy-like Jane. Although he does so jokingly, Rochester suspects supernatural agency. When he formally meets Jane, he tells her, "When you came on me in Hay Lane last night, I thought unaccountably of fairy tales, and had half a mind to demand if you had bewitched my horse" (107). Rochester then asks her pointed questions about her parents, emphasizing Jane's changeling nature. When Jane tells him significantly that she has no parents and cannot remember any, Rochester draws the conclusion that she is in fact a fairy: "I thought not. And so you were waiting for your people when you sat on the stile?" (107). When Jane asks him what he means, he says, "For the men in green: it was a proper moonlight evening for them. Did I break through one of your rings ...?" (107). This reference to breaking fairy rings, while minor, directly parallels the knight's intrusion upon the elf-queen's dancing ring at the beginning of the Wife's tale. Jane denies these half-joking accusations that she is a fairy, but Rochester continues to refer to her fairy-like nature throughout the book. He calls her "elfish," a "sprite," "a fairy ... from elfland," an "elf," and many other fairy-like names (229, 230, 235, 275).[10]

Like the knight in the Wife's tale, Rochester believes that he has finally found in Jane a way to escape from his doom without paying for his crimes or changing his lifestyle. He hides his marriage from her and intends to wed her in an illegal ceremony. These actions demonstrate a continued disregard of the consequences of his actions upon women. Maynard argues that "there is no question that [Rochester's] way of overcoming [Jane's] scruples is in itself a kind of attempted rape" (112). Like the knight, he thinks he has cheated the consequences of his crime. Even when Jane discovers his secret, Rochester continues to pressure her into intimacy, hoping that she will still provide the escape from Bertha, the bane of his existence.

Contrary to his hopes, however, Jane refuses to release him from his responsibilities. Like the knight, Rochester admits he is wrong but resists his obligations because he is horrified by the disgrace of a mad, disgusting wife. His dismay over relinquishing Jane and his accompanying horror of remaining bound in marriage to Bertha creates a compelling parallel to the knight's reluctance to marry the hag/elf queen in the "Wife of Bath's Tale." Both men obstinately seek to ignore circumstances and return to their own choice, their own self-determination. Jane's refusal to marry Rochester and her decision to flee foils Rochester's attempt to avoid the consequences of his actions. As Pat MacPherson points out, "female flight" is, in Jane's world, the one way to tame "impetuous male desire" (38). When Jane leaves, she leaves Rochester in misery, married, like the knight, to a woman with whom he is disgusted. This harsh treatment *forces* him, as it forces the knight, to come to terms with what he has done and honestly evaluate his situation.

Rochester's dilemma echoes the choice given to the knight in other ways as well. He is forced to choose between a repulsive Bertha, with whom a relationship would be legitimate, or an attractive Jane, with whom any relationship would be illegitimate. This is not so different, in Victorian terms, from a beautiful but unfaithful wife and an ugly but chaste one. Furthermore, much in the story suggests that, like the two possible wives between whom the knight must choose, Jane and Bertha are alter egos, merely different sides of the same coin. After noting the innkeeper's parallel references to "witch" (Bertha) and "bewitchment" (Jane), Martin argues that within the context of a fairy tale, "One can only suggest that both Jane and Bertha are witches, that they are two sides of the same self. Jane is the attractive young witch ...; Bertha is the hag...." (92). As in the Wife's tale, it is the choice between enchanted feminine alter egos that brings resolution to male crime. In both stories, men guilty of crimes against women wrestle with a dilemma imposed upon them by fairy women, and in both tales, the men must abandon their independence and self-determination for the dilemma to be resolved.[11]

Later, while trying to save Bertha in a fire, Rochester is crippled and blinded. This act signals both his acceptance of obligation and his loss of self-determination. By trying to save Bertha, he accepts his duties as a husband. If he simply let her die, then he could remarry. At the same time, by sacrificing his eyesight and by becoming crippled, he loses self-control and independence. He thus symbolically and literally relinquishes self-determination at the same time that Bertha dies and he is accordingly released from his doom. It is only in this state, when he has given up his self-determination, that Rochester becomes a candidate for redemption. Richard Chase argues correctly that reconciliation can be made in the novel only "after the spirit of the masculine universe is controlled" (110). Like the knight, Rochester finds the answer to happiness only in his submission.

Rochester and Jane are reunited at Ferndean, an environment that reeks of Faery. Jane tells us that it is "deep buried in a wood," and that "Even when within a short distance of the manor-house you could see nothing of it; so thick and dark grew the timber of the gloomy world about it" (378). As she approaches the house, she says, "The darkness of natural as well as sylvan dusk gathered over me" (379). It is in this fairy-like environment that a just resolution to the male crime takes place. Brontë emphasizes Rochester's loss of self-determination. When Jane sees him, she calls him a "caged eagle" and "sightless samson" (379). She speaks of "the subjugation of that vigorous spirit" and calls him "a lamp quenched, waiting to be relit" (386). Like the knight, Rochester has given up self-control and independence. He is now dependent upon the Jane's mastery, and Jane readily welcomes the task. She says, "It was not himself that could now kindle the lustre of animated expression: he was now dependent on another for that office" (386). And like the knight, Rochester welcomes his dependence and doesn't regret his loss of self-determination. He says to Jane, "Hitherto I have hated to be helped—to be led: henceforth, I feel, I shall hate it no more.... Jane's soft ministry will be a perpetual joy" (392). At the same time, Rochester significantly points out again the fairy-like nature of Jane's existence. As they are reconciled, and as he expresses his joy, he calls her a "mocking changeling—fairy-born and human bred" (386). This and other references reemphasize the notion that fairy-magic has prompted this resolution. Jane accepts his dependence (her mastery) and promises him the happiness which be has sought. She tells him, "I love you better now ... than I did in your state of proud independence" (392), and she promises to marry him. Like the knight, Rochester gets the best half of each choice; he has his beloved Jane, and he has her in a legitimate relationship. With an attitude of sincere penitence which might just as easily be evinced by the knight in "The Wife of Bath's Tale," Rochester ends his role with the following words and actions: "'I humbly entreat my Redeemer to give me strength to lead henceforth a purer life than I have done hitherto!' Then he stretched out his hand to be led" (395). Thus, Brontë also uses the world of faery to address male crime. Condemned by his crime against a woman, Rochester is tempted by what he thinks is a chance of escape. Initially, he sees the fairy-like Jane as a means of delivering himself from his doom without any major changes to his lifestyle. He soon finds out, however, that he can escape the consequences of his crime only by giving up his choice, independence, and "maistrie" to Jane, his elfish mistress. As with the knight in "The Wife of Bath's Tale," his submission alone allows him the best of all possible outcomes. Like Chaucer's wife, Brontë finds in the feminine world of faery a powerful tool for undermining dominant patriarchal values. In *Jane Eyre*, she uses the same powerful symbolic structure as Chaucer's medieval rape story to illuminate her own concerns about the more subtle, yet equally damaging, gender oppression of the nineteenth century.

Notes

1. For a fuller discussion of Victorian medievalism, see Alice Chandler's *A Dream of Order: The Medieval Ideal in Nineteenth-Century English Literature*. Chandler writes that "the partly historical but basically mythical Middle Ages that had become a tradition in literature served to remind men of a Golden Age. The Middle Ages were idealized as a period of faith, order, joy, munificence, and creativity" (1).

2. The list in the Nussey letter is short, and in it Brontë shows a strong sensitivity to the moral appropriateness of some literature. She goes so far as to defend Shakespeare and Byron, for example, as if Nussey would have been shocked by these scandalous writers. And even though she defends them as "great," Brontë nonetheless tells Nussey to "Omit the comedies of Shakespeare and the Don Juan, perhaps the Cain of Byron, though the latter is a magnificent poem, and read the rest fearlessly" (Gaskell 115). These words

demonstrate her conscious sense of the propriety in the works on the list rather than her aesthetic sense of their greatness. Furthermore, Brontë recommends histories which she admits she herself has not read (115). Clearly, the list is one which aspiring young female intellectuals should read rather than what Brontë herself read. Since Chaucer was considered bawdy and risque even by most Victorians who liked him, he clearly wouldn't have been included on such a list.

3. *The Poetical Works of Alexander Pope* (London: Thomas M'Lean, 1821). for example, includes the full "modernization" of the prologue to "The Will of Bath's Tale." It is perhaps appropriate for me to express here my appreciation to Cindy Burgess and the rest of the staff at Baylor's Armstrong-Browning Library for providing me with both cooperation and access to the library's rare book collection.

4. See Noah's wife in the Wakefield cycle's *Processus Noe* for another example of the medieval type of the shrew, a domineering and independent woman. Noah's wife is a sympathetic figure, especially next to the abusive and quarrelsome Noah. Such wives are often found in medieval Dutch plays as well: see *Boss For Three Days*, Therese Decker's translation of *Drie daghe here*, in the Fall 1997 edition of the *Canadian Journal of Netherlandic Studies* for a good example.

5. In "Biographical and Historical Contexts" in *The Wife of Bath*, Peter Beidler writes, "There is an ambiguous legal record in which a woman named Cecilia Chaumpaigne, in consideration of a payment of tell pounds, releases Geoffrey Chaucer from the charge of *raptus*. The import of the charge and the circumstances surrounding it are sufficiently vague that various scholars have attempted in clear Chaucer of the charge of sexual rape by pointing out that *raptus* might have meant something more like our modern 'abduction.' In fact, we know neither that he was guilty of raping, or attempting to rape, Cecilia, nor that he was not guilty." (6)

6. In "*Jane Eyre* and the World of Faery," Robert Martin tells us that "One must not take Jane's 'serious' comments about the departure of the men in green too seriously" (92). Martin, however, has a vested interest in keeping faery in the novel; he does all excellent job of tracing the structural influence of such tales as "Cinderella," "Briar Rose," "Beauty and the Beast," and "Rapunzel" through the structure of *Jane Eyre*. Jane's comments might on the surface undermine his belief that "the world of faery" is an important part of the novel. I see no such contradiction. Jane's remarks clearly apply to the world around her, the national, patriarchal world against which she finds herself struggling. She is herself the representative of "faery" in the novel, and it is precisely her reintroduction of the faery and female perspective which makes her story so profoundly meaningful. Jane's comments do not prevent "faery" from being a part of the novel, only from existing in the oppressive patriarchal system into which she is introduced and which she seeks to destroy.

7. Chaucer ties into an established anti-clerical polemic with this reference. In the late medieval period, Friars are frequently portrayed as sexual predators who use their chastity and poverty as a front to lull their victims into a false sense of security. The anonymous author of *Preste, Ne Monke, Ne Yit Chanoun*, for example, warns his audience never to let a Friar into their homes unless he has been castrated (ll. 85–8), because Friars will sexually assault the women of the house:

For may he til a woman wynne
In priveyte, he wyl not blynne
Er he a chime put hir with-inne-
And perchaunce two at ones!
Thof he loure under his hode,

With semblaunt quaynte and mylde,
If thou him trust, or dos him gode,
By God, thou art bygylde. (ll. 89–96)

8. The Wife's tale is one of a series of tales that use the theme of the "loathly lady" and the choice that turns her into a beautiful maiden. Perhaps the most famous is "Sir Gawain and Dame Ragnell," in which the secret to the transformation is simple courtesy. Chaucer's version shares much with these tales, but it differs from most in that the enchantment is voluntary. For more discussion of the "loathly lady" form, see G. F. Dalton's "The Loathly Lady" or Edward Vasta's "Chaucer, Gower, and the Unknown Minstrel: The Literary Liberation of the Loathly Lady."

9. The eventual happy ending for the rapist knight is the most controversial element of the Wife's tale for many feminists. Elaine Turtle Hansen gives a representative perspective: "The knight is not only spared and reformed but eventually rewarded, it seems, for his crime" (281).

10. Moglen notices this as well, although she marks a different set of terms. She writes, "[Rochester] enjoys this sense of her, insists upon it: repeatedly describing her as 'elfin,' a 'nonnette,' 'a fairy,' 'his god genii,' 'a dream or shade,' a 'strange ... almost unearthly thing.'" (118).

11. In their classic feminist text, *The Madwoman in the Attic* (a title apparently taken from Bertha's character in *Jane Eyre*) Sandra M. Gilbert and Susan Gubar notice this very similarity between the stories, although they do not speak of the larger structural and thematic similarities. They write, "When [Chaucer] gave the Wife of Bath a tale of her own, he portrayed her projecting her subversive vision of patriarchal institutions into the story of a furious hag who demands supreme power over her own life and that of her husband: only when she gains his complete acceptance of her authority does this witch transform herself into a modest and docile beauty. Five centuries later, the threat of the hag, the monster, the witch, the madwoman, still lurks behind the compliant paragon of women's stories" (79).

Works Cited

Beidler, Peter. "Biographical and Historical Contexts." *The Wife of Bath*. Ed. Peter Beidler. New York: Bedford Books, 1996. 3–27.

Brewer, Derek. *Chaucer: The Critical Heritage*. London: Routledge & Kegan Paul, 1978.

Brontë, Charlotte. *Jane Eyre*. 1847. Ed. Richard J. Dunn. New York: W. W. Norton & Co., 1987.

Buber, Martin. *The Legend of the Baal-Shem*. Trans. Maurice Friedman. New York: Schocken Books, 1969.

Chandler, Alice. *A Dream of Order: The Medieval Ideal in Nineteenth-Century Literature*. Lincoln: U of Nebraska P, 1970.

Chase, Richard. "The Brontës: or Myth Domesticated." *Forms of Modern Fiction*. Bloomington: Midland Book Edition, 1959. 102–19.

Chaucer, Geoffrey. *Canterbury Tales*. Ed. A. C. Cawley. New York: Alfred A. Knopf, 1958.

Dalton, G. F. "The Loathly Lady." *Folklore* 82 (1971): 124–31.

"Drie Daghe Here." Trans. Therese Decker. *Canadian Journal of Netherlandic Studies*. XVIII: ii (Fall 1997): 19–31.

Gaskell, E. C. *The Life of Charlotte Brontë*. New York: D. Appleton & Co., 1857.

Gerin, Winifred. *Charlotte Brontë*. Oxford: Clarendon Press, 1967.
Gilbert, Sandra M. and Susan Gubar. *The Madwoman in the Attic*. New Haven: Yale UP, 1979.
Hansen, Elaine Tuttle. "'Of his love daungerous to me': Liberation, Subversion, and Domestic Violence in the Wife of Bath's Prologue and Tale." *The Wife of Bath*. Ed. Peter Beidler. New York: Bedford Books, 1996. 273–89.
MacPherson, Pat. *Reflecting on Jane Eyre*. New York: Routledge, 1989.
Martin, Robert. "Jane Eyre and the World of Faery." *Mosaic* 10 (1977): 85–95.
Maynard, John. *Charlotte Brontë and Sexuality*. Cambridge: Cambridge UP, 1984.
Moglen, Helene. *Charlotte Brontë: The Self Conceived*. New York: W. W. Norton & Co., 1976.
Pope, Alexander. *The Poetical Works of Alexander Pope*. London: Thomas M'Lean, 1821.
"Preste, Ne Monke, Ne Yit Chanoun." *Medieval English Political Writings*. Ed. James M. Dean. Kalamazoo: Western Michigan UP, 1996. 45–52.
Spurgeon, Caroline F. E. *Five Hundred Years of Chaucer Criticism and Allusion*. New York: Russell & Russell, 1960.
Vasta, Edward. "Chaucer, Gower, and the Unknown Minstrel: The Literary Liberation of the Loathly Lady." *Exemplaria* 7:2 (1995 Fall): 395–418.

JAMES BUZARD

The Wild English Girl: Jane Eyre

> Thus from a Mixture of all kinds began,
> That Het'rogeneous Thing, an *Englishman* ...
>
> —Daniel Defoe, "The True-Born Englishman"[1]

> I was a discord in Gateshead Hall; I was like nobody there; I had nothing in harmony with Mrs Reed or her children, or her chosen vassalage. If they did not love me, in fact, as little did I love them. They were not bound to regard with affection a thing that could not sympathize with one amongst there; a heterogeneous thing, opposed to them in temperament, in capacity, in propensities; a useless thing, incapable of serving their interest, or adding to their pleasure; a noxious thing, cherishing the germs of indignation at their treatment, of contempt of their judgment.
>
> —Jane Eyre[2]

I

Readings of *Jane Eyre* and of Charlotte Brontë's work as a whole have derived much energy from the idea that Brontë had to drop the pretense of *The Professor*'s masculine narrator in order to "find her voice," and that she found and used that voice triumphantly in her impassioned second novel.

From *Disorienting Fiction: The Autoethnographic Work of Nineteenth-Century British Novels.* © 2005 by Princeton University Press.

This chapter will consider the phenomenon of voice in *Jane Eyre* as a much more paradoxical and ambivalence-generating issue than critics have been inclined to regard it. It seems to me that *Jane Eyre* cultivates considerable suspicion about the powers and tendencies of the voice, holding apart Jane the speaker and Jane the retrospective narrator and deeming the latter to possess advantages of perspective that the former was too young, too degraded, too enraged, too narrow-sighted to have access to. In this, the novel exploits a possibility inherent in all first-person narration, heightening the effect of the split between narrating and narrated selves. Its tense, play with writing and speech also harks back to Scott and the authors of the National Tale, for whom Celtic-speaking voices could be "heard" only if translated into the silent markings in an English or self-anglicized text: *Jane Eyre* is an *English* National Tale that subjects the speech of its narrator's former self to just such translation.[3]

Yet the crucial business of the telephonic communication between Jane and Rochester at the close of the novel routes us *back* to the domain of the voice and disrupts any simple progress from voice to print, from local to abstracted national consciousness. Moreover, throughout the narrative, we may detect intimations of a persistent aural dimension whenever we find Jane Eyre being placed in situations that emphasize her status as a figure of ire, as someone who longs to fly off into *air*, as a dispossessed *heir(ess)*, and, most tenuously yet most intriguingly of all, as having something to do with *Eire* or *Erin*. Circulating amidst these possible associations is the suggestion that it just might matter how one *pronounces* the heroine's name, as if the recommended method for dealing with *Jane Eyre* were to read it aloud to hearers within the reader's immediate vicinity, not to peruse it in solitary silence. The national consciousness Brontë seeks to cultivate cannot be permitted to remain simply abstract; it has to reincorporate the elements of locality (the body, the voice) rather than simply trade these in for an anonymous comradeship whose image is "the reading public." As in *The Professor*, though now working from the inside out (that is, from local to national) instead of from the outside in (from expatriation to repatriation), *Jane Eyre* describes a quest for a positive national identity that will supplement and transcend other identities but not obliterate them, that will sustain the condition of being other than one thing. This means, as in all Brontë's work, confronting and resisting the allure of those one-making tropes of purgation or conversion to which a significant segment of Brontë's own imaginative energy is undeniably attracted. It means actualizing, through the resources distinctive to narrative—chiefly the relationships between discourse- and story-spaces, silent print and evoked voices—the powers distinctive to Englishness as a "heterogeneous thing." The shift to a female narrator enables *Jane Eyre* to succeed *The Professor* as a revisionary romance in which the protagonist develops into the kind of heroine capable of saving the novel's hero and of complementing Defoe's one-sided account of the hybrid Englishman with an Englishwoman no less mixed in her nature than he. But, as I indicated above, Brontë's aim is a strictly regulated heterogeneity that has to turn aside from engagement with forms of otherness deemed unmanageable or threatening to the integrity of the system of differences constituting the national culture.[4]

The general tendency in *Jane Eyre* to move from the domain of voice to authorship and print and then, jarringly, back through voice again, fits the pattern of return on which—as many have noted—much of the novel is organized. He.e again Brontë mobilizes, and provides repeated thematic echoes of, an intrinsic potentiality of her form. Not only does retrospective first-person narration lend itself to figuration as a return to the past; the plot of *Jane Eyre*, too, is filled with returns. On the novel's very first page, Jane refers to her childhood dislike of returning from cold walks outside to the morally cold interior of Gateshead. Later on, when in Rochester's employment, she leaves Thornfield to go back to Gateshead to visit the dying Mrs. Reed and learn of her uncle John's earlier attempts to locate her; this departure from Thornfield allows both for a space of reflection on what has been happening there and for a first-ever return to Thornfield itself, where Jane is now courted in earnest by Rochester. Later, fleeing Thornfield after the revelation of Rochester's existing marriage, Jane makes a paradoxical "homecoming" to a set of relatives she has never known she had, the Riverses at Moor House. We can call this a return or recovery, or call the Riverses Jane's "long-lost" relatives, to the extent that we invest in the idea that blood relation makes abiding claims having nothing to do with an individual's actual experience: it is the *cri du sang* that draws Jane at her time of utter "friendlessness" toward this home she never knew she had.[5] A little later, though, pressed to leave England on St. John Rivers's missionary campaign, Jane hears the far-off pleadings of Rochester and returns once more to Thornfield to find it a ruin.

Only after undergoing all these trying and recuperative returns can Jane the character move *beyond* this pattern of return, to Ferndean, where she enters into her definitively new state as savior of Rochester, as wife and mother, and, of course, as an author capable of enacting the very different *kind* of return constituted by the first-person narrative. Rochester himself has all the while been moving through a pattern of return, as well: his first appearance in the novel and first encounter with Jane—we learn much later—coincides with his return to England after ten long years of hopeless wandering. He contrasts the "quiet little figure" of Jane he sees on that day to a catalogue of female foreignness—not only the Creole Bertha but, in efficient succession, the Parisian Celine, the Italian Giacinta, and the German Clara—with whom he has spent his years as a "Will-o'-the-wisp," just as he will later contrast her to the anticultural Englishwoman Blanche Ingram (JE 348). If he were to marry Blanche, their marriage would offer a precise opposite to the possibility Rochester and Jane's marriage holds out: instead of a model of English culture balancing the claims of individual and collectivity (see my discussion in chapter 6), a jail or "Bridewell," as the charade enacted in the Thornfield drawing room suggests (JE 208–9).

Had all these returns in the plot not occurred, the authoritative Jane who revisits her past by narrating it would never have come into being. Jane's authority to author her own life is secured every time she can demonstrate the vital difference between her former and her present selves, and between successive stages of her former character. Revisiting Gateshead, for example, Jane finds "the inanimate objects ... not changed[,] but the living things ... altered past recognition":

> On a dark, misty, raw morning in January, I had left a hostile roof with a desperate and embittered heart—a sense of outlawry and almost of reprobation.... The same hostile roof now again rose before me: my prospects were doubtful yet; and I had yet an aching heart. I still felt as a wanderer on the face of the earth; but I experienced firmer trust in myself and my own powers, and less withering dread of oppression. The gaping wound of my wrongs, too, was now quite healed; and the flame of resentment extinguished. (JE 256)

Over the next few pages, Jane the narrator is at pains to assert how fully her character-self had *already* liberated herself from the psychological barriers imposed on her at the aptly named Gateshead, that factory for making "mind-forg'd manacles." Her cousins' contempt "had no longer that power over me it once possessed"; "their airs gave me no concern either for good or bad"; "Eliza did not mortify, nor Georgiana ruffle me" (JE 257). That narrator remembers being "surprised to find how easy [she] felt" when subjected once again to her cousins' barbs. Looking back, she shows her achieved detachment by generalizing philosophically on her earlier experiences of both the original oppression and the later recognition of how much she had overcome its effects:

> It is a happy thing that time quells the longings of vengeance, and hushes the promptings of rage and aversion: I had left this woman

> in bitterness and hate, and I came back to her now with no other emotion than a sort of ruth for her great sufferings, and a strong yearning to forget and forgive all injuries—to be reconciled and clasp hands in amity. (JE 259)

This outlook that subordinates personal experience to the function of illustrating maxims ("It is a happy thing that time ... ") is plainly opposed to the perspective conjured up at the novel's beginning, in the famously terse remark "There was no possibility of taking a walk that day" (JE 13). There Jane the narrator returns momentarily to the mentality of her child-self, so deeply inside the deadening nightmare of Gateshead life that she has no thought of any viewpoint *outside* it that might contextualize her circumstances. To the child Jane, those circumstances are the extent of the real and the possible, until the moment ("that day") when she begins to question her fate.

Not only does the narrative of *Jane Eyre* enact a return and describe several, it also includes reflection on the idea of return. Around the middle of the novel, telling of her journey back to Thornfield after the return to Gateshead, Jane the narrator writes:

> How people feel when they are returning home from an absence, long or short, I did not know: I had never experienced the sensation. I had known what it was to come back to Gateshead when a child, after a long walk ... and later, what it was to come back from church to Lowood.... Neither of these returnings were very pleasant or desirable: no magnet drew me to a given point, increasing in its strength of attraction the nearer I came. The return to Thornfield was yet to be tried. (JE 272)

Shortly after this, Jane will blurt out to Rochester, "wherever you are is my only home" (JE 276).

It scarcely needs to be said that this novel's much-exampled commitment to the idea of return derives in great part from the model of Pilgrim's Progress and the Christian tradition narrating life as a journey of the soul toward its spiritual home. This and other novels' secularization of such time-honored topoi is well known. But Brontë's adaptation of the model in *Jane Eyre* leads its journeying protagonist along a path that stretches not simply from homelessness to home, but from a series of *antihomes* to the idealized home these define by opposition. The right kind of home turns out to be the kind of place to which one can make the right kind of return, which of course implies that one needs to be displaced from it first.

The novel opens by evoking a return that doesn't happen: Jane and the Reeds don't take a walk "that day," so they don't come back to Gateshead. On the same page we find those unpleasant memories of past returns from such walks, which Jane "never liked" because "dreadful to [her] was the coming home in the raw twilight" (JE 13). These maneuvers set up twin negative versions of the pattern governing the entire narrative: one state of affairs to which there is no possibility of a return because one doesn't get out of it, and another in which the getting out of it is rendered valueless because there must always be a return to exactly the same (miserable) situation one has left. In contrast, all *productive* returns in *Jane Eyre*, including the return involved in retrospective first-person narration, make themselves felt as returns-with-a-difference, the identity that establishes the event as a return being qualified by a difference that insists upon recognition. We have seen (in chapter 4) Scott making powerful use of such qualified returns in *Waverley*, where the re-presentation of Tully-Veolan to the Baron of Bradwardine and Waverley's own gaze at the dual portrait of himself and Fergus MacIvor seem designed to problematize Scott's own effort to represent "Scotland" as its self-designated autoethnographer. In *Jane Eyre*, the identity over time that is vouched for by the *name* the character and narrator share, the identity that makes the novel the "autobiography" its subtitle claims it to be, is complicated by the oppositional logic in which Brontë conceives of the novel's several determinative social environments. The allegorical-sounding Gateshead, Lowood, Thornfield, and Whitcross are differentiated from each other in several ways, but each supplies a variety of anticulture against which the final ideal of a genuine culture (figured in Jane's account of her married state) can be imagined: a utopian vision somehow magically capable of sustaining *both* a Protestant, protofeminist individualism and a condition of intersubjective integration that I likened (in chapter 6) to Hegel's "the I that is a we and the we that is an I."

The differences between the Gateshead Jane and the narrating Jane suggest that Brontë is traveling in the conceptual territory mapped out by the later, post-Boasian anthropologists of the so-called Culture-and-Personality School, for whom human character came to seem almost wholly malleable.[6] The deformative cultures that successively shape the young Jane are made visible in the older Jane's backward-looking narrative by the productive tension between ethnography's Observer and Participant functions, a tension that endows first-person narration with the specific force of a "cultured" self's return to lived-through versions of anti-culture and to the antiselves they manufactured or were designed to create. With the exception of Whitcross, where Jane briefly inhabits a condition that is anticultural in the sense of being wholly *outside* the domain of civilization, the stages of Jane's life-travels represent protoethnographic perversions of the utopian culture at which she will finally arrive. Systematically pressuring their inmates to conform to and internalize normative models of character, Gateshead, Lowood, and Thornfield are all *cultures*: both the forms of selfhood they seek to produce in Jane and the forms they actually produce bear the inscription of their acculturating power. At Gateshead in particular, her "native environment," Jane in childhood exhibits pathologies of character and mentality that take their shape very precisely, *even in rebellion*, from the totalitarian regime in which she has been raised. To borrow a phrase of Christine Froula's, one could say that *Jane Eyre* practices autoethnography in the form of a portrait of the artist *as* her culture.[7]

That claim requires two immediate qualifications, however. First, the claims of the blood never entirely disappear from Brontë's exploratory fiction of cultural determinism: they are there all the time, unforgettably embodied in the figure of Bertha Mason, and where Jane is concerned they return in force at her severest moment of exile from all forms of culture whatever, at Whitcross. Second, reading *Jane Eyre* as an autoethnographic "portrait of the artist as her culture" does not entail the claim that, chameleon-like, Jane the character assumes a completely different hue every time she is placed in a new environment. On the contrary, the novel emphasizes the accretive, sedimentary nature of the acculturation process, showing how habits of response instilled at Gateshead persist and crop up under later, different conditions, alongside traits of more recent vintage. Chief among these habits is the tendency to regard human relations through the lens of a fundamental antinomy wherein all social existence presents itself as unmitigated servitude and the only possible freedom as utter isolation. Like the antinomy "race versus culture," that of "society versus freedom," Brontë suggests, is a symptom of social pathology, not a "problem" for which one should seek a "solution" by proving the final predominance of one side.

Brontë's emphasis in *Jane Eyre* upon the power of culture is counterbalanced by all those vital elements in the text that come from domains *outside* the merely cultural: God, whose law Jane resolves to keep, in the face of Rochester's antinomian urgings; the monitory spirits who visit Jane when she is in extremis at Gateshead and later at Thornfield; the mad savagery of Bertha Mason; the cri du sang that brings her to the Riverses; St. John Rivers' divine vocation; the "natural sympathies" that ultimately reunite Jane with Rochester; above all, the fundamental "restlessness" Jane comes to discover inside herself, a literally "hyperbolic" drive to "overpass [the] limit" of any condition (JE 125). The visitations of these forces from beyond the social world break into and disrupt the otherwise dominant naturalizing ideologies of culture. Jane says of the strange visionary light that sometimes comes over her that it strikes her "into syncope" (JE 358), a word suggesting not just loss of consciousness but a violent truncation or interruption of consciousness's normal flow: the word derives from the Greek *sunkoptein*, to chop up or cut off. So steadily peremptory is the authority of culture (whether that authority is wielded by John Reed, Mr. Brocklehurst, Edward Rochester, or St. John Rivers) that it appears to require nothing less than repeated recourse to the heavy machinery of supernaturalism to put a check upon it. At the same time, the built social environment of a national culture appears to afford us our only means of curbing the dangerously alluring powers of the "beyond." Interrupting and interrupted in turn, the forces of culture and their opposites weave the fabric of Brontë's autoethnography. In the process, Jane the character's spoken voice is *shown* to us as possessing a power that cannot be permitted free rein, even when Jane speaks out in justified indignation against her oppressors. To appreciate the way Brontë makes Jane's writing an instrument for containing and even breaking off the flow of Jane the character's speech, it will be useful to contrast this novel with Anne Brontë's earlier novel of a downtrodden but ultimately triumphant governess, *Agnes Grey*.

Both of these works participate in a particular brand of autobiographical narrative we might call "me-narrative," the driving impulse of which is to assert and exercise the *right* to tell one's own tale. Not all first-person accounts of a life exhibit this distinctively modern tendency (whose current avatars choke the airwaves and dull the mode's critical potency). Me-narrative beseeches readers to examine things from the narrator's point of view, aiming not simply to convey information about, or lessons derived from, a life, but above all else to authenticate and justify that life. Like Coleridge's ancient mariner, me-narrators are under a powerful compulsion to narrate, to command attention and sympathy: they exhibit none of that seeming undermotivation we observed in Scott's *Rob Roy* and Brontë's *The Professor*. Their hunger for justification leads them to court and apostrophize their reader, appealing to the absent, faceless public as if it were a single listener physically before the writer, capable of responding to imploring voice and looks rather than merely reading a text. And yet they may align the relationship between writing and speech with that between past powerlessness and present authority. A me-narrator like Anne Brontë's Agnes Grey sets about her task with a certain eagerness because being able to write her life story compensates for the muteness once imposed upon her as a dependent subordinate. Her previous life one long affair of *l'esprit de l'escalier*, Agnes "burned to contradict" the false monologues of the powerful: "I was used to wearing a placid smiling countenance when my heart was bitter within me," Agnes tells us.[8] The definitive effect of her text occurs whenever she points, as she repeatedly does, to the gap between the character in the past and the narrator in the present. Recalling one of the many snubs she received at her employers' hands, for instance, Agnes writes, "I wished to say something in my own justification, but in attempting to speak, I felt my voice falter, and rather than testify any emotion, or suffer the tears to overflow, that were already gathering in my eyes, I chose to keep silence, and bear all, like a self-convicted culprit" (AG 47–48). Protected now by the screens of time and text, the narrator's "voice" does not falter, but "speaks out"—in print. In order to utter all that she could not say in the face-to-face exchanges that the book recounts, the me-narrator has to turn her thwarted voice into silent words on a page, which now affirm, for anyone who might happen to be reading—and will her past oppressors be among them?—that she was in the right, though sorely misused. The me-narrator protests those past situations of silencing but requires them as the basis of her authority as a writer.

Apart from the authority to narrate, the me-narrator insists upon her right to desire. To write is to "give voice" to longings once condemned to remain unspoken. Drawn to the good curate Mr. Weston yet blocked from seeing him by Rosalie, the coquette in her charge, Agnes Grey consoles herself with the reflection that, "though he knew it not, I was more worthy of his love than Rosalie Murray, charming and engaging as she was" (AG 145). "Nobody knew him as I did," she boldly, inwardly resolves; "nobody could appreciate him as I did; nobody could love him as I ... could, if I might" (AG 147). Jane Eyre has her comparable moment when she is compelled to sit in the drawing room of Thornfield and watch Rochester pay court to Blanche Ingram. "He is not to them [Blanche and the others] what he is to me," she writes that she then thought: "he is not of their kind.... I understand the language of his countenance and movements: though rank and wealth sever us widely, I have something in my brain and heart, in my blood and nerves, that assimilates me mentally to him." But all the while that this volcano of self-justification smolders silently in their midst, the denizens of the drawing room go on with their deadening rites: in the text, Jane's inner monologue is broken off with the devastating "Coffee is handed" (JE 199).

Me-narratives about once-silenced characters may be placed on a continuum whose opposite poles would involve either complete acceptance of the trade-off of voice for print (of then for now) or lasting dissatisfaction with that exchange. In the former case, the deferred gratification offered to the narrator in surrogate form would not generate any turbulence but would insert itself smoothly and frictionlessly into the psychic slot once occupied by the silenced character's resentment, describing an airtight economy whose chief products are forgiveness and the psychological liberation of the forgiving self. In the latter, no amount of emphasis on the advantages of "distance" from past sufferings would quell the desire to go back, not just through the medium of reflection and writing but *actually*, to relive and revise painful scenes by speaking up. Neither *Agnes Grey* nor *Jane Eyre* belongs at either end of this continuum, but it is obvious that Anne Brontë's novel deserves a spot far closer to the "accepting" side than is warranted for her older and more famous sister's masterpiece. Even in *Agnes Grey* it is occasionally possible to detect that turbulence I refer to, whenever Agnes the character's stifled desire and rage finds a substitute agent in some creature lower in the hierarchies of society or nature than is Agnes herself. A nursemaid named Betty, for instance, provides the much put-upon governess with some vicarious satisfaction when she confesses herself untroubled by the former's scruples about corporal punishment: "I don't vex myself o'er 'em as you do," Betty says: whenever the monstrous children of the household deserve it, "I hit 'em a slap sometimes; and them little uns—I gives 'em a good whipping now and then—there's nothing else ull do for 'em" (AG 41). In another passage, Agnes recalls her mistress's cruel, vulgar brother and admits that "poor as [she] was, [she] would have given a sovereign any day" to see one of the dogs he regularly brutalized bite him (AG 43). But for the most part, Agnes Grey is content with her bargain, grateful for that state of affairs in which "shielded by [her] own obscurity, and by the lapse of years, and a few fictitious names," she need "not fear to venture, and [may] candidly lay before the public what [she] would not disclose to the most intimate friend" (AG 1). Her narrative remains a tale of quiet virtue rewarded: potentially messy feelings are efficiently borne away by proxies, purifying the heroine in preparation for her inevitable marriage to Mr. Weston, which comes about without Agnes's having to say a word.

Where *Jane Eyre* is concerned, the critical template established by Gilbert and Gubar's *The Madwoman in the Attic* has accustomed us to regarding Bertha Mason as the vehicle for Jane's own inexpressible fury over the false liberation Rochester promises her in "wedlock." But here the use of a substitute as vehicle and sacrificial victim, a device whose troubling implications postcolonial readings have alerted us to,[9] seems but one manifestation among many of Brontë's self-consciousness with regard to the tropes and modes basic to her own fictional practice. For *Jane Eyre* is a me-narrative featuring a character whom many attempt to silence but who seems determined to anticipate the advent of her authorship by speaking out a good deal. "*Speak* I must," writes Jane the narrator, referring not to her writing as a kind of long-deferred speech but to what she could not stop herself from doing many a time in the past (JE 45). Among the simplest gratifications on offer in this complex book is the vicarious pleasure we get when the young

Jane fires off salvoes of righteous retaliation, as for example when she explodes with "How dare I, Mrs Reed? How dare I? Because it is the *truth*.... I will tell anybody who asks me questions, this exact tale. People think you are a good woman, but you are bad; hard-hearted"—and so forth (JE 45–46). Jane's self-quotation at moments like this appears to take us straight to that burning core of resentful authenticity, that sense of "Eyre" as *ire*, which scorns the charge of lying and turns it back upon the authorities of the warped system that imprisons her. Here is that titanic anger whose rupturing of the surface of Brontë's fiction has given critics of opposite tendencies cause for distress or celebration but which in any event has occupied much critical attention ever since *Jane Eyre* was published. Another often-cited instance occurs later on, when, thinking Mr. Rochester intends to see his feigned courtship of Blanche Ingram through to its culmination, Jane bursts forth:

> "I tell you I must go!" I retorted, roused to something like passion.
> "Do you think I can stay to become nothing to you? Do you think I am an automaton?—a machine without feelings? and can bear to have my morsel of bread snatched from my lips, and my drop of living water dashed from my cup? Do you think, because I am poor, obscure, plain, and little, I am soulless and heartless?—You think wrong!—I have as much soul as you,—and full as much heart!" (JE 284)

In such passages, "Eyre" means both *ire* and *air*, the breath of the vehement speaker-on-her-own-behalf.

Without disputing Jane the character's right to be as angry as she frequently was, however, we may observe that it is Jane the narrator's regular practice to subject her earlier and now self-quoted outbursts to the countervailing effort to frame and control them, to keep the indignant voice, however just its cause, from having uncontested sway.[10] In the early stages of the novel, the me-narrator's drive to speak out on her own behalf is both staged and examined, in acts of oral autobiography first delivered "without reserve" (JE 69) and then with a greater attempt to guard "against the indulgence of resentment" (JE 83). At Lowood, seizing upon Helen Burns's request for information about her circumstances, Jane gives voice to that "exact tale" she had threatened to relate about the Reeds' abuse of her: "I proceeded forthwith," the narrator recalls, "to pour out, in my own way, the tale of my sufferings and resentments. Bitter and truculent when excited, I spoke as I felt, without reserve or softening" (JE 69). Two chapters later, under the beneficent influence of Helen and the teacher Miss Temple, Jane offers a different kind of narrative in defending herself against Mr. Brocklehurst's charge of mendacity.

> I resolved in the depth of my heart that I would be most moderate: most correct; and, having reflected a few minutes in order to arrange coherently what I had to say, I told her all the story of my sad childhood. Exhausted by emotion, my language was more subdued than it generally was when it developed that sad theme; and mindful of Helen's warnings against the indulgence of resentment, I infused into the narrative far less of gall and wormwood than ordinary. Thus restrained and simplified, it sounded more credible: I felt as I went on that Miss Temple believed me. (JE 83)

In such passages, Jane the character begins the journey toward her later narrative authority, trying out in speech the narrator's role that can be accomplished only upon accession to the abstracting and "distancing" medium of print (though not with perfect security even then).

Later in the novel, when Jane has left Lowood, she begins to learn a new reason to contain her own speaking voice. After a childhood crushed by authorities who do not want to hear what she has to say (the Reeds, Mr. Brocklehurst), she enters into womanhood to find herself subject to masculine authorities who may pressure her to speak of herself for purposes not in her own interest. Rochester, who makes a show of divulging his sordid past to Jane but who actually conceals the most important fact about himself, tries to use this false candor as a lure to make Jane reveal herself to him—and, when that fails, resorts to the disguise of a Gypsy fortune-teller to enable himself to plumb Jane's secret soul unimpeded. This is the man who announces "I am disposed to be gregarious and communicative" but who really wants to know his new governess without fully being known by her, the master who says, "It would please me now to draw you out: to learn more of you—therefore speak" (JE 151). Her experiences with Rochester doubtless prepare Jane for St. John Rivers's later protest, "if I know nothing about you or your history, I cannot help you," so that she furnishes him with only the sketchiest of accounts, saying, "I will tell you as much of the history of the wanderer you have harboured, as I can tell without compromising my own peace of mind—my own security, moral and physical, and that of others" (JE 388). Sure enough, when he has learned her true identity and parentage, Rivers turns out to be yet another incarnation of those powers that have sought from the beginning to cast Jane in scripts of their own construction, asking for her voice only insofar as it can be made to endorse those scripts.

And there is still a further reason, virtually absent from *Agnes Grey*, why *Jane Eyre* cultivates skepticism about this voice to which part of the imagination informing the text also longs to return. When young Jane talks so stirringly back to her aunt, she also feels that her utterances are "scarcely voluntary ... as if my tongue pronounced words without my will consenting to their utterance: something spoke out of me over which I had no control" (JE 36). Her tirade is followed—or broken off—by the narrator's recollection, "Ere I had finished this reply, my soul began to expand, to exult, with the strangest sense of freedom, of triumph, I ever felt. It seemed as if an invisible bond had burst, and that I had struggled out into unhoped-for liberty" (JE 46). An invisible bond has burst, but the thing struggling out into unhoped-for liberty is actually larger and other than the "I." In *Jane Eyre*, me-narrative is complicated by the vision of desire as an impersonal force that disdains to be thought the servant of this or that self, and that uses the self as its agent and vehicle. Let loose upon Jane's tongue, this desire would rupture not only the invisible bonds of social constraint but the integrity of self as well (as it seems to have done to Bertha Mason): only the cultured self's inscription in a "system of desire" may constrain it.[11] What Jane has achieved by the end of the story is not just the freedom to speak-in-print, but also the recognition that this power that welled up within her and that often impelled her to speak was not in any final or complete way *her own*.

When this alien "something" in Jane forces its way into her words and out of her mouth, the result is a displacing or uncanny effect that parodies the signature effect the text regularly aims at, namely that of an *autoethnographic uncanny* arising every time Jane the narrator makes her presence strongly felt alongside her younger speaking self. Those raging moments in her youth placed Jane (she later writes) "beside myself; or rather out of myself" (JE 19): within the story-space of the novel is reproduced in distorted form the fundamental narrative dichotomy of discourse- and story-spaces. Imprisoned for her insolence in the unused "red-room" at Gateshead, Jane remembers, "My heart beat thick, my head grew hot; a sound filled my ears, which I deemed the rushing of wings: something seemed near me; I was oppressed, suffocated: endurance broke down—I uttered a wild, involuntary cry—I rushed to the door and shook the lock in desperate effort" (JE 24). At this moment of greatest vulnerability to the "something" newly felt within herself, the child Jane tries to burst out of the room, just as that power has burst out of *her* in the form of that involuntary, inarticulate cry.[12] "I never forgot the, to me, frightful episode of the red-room," she writes, "in detailing which, my excitement was sure, in some degree to break bounds" (JE 83). If revisiting such episodes by narrating them can arouse the same bound-breaking energy then let loose, the medium of writing or print must assume the function of distancing and containing desire even while "recalling" it.

One can see it playing this role in the famous scene at Thornfield in which Jane begins to frequent the rooftop to soothe that "restlessness" within her that being a governess has failed to quell. Summarizing her earlier self's burning dissatisfaction, her desire to "overpass [the] limit" of her horizons of possibility, the narrator fully sympathizes with those feelings and embarks upon her famous plea for understanding of the fact that women require "exercise for their faculties, and a field for their efforts as much as their brothers do" (JE 125). Without negating or qualifying the justice of her earlier discontentment, Jane the narrator nevertheless gives us her retrospective account of her feelings on such occasions, rather than exposing us to them in the form of self-quoted involuntary cries or anguished soliloquies. She knows that more expresses itself in the utterance of discontentment than is subject to control by the discontented one who utters: she substitutes her narrative for the "tale" her frustrated self then heard with her "inward ear ... a tale that was never ended—a tale [her] imagination created, and narrated continuously; quickened with all of incident, life, fire, feeling, that [she] desired and had not in [her] actual existence" (JE 125). It is this inward, endless tale of a bottomless desire to which Bertha's "distinct, formal, mirthless" laugh (JE 122) offers pitiless punctuation and the novel's ending dream of a genuine culture offers utopian resolution.

We also see the form of self-splitting that parodies the autoethnographic uncanny in those much-noted instances of mirroring—simultaneously self-recognizing and self-alienating—when Jane the character looks at some vision of herself and we look at that looking through the retrospective narrator's lens. In the red-room, the child Jane "had to cross before the looking-glass" and saw a "strange little figure there gazing at me, with a white face and arms specking the gloom and glittering eyes of fear moving where all else was still" (JE 21). To her own self she "had the effect of a real spirit: [she] thought [the figure in the mirror] like one of the tiny phantoms, half fairy, half imp" she had heard of in tales told by a Gateshead servant (JE 21–22). Later the effect acquires additional layers of mediation, in the scene in which Jane tells Rochester about her "dream" of seeing "a woman, tall and large" (Bertha) trying on Jane's wedding veil the night before Jane's nuptials and then turning to look at herself in a mirror that is so positioned as to afford Jane a view of the woman's reflected face, as if standing before that mirror herself (JE 317). If the first instance records an experience that set a seal upon Jane's recently commenced break from complete absorption in her native social environment, the second not only displays the existence of another "Mrs. Rochester" but also suggests that Jane's mistake in thinking she has found a properly nurturing new environment at Thornfield threatens to put her in essentially the same position as her predecessor and dark double.

A third moment transmutes these earlier two, in preparation for Jane's recovery of both identity and culture on a higher plane. This occurs in the passage in which St. John Rivers presents Jane, heretofore known to him as "Jane Elliott," with a piece of paper bearing her true name in her own hand. "He got up," Jane recalls, "held it close to my eyes: and I read, traced in Indian ink, in my own handwriting, the words 'Jane Eyre'—the work doubtless of some moment of abstraction" (JE 426). Instead of seeing her ghost-like, Gateshead-crushed antiself or her monstrous, Thornfield-imprisoned doppelgänger, Jane sees in her written name the prospect of the self she might become. We discern here the progressive move, typical of me-narrative, from voice to print, from local bonds to the author's power of "abstraction,"[13] but we should not overlook the fact that this moment of self-representation in and as *text* coincides precisely with the countervailing and (in this novel) the powerfully localizing force of the blood ties Jane discovers to exist between her and the Riverses.[14]

The book Jane Eyre writes about her life functions as a cage or box—perhaps as a jail—for the voice imperfectly controlled by her former self. In the context of 1840s Britain, that voice does not simply express the insatiable yearnings of the Id or the Dionysian element in human nature, but more specifically those increasingly identified with the *Celt*. We have seen how, in *Waverley*, Scott self-consciously aligns his practice as an autoethnographer with the dispensing of English justice after the Jacobite Rebellion and presents his translating book as the modern British container (perhaps the coffin) for the Celtic voice. Approaching the middle of the century, the increasingly prestigious, pseudo-scientific distinction between supposed Germanic and Celtic traits was making ever more widely available the explanation of Ossianic melancholy as a symptom of a whole race's susceptibility to unfulfillable desire. The Celt, the limit of whose powers had been shown time and again in the history of the British Isles, who had been driven to the fringes of Britain and beyond the Pale in Ireland, was the pawn of a longing *without* limit, both symptom and cause of his historical failures. The "Celtic sadness" stemmed from the "Celtic longing for infinite things."[15] In the context in which such stereotypes were coming to acquire the authority of science, Brontë appears to be placing within her model English heroine the boundless and self-defeating hunger suited to this racialist stereotype.

To make this connection is not to suggest that Brontë does anything so positive as try to identify Jane as covertly Irish; but Irishness remains the limit-case in her exploration of a possibly heterogeneous Englishness. It seems no accident that the final ploy of Rochester in his effort to get Jane to declare her feelings for him is the lie that upon his marriage to Blanche Ingram Jane will be sent off "to undertake the education of the five daughters of Mrs Dionysius O'Gall of Bitternut Lodge, Connaught, Ireland." Rubbing salt in the wound, Rochester says, "You'll like Ireland, I think: they're such warm-hearted people there, they say," adding, "and when you get to Bitternut Lodge, Connaught, Ireland, I shall never see you again, Jane: that's morally certain. I never go over to Ireland, not having myself much of a fancy for the country" (JE 282). Having before her the example of a father who had made the one-way journey out of Ireland to England and Englishness, Brontë can think of no prospect more cruel than that her English heroine be condemned to make a one-way journey in the opposite direction.[16] In her autoethnographies of English culture as a heterogeneous thing, it remained an open question whether an expansive Englishness could really come to include Irishness—in other words, whether the latter could ever provide the position of an *insider's outsidedness* for the English, rather than remaining simply, ineluctably beyond the pale (as racialist explanations would have it).

II

Foucauldian perspectives on *Jane Eyre* have highlighted those elements in the narrative that are devoted to the production of a model modern subject. It is certainly, forcefully true that the initial chapters, larded as they are in terminology drawn from the lexicon of political theory and starkly contrasting two social environments in a manner comparable to Foucault's at the start of *Discipline and Punish*, seem to indicate that the private history of Jane Eyre will encode an allegory about the birth of modern subjectivity out of the ruins of the ancien regime. Foucault's opposition of a premodern social order focused on the body of the king and a carceral modernity aimed at the production of self-regulating subjects is almost too neatly anticipated in the opposition of Gateshead to Lowood, the former run according to the fiat of its rulers and devoted to the commemoration of a dead father-king, the latter a highly regimented "Institution" in which natural differences are suppressed and every movement of the day strictly scheduled. Yet while Jane does acquire at Lowood lessons in the cultivation of interiority that stand her in good stead for the rest of the narrative, it would be a mistake, in view of the rapturous vision of intersubjectivity that ends the novel, simply to conclude (whether one approves of liberal individualism or mistrusts it) that such individualism is *in itself* the novel's aim: to read *Jane Eyre* in this way is to miss its devotion to producing reciprocally defined ideals of selfhood and culture as heterogeneous things. It is also to operate at a level of generality on which different modernities, including the specific United Kingdom variety I am investigating here, remain analytically invisible. Brontë draws upon the national allegories of the Waverley Novels and the National Tales of her father's generation, but where Scott produces narratives about a male character's accession to a modernity and a maturity that balance nostalgic antiquarianism with the virtues of a commercial, voluntarist social order, Brontë's revisionary romance seeks the freedom to realize the powers of the female self within the constraints of an intersubjective order, a genuine culture, far more positive and forceful than the pale contractual models of society permitted under classical commercial liberalism.

To be sure, the early chapters offer considerable support for a reading of Jane as the rights-bearing liberal subject just beginning to emerge. On the momentous "that day" of the novel's abrupt opening, Jane shatters her bonds of servitude, casting off the mental blinders imposed on her by Gateshead the moment she questions the legitimacy of its rule and demands to know, "Why is he [John Reed] my master?" (JE 19). Here we see Jane as the subject of a society recognizing no rights, only revocable "privileges," and as having "no appeal" against capricious authority. John Reed appears to Jane as a "tyrant" and "slave-driver;" akin to the more bloodthirsty of the "Roman emperors" (JE 17). A "rebel slave," she "resist[s] all the way" against his "violent tyrannies"; she cries "Unjust!—unjust!" against the "insupportable oppression" she endures, longing to mount an "insurrection" (JE 22, 19).[17] Thrown like some sacrificial virgin into the mausoleum of the dead patriarch—the red-room where Mr. Reed had lain "in state"—she perceives a chair looking "like a pale throne" and the massive bed standing "like a tabernacle" in the center of the room. The images recall how absolutism legitimated itself (and the heirs fathered on such beds) through appeals to divine right. When Jane sees them, both the furniture and the chamber that contains it are things of "vacant majesty": absolutism's era has passed, and we are on the cusp of something new, but Mrs. Reed carries on oblivious of the fact that the girl she harbors and maltreats belongs to a future in which she and her kind will have no place. At the novel's start, she sits like a queen in her court, "her darlings" "clustered round her" like fawning courtiers (JE 13). Peremptory and arbitrary, she will not submit her rule to the scrutiny of "cavillers or questioners" and will not even answer Jane's plea to know what she has done to deserve punishment (JE 13). Gateshead life amounts to a weird cultural "survival," a holdover from a bygone epoch in human development.[18] We learn enough about the kindness of the deceased Mr. Reed (e.g., JE 24) to infer that absolutism could in former days be benevolently practiced, but we also note the close coincidence of his death and Jane's birth, which seems to suggest that Jane embodies a principle whose entry into the world is inimical to absolutism per se, whether benevolent or not. Reproved by John Reed as a "bad animal," little Jane is the rough beast of a new era whose hour has come round at last.

Writing of her incarceration in the red-room, Jane sums up her newfound awareness of her position at Gateshead in that famous passage I have used as one of the epigraphs to this section, a passage that rings the changes upon some of the best established metaphors for describing fixed, hierarchical social orders. Jane's identification of herself as "a discord" derives from traditional appeals to natural and social hierarchies (or chains of being, in the related trope), appeals stretching back at least to Plato's *Republic* and descending by way of such famous instances as the "untune that string" speech in Shakespeare's *Troilus and Cressida*: according to these, justice in the soul and in society is the harmony of lower, middle, and higher elements. Calling herself "a noxious thing," Jane invokes the time-honored figure of the "body politic," which, like the trope of social harmony, defines individual members of societies entirely in terms of their function as parts within and servants of the total structure. The statements that she was "like nobody" and "a useless thing" at Gateshead proceed from this, for in beginning to assert needs not congruent with her allotted role, Jane is laying claim to a dimension of selfhood not even visible (or so the tendentious modern argument runs) in traditional societies. A self whose worth and identity are drawn from inner reservoirs of thought and feeling strictly partitioned from given role or level does not even figure in absolutism's calculus, has no weight on its evaluative scales; modern selfhood is *definitively* "useless" by the ancient standard. When she labels herself "a heterogeneous thing," Jane is not signaling that she, homogeneous within herself, does not belong in the otherwise homogeneous social universe of Gateshead but, rather, that modern selfhood is *intrinsically* heterogeneous, founded as it is upon the distinction between role and core. More specifically than this, she alludes to the distinctive heterogeneity of the English that Defoe (in this chapter's other epigraph) expressed solely in racial terms but which Brontë explores in more registers than merely that one.

In the twilight of its epoch, with its hold beginning to weaken, absolutism becomes both more violent and more erratic in its attempt to retain power. One sign of its decadence is the latitude Mrs. Reed grants to her torturer or chief of secret police—her son John—to keep order by any means. On his watch, the unconditional authority of the monarch extends itself in efforts to exercise surveillance and control over absolutely every aspect of its subject's existence, and, in striving toward totalitarianism,

Gateshead life becomes the anticulture that sets in motion Jane's quest for its structural opposite. But first Jane has to surmount the other antithesis inscribed in her by the very oppression she longs to escape, the opposing idea of a freedom as unconditioned and solitary as Gateshead society is intrusive and "airless." Jane the narrator's account of the crisis that precipitated her expulsion from the negative Eden of her childhood both analyzes her Gateshead-nurtured pathology of thinking in terms of extremes without middles (as in *society vs. freedom*) and suggests the terms in which such dichotomous structures have *themselves* been opposed and overcome in the mature authorial Jane.

When, in chapter 1, Jane manages to steal a few minutes' solitude behind the "folds of scarlet drapery" in the drawing-room window seat, she daydreams herself away to the barren climes reachable only by the subjects of the book in her hand, "Bewick's *History of British Birds*." Her imagination dilates upon "the haunts of the sea-fowl ... 'the solitary rocks and promontories' by them only inhabited," upon "the vast sweep of the Arctic zone, and [its] forlorn regions of dreary space": the oppression of Gateshead stimulates in reaction the imagination of freedom as flight from all human habitation, a one-way flight into the "death-white realms" of the north (JE 14). Before John Reed has a chance to reassert his punitive power by literally throwing the book at her, Jane flies off in reverie from human society in its entirety, as yet incapable of envisioning any form of society other than Gateshead's crushing despotism. She escapes in imagination to a state of uncompromised animal purity achievable, if anywhere, only on a landscape as barren to human purposes as those ice floes. As Jane describes the several "vignettes" in Bewick on which her imagination alighted, we note the way her former self inclined toward those images showing unpopulated land- or seascapes, scenes or events remote from or inimical to human good: "the broken boat stranded on a desolate coast"; the "wreck just sinking"; "the quite solitary churchyard" (JE 15). The only individual human figure she pauses over ("the fiend pinning down the thief's pack") is bent on nefarious purposes, and him Jane "passe[s] over quickly," fleeing his company. She seems to perceive as the essential character of all human society what the final vignette shows her in depicting a "black, horned thing" sitting "aloof on a rock, surveying a distant crowd surrounding a gallows" (JE 15). Young Jane herself—rough beast—might *be* that strange creature, the deformed or deviant subject who looks on with jaundiced eye at this rite whereby communities achieve cohesion by the elimination of the deviant. Here is a vision of anticulture to rival Joseph de Maistre's chilling celebration of the executioner as the figure on whom "all greatness, all power, all subordination rest," the "terror and the bond of human association."[19] We recall how, at the start of the novel, Jane was banished from the Reed family circle, "exclude[d] from privileges intended only for contented, happy, little children" (JE 13), and how she refers to herself as "the scape-goat of the nursery" (JE 23).

If *Jane Eyre* were simply an instruction manual in docile liberal subjectivity, we would expect to see in the ensuing sections of the novel an unambiguous endorsement of all those forces encouraging Jane to develop the inner landscape of her soul and recommending the taking of refuge therein. It is true that in the opening chapter, Jane describes herself as "shrined in double retirement" (JE 14) when she sequesters herself with Bewick in the window seat, drapery on one hand and window panes on the other, and that this self-enshrining both contrasts with the deference paid to absolutist authority in the "tabernacle" of the red-room and points forward to the Lowood portion of the novel, where, encouraged by Helen Burns and instructed by Miss Temple, Jane begins to learn the self-discipline necessary for the construction of her own private temple of interiority. Thus far, the details line up in support of a reading of the novel as more or less enacting, in a Foucauldian key, the process described in Keats's "Ode to Psyche." But the admiration Jane the narrator expresses for Helen and for Miss Temple is anything but unqualified: both figures offer too extreme a swing of the pendulum away from Gateshead-Jane's wild rebelliousness, a self-composure that relinquishes all claim whatever upon the order of society or even (in Helen's case) upon mortal existence.

Helen receives the novel's implicit approval when she argues that the forgetting of grievances is necessary to psychological liberation, but not when she turns forbearance into utter passivity: her capacity to "live in calm, looking to the end" of life (JE 70) differs completely from Jane's later, hard-won independence, which is sustained on the principle that "God did not give me my life to throw away" (JE 461). Helen Burns's life is thrown away, and the girl acquiesces to the act. Where Miss Temple is concerned, all the respect and gratitude Jane feels for her do not dispel the memory of the "petrified severity" she imposes upon herself when she withdraws in silence from the noisy tyranny of Mr. Brocklehurst: Jane recalls how, under the hail of his abuse, Miss Temple "gazed straight before her, and her face, naturally pale as marble, appeared to be assuming also the coldness and fixity of that material; especially her mouth closed as if it would have required a sculptor's chisel to open it" (JE 75). This is making oneself into a temple of interiority in a wholly negative sense, a self-petrification and self-silencing that represents but the extreme reversal of the Gateshead Jane's bound-breaking fits and cries. Together, Gateshead and Lowood offer complementary situations of extremes without middles, the hallmark of anticultural situations. When disease brings the icy hand of death to Lowood, it comes in a "bright May" teeming with dowers (JE 90); the relaxation of Brocklehurst's disciplinary system that occurs during this crisis sends Jane careening back into a state of total license in which a new companion (an anti-Helen) gives "ample indulgence" to Jane's faults, "never imposing curb or rein on anything" she says or does (JE 90–91). When Miss Temple marries and leaves the school, Jane backslides to a position from which she "gasp[s]" for an impossibly abstract "liberty," then scorns her own desire and calls out cynically for "a new servitude" (JE 99). Genuine culture, when it is finally attained, will offer itself as mediating these hypostatized alternatives: Burke's ideal of a "*social* freedom ... in which Liberty is secured by the equality of Restraint."[20]

At Thornfield, Jane is so worked upon by Rochester's deceit as to believe that she has found the means of obtaining all the freedom and self-realization she is entitled to there by marrying the master, in the style of Richardson's *Pamela*. Yet, along with many other disturbing signs, the recurrence of situations of stark antithesis or extremes without middles identifies the place, in keeping with its name, as another variety of anticultural wasteland. Shortly after arriving at Thornfield, Jane gazes from the rooftop and then hears the "curious laugh" of the incarcerated wife she knows nothing about: she looks out upon a broad horizon and "a propitious sky, azure, marbled with pearly white"—a sky that seems to promise her greater reach and range than she has yet known—then immediately down through the trapdoor back to the attic: "I could scarcely see my way down the ladder," she writes, "the attic seemed black as a vault compared with that arch of blue to which I had been looking up" (JE 122). Jane's later discovery of what was always the truth about Thornfield brings on one more passage of heightened oppositions, similar to the kind we saw in the Lowood portion of the novel. Jane writes that her "cherished wishes, yesterday so blooming and glowing ... lay stark, chill, livid corpses that could never revive": "A Christmas frost had come at midsummer; a white-December storm had whirled over June; ice glazed the ripe apples, drifts crushed the blowing roses; on hay-field and corn-field lay a frozen shroud: lanes which last night blushed full of flowers, to-day were pathless with untrodden snow; and the woods, which twelve hours since waved leafy and fragrant as groves between the tropics, now spread, waste, wild, and white as pine-forests in wintry Norway" (JE 330).

Brontë's fiction implicitly suggests that oppositions like the one between discourse- and story-space in narrative become autoethnographically productive to the extent that they generate tension at their boundary and begin to suggest that significant kinds of trespassing are going on across it. One striking method for enabling this tension or trespass is Jane the narrator's occasional lapse into the present tense when representing past moments of particular emotional intensity. Recalling her first, silent admission of love for Rochester while watching him amidst the ladies and gentlemen in the drawing room, the narrator elides the inner monologue she engaged in then and her retrospective account of the scene: the character thinks, "He is not to them what he is to me" and "while I breathe and think I must love him," and then the narrator writes, "Coffee is handed. The ladies ... have become lively as larks" (JE 199). For a little less than a page, the temporal frontier between the two Janes vanishes. Later, describing her return to Thornfield from Gateshead, where she was impressed by her lack of vengefulness toward the Reeds, Jane assumes the present tense once more, in a passage that points forward to the winter-in-summer one quoted just above. Once more thinking of her feelings for Rochester, the writer gives us this:

> They are making hay, too, in Thornfield meadows: or rather, the labourers are just quitting their work, and returning home with their rakes on their shoulders: now, at the hour I arrive. I have but a field or two to traverse, and then I shall cross the road and reach the gates. How full the hedges are of roses! But I have no time to gather any; I want to be at the house. I pass a tall briar, shooting leafy and flowery branches across the path; I see the narrow stile with stone steps; and I see—Mr Rochester sitting there, a book and pencil in his hand: he is writing. (JE 274)

At such moments we confront the double uncanniness of a narrator whose usual effect is to stress her difference from her narrated self, now dropping into the perspective of that former self. The compulsion to relinquish authorial control and fully to inhabit that earlier viewpoint, felt in the insistent "now, at the hour I arrive," is felt even more strongly and strangely when we notice that all of a sudden it is Rochester who is writing, not Jane. The remembered pleasure of seeing him again is accompanied by the disturbing thought that he was even then writing Jane as a character into his plot, subordinating her to his duplicitous narrative. This is the false summer of Jane's hopes.

A third such passage, the most arresting and sustained, occurs immediately after Jane has fled the fraudulent promise of Thornfield and finds herself "absolutely destitute" "at a place called Whitcross" (JE 362). If we recall Jane's Gateshead-inspired longings to be free of all human society, we will be prepared to read the ensuing episode as a terrible vision of those very longings realized. "Not a tie holds me to human society at this moment," she writes, "not a charm or hope calls me where my fellow-creatures are—none that saw me would have a kind thought or a good wish for me" (JE 362). The narrator's adoption of the present tense in this instance strongly suggests that she is rehearsing a central problem of romanticism, the desire for a spontaneity and fullness of being thought to exist among the unreflective animals. The relationless liberty imagined to be found outside of human culture would be a condition without past and future, an atemporal unconsciousness such as Wordsworth ascribed to the hares "running races in their mirth" while he brooded upon mutability, in "Resolution and Independence." At Whitcross, experience loses its layered temporality as the narrating Jane disappears behind her narrated self. "I have no relative but the universal mother, nature," she declares, "I will seek her breast and ask repose" (JE 363). But in the words of John Jarndyce in Dickens's *Bleak House*, "the universe makes an indifferent parent." "[N]o town, nor even a hamlet," but a mere "stone pillar set up where four roads meet," Whitcross is Jane's crossroad. Like Wordsworth, like Coleridge in such poems as "The Eolian Harp," she will turn back from the path of self-annihilating boundless desire, affirming that *human* freedom is constituted in and through time and the claims of others, that the apparent freedom of the beasts is subjection *to* time. With this affirmation comes the resumption of past-tense narration and the capacity to analyze the desire rather than simply to submit to it. Jane writes that, alone upon the moor, she "wished [she] could live in it and on it": "I saw a lizard run over the crag," she remembers; "I saw a bee busy among the sweet bilberries. I would fain at the moment have become bee or lizard, that I might have found fitting nutriment, permanent shelter here. But I was a human being" (JE 364). Saved by the providential light that guides her to her unsuspected relatives, Jane recovers her self and name not upon the moor but at "Moor House," and she recovers these, as we have seen, in writing.

With Diana and Mary Rivers she finds "perfect congeniality of tastes, sentiments, and principles," and through them learns to "comprehend the feeling" of their "perfect enthusiasm of attachment" to the particular landscape they inhabit, and also to "share both its strength and truth." They teach Jane "the fascination of the locality" and in doing so the value of locality as such (JE 391). St. John, in contrast, "considers himself an alien from his native country" (JE 395), and turns from local attachment to its extreme opposite, abstract, universalizing philanthropy. Like Jane in being prone to "insatiate yearnings and disquieting aspirations," he manifests the same cruel self-conquering discipline shown earlier by Miss Temple (JE 394). Jane watches him "sitting as still as one of the dusky pictures on the walls;

keeping his eyes fixed on the page he perused, and his lips mutely sealed.... Had he been a statue instead of a man, he could not have been easier [to examine]." With "Greek face" and forehead "colourless as ivory," he marbleizes himself in acts of "despotic constriction" against the sensuous appeal of Rosamund Oliver, the "Rose of the World" (JE 386, 407, 419). Had he married Rosamund and acquired control of her father's sizeable fortune, he might have exercised his formidable gifts in England. It is against the backdrop of St. John's boundless and self-consuming vocation that Rochester's call to Jane comes into focus as effecting a bond *both* translocal and demarcatable, a voluntary union animated by the energy of a quasi-religious *calling*: a national culture.[21]

The appellation "Moor House" encodes the refusal of singleness required of deliberately heterogeneous things: it beckons toward the natural expanse and the domestic enclosure alike. We saw such a gesture at the beginning of the novel, in that suggestive tableau of Jane in the Gateshead window seat, "shrined in double retirement." She sat there dreaming in the most conventional of metaphors for a state of perfect liberty, but the book she used to imagine herself flying away from social toils was a book of *British* birds.[22] Can there exist a creature both British and as free as a bird? An ideal culture would give its members the feeling that their natural longings and their social needs were being satisfied in equal measure. In the Gateshead window seat, only glass divides Jane from the domain of "the natural"—but she can see it; only a curtain divides her from that of "the social"—she can temporarily block it out but never escape it while living, and so must begin the search for a home she might fly in. But she can find it, evidently, only at the cost of proving true what she suspected and dreaded about cultures when she fixed her eye upon that final vignette from Bewick. Both narrative closure and national closed unity *do* turn out to require the elimination of some element—Bertha, of course, but also Irishness, perhaps?—*too* deviant to be admitted within the culture of heterogeneous things without blasting it apart.

Notes

1. Defoe, *The True-Born Englishman and Other Writings*, ed. P. N. Furbank and W. R. Owens (Harmondsworth: Penguin, 1997), 35; Benedict Anderson uses this passage as an epigraph to *Imagined Communities*.

2. Brontë, *Jane Eyre* (1847: Harmondsworth: Penguin, 1996), 23: henceforth JE.

3. Whereas most of the internal evidence suggests that the events Jane narrates took place in the 1820s, one anomalous reference to Scott's *Marmion* (1808) as a "new publication" (JE 414) would make Jane's story contemporaneous with the non-English National Tales of Owensen, Maturin, and others.

4. Brontë is thus well ahead of the trend Robert J. C. Young locates in the later

nineteenth century "for the English to invoke Defoe's account of 'that Het'rogeneous Thing, An Englishman', and to define themselves as a hybrid or 'Mongrel half-bred Race'": Robert J. C. Young, *Colonial Desire: Hybridity in Theory, Culture, and Race* (London: Routledge, 1995), 17. In her interesting *Imperialism at Home: Race and Victorian Women's Fiction* (Ithaca: Cornell University Press, 1996), Susan Meyer attributes to Brontë too uncomplicated an investment in the trope of purification and thus constructs a neater opposition between "plague-cursed colonial environments" and a bourgeois ideal of "England, cleanliness, and home" than I would draw (87; cf. chap. 2). Cf. Firdous Azim, *The Colonial Rise of the Novel* (London: Routledge, 1993), for the argument that Jane's ties to the colonial domain "Creolise" her into a figure "whose inscription within English society remains heterogeneous" (177): Azim misses the national allegory through which *Jane Eyre* recommends a *restricted* heterogeneity as a formula for modern Englishness.

5. Cf. Ruth Perry, "De-Familiarizing the Family; or, Writing Family History from Literary Sources," *Modern Language Quarterly* 55/4 (Dec. 1994), 415–27.

6. Cf. George W. Stocking Jr., ed., *Malinowski, Rivers, Benedict and Others: Essays on Culture and Personality* (Madison: University of Wisconsin Press, 1986), and David Simpson's recent revisiting of the issue in *Situatedness, or, Why We Keep Saying Where We're Coming From* (Durham, N.C.: Duke University Press, 2002), chap. 3.

7. Cf. Froula, *Modernism's Body: Sex, Culture, and Joyce* (New York: Columbia University Press, 1996).

8. Anne Brontë, *Agnes Grey* (1847; Oxford: Oxford University Press, 1998), 145; henceforth AG.

9. Cf. Gayatri Chakravorty Spivak, "Three Women's Texts and a Critique of Imperialism," *Critical Inquiry* 12 (1985), 243–61.

10. Compare those passages toward the end of *Shirley*, when the title character's expressions of scorn for her narrow-minded uncle Sympson are so little checked that one starts to feel rather sorry for the man.

11. Christopher Herbert, *Culture and Anomie: Ethnographic Imagination in the Nineteenth Century* (Chicago: University of Chicago Press, 1991), 51.; cf. *Patricia Ticineto Clough, Autoaffection: Unconscious Thought in the Age of Teletechnology* (Minneapolis: University of Minnesota Press, 2000), on autoethnographic sociology's programmatic "forgetting ... of the unconscious and desire altogether, so that what began as a criticism of the authority produced in ethnographic writing comes back at times as a naive production of autobiographical authority" (16–17).

12. This was one instance in which Brontë may have felt she could not trust the partitioning force of print: the words "I uttered a wild, involuntary cry" appear in manuscript but were deleted from the published text; they have been "restored" in the Penguin and some other editions of the novel.

13. Cf. Sharon Marcus, "The Profession of the Author: Abstraction, Advertising, and *Jane Eyre*," *PMLA* 110/2 (1995), 206–19.

14. For Brontë, blood makes a double-edged claim: her siblings afforded her the very quintessence of locality (voices and faces intensely present), but where her parents were concerned blood ties could be powerfully dislocating, a constant reminder of far-off places (Cornwall, Ireland) involved in the formation of her identity.

15. Cf. Fredric Faverty, *Matthew Arnold the Ethnologist* (Evanston: Northwestern University Press, 1951), 154.

16. Cf. *The Letters of Charlotte Brontë*, Vol. 1 (1829–47), ed. Margaret Smith (Oxford: Clarendon Press, 1995), 269, for Brontë's sole (and oblique) reference to her father's Irishness, and *The Letters of Charlotte Brontë*, Vol. 2 (1848–51), ed. Smith (Oxford:

Clarendon, 2000), 497 ff., for her interesting correspondence with an Irish fan, "K. T."

17. It was this language, concentrated in the early scenes, that led the reviewer for the *Christian Remembrancer* to the hyperbole of saying that "[e]very page burns with moral Jacobinism" and that "'Un just, unjust,' is the burden of every reflection upon the things and powers that be": cf. Miriam Allott, ed., *The Brontës: The Critical Heritage* (London and Boston: Routledge and Kegan Paul, 1974), 90.

18. Cf. JE 38, for an image of the passing social order dabbling in the ways of the new one: "[Eliza Reed] had a turn for traffic, and a marked propensity for saving; shown not only in the vending of eggs and chickens, but also in driving hard bargains with the gardener about flower-roots, seeds, and slips of plants; that functionary having orders from Mrs Reed to buy of this young lady all the products of her parterre she wished to sell." Brontë, who had considered Peel a traitor when he capitulated to the anti-Corn-Law faction, objects here to a system of trade rigged in favor of the landed classes.

19. Quoted in Isaiah Berlin, "Joseph de Maistre and the Origins of Fascism," *The Crooked Timber of Humanity: Chapters in the History of Ideas*, ed. Henry Hardy (Princeton: Princeton University Press, 1990), 117.

20. Quoted by Conor Cruise O'Brien in the introduction to Burke, *Reflections on the Revolution in France* (Harmondsworth: Penguin, 1969), 15.

21. As Rochester's servant says of his wounded, regenerate master after the destruction of Thornfield, "he's in England: he can't get out of England. I fancy—he's a fixture now" (JE 476).

22. Or, as actually titled, *A History of English Birds* (1804).

Chronology

1816 Born April 21 at Thornton in Yorkshire, the third daughter of Patrick Brontë and Maria Branwell Brontë.

1820 Father appointed perpetual curate of Haworth, so family moves there.

1821 Mother dies. Sister, Elizabeth Branwell, comes to live with the family.

1824 Charlotte's sisters Maria and Elizabeth enroll at the Clergy Daughters' School, Cowan Bridge. Charlotte and Emily join them. The school becomes the model for the one in *Jane Eyre*. Elizabeth and Maria return home and die of consumption.

1825–1831 Charlotte and Emily return home. Write thousands of pages in miniature books about a kingdom they've created.

1831 Enrolls at Miss Wooler's School, Roe Head.

1832 Completes schooling and returns home to teach sisters.

1835 Returns to Roe Head as a teacher.

1838 Resigns position and returns home.

1839 Turns down marriage proposals from two suitors.

1842 Charlotte and Emily enroll in the Pensionnat Heger, Brussels; aunt Elizabeth Branwell's death brings money to each niece and nephew, enabling both girls to return home.

1843 Returns to Brussels to teach English and to study.

1844	Leaves Brussels; she and sisters attempt to start a school.
1846	Charlotte, Emily, and Anne take on the expense to publish *Poems by Currer, Ellis and Acton Bell*, a pseudonymous collection of their own work. Charlotte's novel *The Professor* completed but no publisher wants it; begins *Jane Eyre* while caring for her father after an eye operation.
1847	Publishes *Jane Eyre*, immediately acclaimed, under the pseudonym Currer Bell.
1848	Brother Branwell, the only son of the family, dies in September; Emily dies in December.
1849	Anne dies. Novel *Shirley* published, also under pseudonym Currer Bell.
1850–1851	Travels and meets her literary hero, Thackeray. Meets and befriends Elizabeth Gaskell, who later writes Charlotte's biography. Rejects marriage proposal from gentleman at her publishing company.
1853	Publishes novel *Villette*.
1854	Marries Arthur Bell Nicholls, her father's curate. Begins novel *Emma*.
1855	Pregnant in January. Dies on March 31.
1857	Gaskell's *Life of Charlotte Brontë* published; *The Professor* published posthumously.

Contributors

HAROLD BLOOM is Sterling Professor of the Humanities at Yale University. He is the author of 30 books, including *Shelley's Mythmaking* (1959), *The Visionary Company* (1961), *Blake's Apocalypse* (1963), *Yeats* (1970), *A Map of Misreading* (1975), *Kabbalah and Criticism* (1975), *Agon: Toward a Theory of Revisionism* (1982), *The American Religion* (1992), *The Western Canon* (1994), and *Omens of Millennium: The Gnosis of Angels, Dreams, and Resurrection* (1996). *The Anxiety of Influence* (1973) sets forth Professor Bloom's provocative theory of the literary relationships between the great writers and their predecessors. His most recent books include *Shakespeare: The Invention of the Human* (1998), a 1998 National Book Award finalist, *How to Read and Why* (2000), *Genius: A Mosaic of One Hundred Exemplary Creative Minds* (2002), *Hamlet: Poem Unlimited* (2003), *Where Shall Wisdom Be Found?* (2004), and *Jesus and Yahweh: The Names Divine* (2005). In 1999, Professor Bloom received the prestigious American Academy of Arts and Letters Gold Medal for Criticism. He has also received the International Prize of Catalonia, the Alfonso Reyes Prize of Mexico, and the Hans Christian Andersen Bicentennial Prize of Denmark.

SALLY SHUTTLEWORTH is professor of modern literature at the University of Sheffield, England. She is a coeditor of George Eliot's *Lifted Veil: Brother Jacob* as well as coeditor of *Embodied Selves: An Anthology of Psychological Texts*.

SUSAN MEYER teaches English at Wellesley College. In addition to publishing *Imperialism at Home: Race and Victorian Women's Fiction*, she has coedited *The New Nineteenth Century*.

SUSAN OSTROV WEISSER teaches English at Adelphi University. She is coeditor of *Feminist Nightmares: Women at Odds* and *Women and Romance: A Reader*.

SANDRA M. GILBERT is professor of English at the University of California, Davis. She is the coauthor of *Madwoman in the Attic: The Woman Writer and the Nineteenth-Century Literary Imagination*. She is the coeditor of the second edition of *The Norton Anthology of Literature by Women: The Traditions in English* and also has written several books of poetry.

MARIANNE THORMÄHLEN is professor of English literature at Lund University in Sweden. She is the author of *"The Waste Land": A Fragmentary Wholeness* and other titles, and the editor of *Rethinking Modernism*.

JEROME BEATY, now deceased, was professor of Victorian literature at Emory University. He authored several titles, including *Misreading* Jane Eyre*: A Postformalist Paradigm*. He edited several titles as well, including the *Norton Introduction to Fiction*.

HEATHER GLEN teaches English at the University of Cambridge, England. Her published work includes *Jane Eyre: New Casebook*; she is also the editor of *The Cambridge Companion to the Brontës* and other titles.

WARREN EDMINSTER teaches English and Philosophy at Murray State University. He is the author of *Preaching Fox: Elements of Festive Subversion in the Plays of the Wakefield Master*.

JAMES BUZARD teaches literature at the Massachusetts Institute of Technology. He is the coeditor of *Victorian Prism: Refractions of the Crystal Palace* and the author of a book as well as of several essays on nineteenth- and twentieth-century British literature and culture.

Bibliography

Beattie, Valerie. "The Mystery at Thornfield: Representations of Madness in *Jane Eyre*." *Studies in the Novel* 28, no. 4 (Winter 1996): 493–506.

Beaty, Jerome. *Misreading* Jane Eyre*: A Postformalist Paradigm*. Columbus: Ohio State University Press, 1996.

Beaty, Jerome. "St. John's Way and the Wayward Reader." In Jane Eyre: *An Authoritative Text, Contexts, Criticisms*. New York: W. W. Norton and Company, 2001.

Berg, Maggie. Jane Eyre: *Portrait of a Life*. Boston: Twayne , 1987.

Betsinger, Sue Ann. "*Jane Eyre* and the Orphan's 'Mother.'" *Brontë Studies* 29, no. 2 (July 2004): 111–123.

Bloom, Harold. *The Brontës* (Bloom's Major Novelists series). Philadelphia: Chelsea House, 2000.

———. *Jane Eyre* (Bloom's Notes series). Philadelphia: Chelsea House, 1998.

Boumelha, Penny. *Charlotte Brontë*. Bloomington: Indiana University Press, 1990.

Buzard, James. "The Wild English Girl: *Jane Eyre*." In *Disorienting Fiction: The Autoethnographic Work of Nineteenth-Century British Novels*. Princeton, N.J.: Princeton University Press, 2005.

DeLamotte, Eugenia C. *Perils of the Night: A Feminist Study of Nineteenth-Century Gothic*. New York: Oxford University Press, 1990.

Edminster, Warren. "Fairies and Feminism: Recurrent Patterns in Chaucer's 'The Wife of Bath's Tale' and Brontë's *Jane Eyre*." *The Victorian Newsletter*, no. 104 (Fall 2003): 22–28.

Emberson, Ian M. "'A Wreck Just Sinking': The Beginning of *Jane Eyre* and the Ending of *Villette*." *Brontë Studies* 28, no. 1 (March 2003): 89–90.

Gana, Nouri. "Forbidden Otherness: Plain Jane's Regress." *Atlantic Literary Review* 2, no. 1 (January–March 2001): 1–23.

Gates, Barbara Timm. *Critical Essays on Charlotte Brontë*. Boston, Mass.: G.K. Hall, 1990.

Gilbert, Sandra M. "*Jane Eyre* and the Secrets of Furious Lovemaking." *Novel* 31, no. 3 (Summer 1998): 351–372.

Glen, Heather. "Triumph and Jeopardy: The Shape of *Jane Eyre*." In *Charlotte Brontë: The Imagination in History*. Oxford: Oxford University Press, 2002.

Gordon, Lyndall. *Charlotte Brontë: A Passionate Life*. London: Chatto & Windus, 1994.

Haller, Elizabeth K. "Guise and the Act of Concealment in *Jane Eyre*." *Brontë Studies* 28, no. 3 (November 2003): 205–213.

Hoeveler, Diane Long, and Lisa Jadwin. *Charlotte Brontë*. New York: Twayne Publishers, 1997.

Ifkovic, David A. "Conflict Resolution by the Brontës: *Jane Eyre*—A Case in Point." *Brontë Studies* 27, no. 2 (July 2002): 171–173.

Kaplan, Carla. *The Erotics of Talk: Women's Writing and Feminist Paradigms*. New York: Oxford University Press, 1996.

Karson, Jill, ed. *Readings on* Jane Eyre. San Diego, Calif.: Greenhaven Press, 2000.

Knight, Charmian. "Reader, What Next?: The Final Chapter of *Jane Eyre*." *Brontë Society Transactions* 23, no. 1 (April 1998): 27–30.

LaMonaca, Maria. "Jane's Crown of Thorns: Feminism and Christianity in *Jane Eyre*." *Studies in the Novel* 34, no. 3 (Fall 2002): 245–263.

Lamonica, Drew. *"We Are Three Sisters": Self and Family in the Writing of the Brontës*. Columbia: University of Missouri Press, 2003.

Lane, Christopher. "Charlotte Brontë on the Pleasure of Hating." *ELH* 69, no. 1 (Spring 2002): 199–222.

Levine, Caroline. "'Harmless Pleasure': Gender, Suspense, and *Jane Eyre*." *Victorian Literature and Culture* 28, no. 2 (2000): 275–286.

Meyer, Susan. "'Indian Ink': Colonialism and the Figurative Strategy of *Jane Eyre*." In *Imperialism at Home: Race and Victorian Women's Fiction*. Ithaca, N.Y.: Cornell University Press, 1996.

Mitchell, Judith. *The Stone and the Scorpion: The Female Subject of Desire in the Novels of Charlotte Brontë, George Eliot, and Thomas Hardy*. Westport, Conn.: Greenwood Press, 1994.

Nestor, Pauline. *Charlotte Brontë's* Jane Eyre. New York: St. Martin's Press, 1992.

Peters, John G. "'We Stood at God's Feet, Equal': Equality, Subversion, and Religion in *Jane Eyre*." *Brontë Studies* 29, no. 1 (March 2004): 53–64.

Plasa, Carl. *Charlotte Brontë*. New York: Palgrave Macmillan, 2004.

Prentis, Barbara. *The Brontë Sisters and George Eliot: A Unity of Difference*. Totowa, NJ: Barnes & Noble Books, 1988.

Schaff, Susan V. "Echoes of Aristotle: Rochester's Rhetorical Ploys in *Jane Eyre*." *Brontë Studies* 27, no. 2 (July 2002): 113–120.

Shuttlesworth, Sally. "*Jane Eyre*: Lurid Hieroglyphics." In *Charlotte Brontë and Victorian Psychology*. Cambridge, U.K.: Cambridge University Press, 1996.

Spiegel, Joanne. "The Construction of the Romance in *Jane Eyre*." *Readerly/Writerly Texts* 9, nos. 1–2 (Spring–Winter 2001): 133–146.

Sternlieb, Lisa. "*Jane Eyre*: 'Hazarding Confidences.'" *Nineteenth-Century Literature* 53, no. 4 (March 1999): 452–479.

Stockton, Kathryn Bond. *God between Their Lips: Desire between Women in Irigaray, Brontë, and Eliot*. Stanford, Calif.: Stanford University Press, 1994.

Symons, Alison. "Criticizing the Critical Male Gaze in *Jane Eyre* and *Villette*." *Atlantis* 29, no. 1 (Fall 2004): 113–115.

Tayler, Irene. *Holy Ghosts: The Male Muses of Emily and Charlotte Brontë*. New York: Columbia University Press, 1990.

Thaden, Barbara. *Student Companion to Charlotte & Emily Brontë*. Westport, Conn.: Greenwood Press, 2001.

Thormählen, Marianne. "The Enigma of St John Rivers." In *The Brontës and Religion*. Cambridge, U.K.: Cambridge University Press, 1999.

Tracy, Thomas. "'Reader, I Buried Him': Apocalypse and Empire in *Jane Eyre*." *Critical Survey* 16, no. 2 (2004): 59–77.

Weisser, Susan Ostrov. "Thornfield and 'The Dream to Repose on': *Jane Eyre*." In *A "Craving Vacancy": Women and Sexual Love in the British Novel, 1740–1780*. New York: New York University Press, 1997.

Winkler, Mary. "'But It Is a True Thing': Vision and Creation in the Work of Charlotte Brontë." In *Seeing and Saying: Self-Referentiality in British and American Literature*, edited by Detlev Gohrbandt and Bruno von Lutz. Berlin: Peter Lang, 1998.

Wylie, Judith. "Incarnate Crimes: Masculine Gendering and the Double in *Jane Eyre*." *Victorians Institute Journal* 27 (1999): 55–69.

Acknowledgments

Shuttleworth, Sally. *Charlotte Brontë and Victorian Psychology*. Pp. 148–182. Copyright © 1996 Cambridge University Press. Reprinted with the permission of Cambridge University Press.

Reprinted from Susan Meyer: *Imperialism at Home: Rare and Victorian Women's Fiction*. Copyright © 1996 by Cornell University. Used by permission of the publisher, Cornell University Press..

"Thornfield and 'The Dream to Repose On': *Jane Eyre*" by Susan Ostrov Weisser. From *A "Craving Vacancy": Women and Sexual Love in the British Novel, 1740–1880*: 53–72. © 1997 by Susan Ostrov Weisser. Reprinted by permission.

"*Jane Eyre* and the Secrets of Furious Lovemaking" by Sandra M. Gilbert. From *Novel* 31, no. 3 (Summer 1998): 351–372. © 1998 Novel Corp. Reprinted by permission.

"The Enigma of St John Rivers" by Marianne Thormählen. From *The Brontës and Religion*: 204–220. © 1999 by Marianne Thormählen. Reprinted by permission.

"St. John's Way and the Wayward Reader" by Jerome Beaty. From Jane Eyre*: An Authoritative Text, Contexts, Criticism*: 491–503. © 2001 by W. W. Norton & Company. Reprinted by permission.

"Triumph and Jeopardy: The Shape of *Jane Eyre*" by Heather Glen. From *Charlotte Brontë: The Imagination in History*: 50–64. © 2002 by Heather Glen. Reprinted by permission.

"Fairies and Feminism: Recurrent Patterns in Chaucer's 'The Wife of Bath's Tale' and Brontë's *Jane Eyre*" by Warren Edminster. From *The Victorian Newsletter* no. 104 (Fall 2003): 22–28. © 2003 by *The Victorian Newsletter*. Reprinted by permission.

"The Wild English Girl: *Jane Eyre*" by James Buzard. From *Disorienting Fiction: The Autoethnographic Work of Nineteenth-Century British Novels*: 196–217. © 2005 by Princeton University Press. Reprinted by permission.

Every effort has been made to contact the owners of copyrighted material and secure copyright permission. Articles appearing in this volume generally appear much as they did in their original publication with few or no editorial changes. Those interested in locating the original source will find bibliographic information in the bibliography and acknowledgments sections of this volume.

Index

Note: Literary characters are listed by first name.

VIVA Modern Critical Interpretations

Available Titles in the Series

Viva

Alice's Adventures in Wonderland

9788130906362 Rs. 145

Animal Farm

9788130906355 In Print

As You Like It

9788130918723 Rs. 195

The Adventures of Huckleberry Finn

788130907390 Rs. 165

Beowulf

9788130907406 In Print

Beloved

9788130918884 Rs. 195

Black Boy

788130906737 Rs. 125

Brave New World

9788130906348 In Print

Cat on a Hot Tin Roof

9788130906393 Rs. 99

VIVA Modern Critical Interpretations

Available Titles in the Series

Viva

Crime and Punishment
9788130906409 Rs. 175

The Chronicles of Narnia
9788130907468 Rs. 145

The Crucible
9788130906416 Rs. 125

Darkness at Noon
9788130906423 Rs. 145

David Copperfield
9788130918730 Rs. 145

The Death of Artemio Cruz
9788130907475 Rs. 145

Death of a Salesman
9788130906744 Rs. 125

The Divine Comedy
9788130918846 Rs. 175

Don Quixote
9788130904658 Rs. 125

VIVA Modern Critical Interpretations

Available Titles in the Series

Viva

Dracula

9788130906430 Rs. 195

Emerson's Essays

9788130906577 Rs. 175

Emma

9788130918839 Rs. 165

A Farewell to Arms

9788130918754 Rs. 175

Frankenstein

9788130907413 Rs. 145

The General Prologue to the Canterbury Tales

9788130918747 Rs. 175

The Glass Menagerie

9788130907482 In Print

The Grapes of Wrath

9788130906751 Rs. 145

Great Expectations

9788130904597 Rs. 175

VIVA Modern Critical Interpretations

Available Titles in the Series

Viva

The Great Gatsby
9788130906454 Rs. 145

Gulliver's Travels
9788130906461 Rs. 195

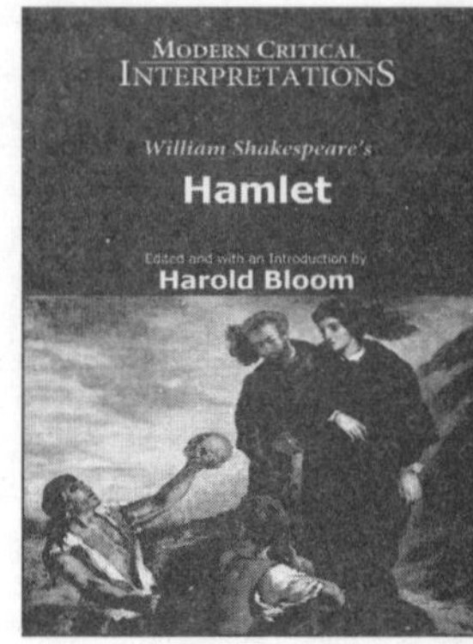

Hamlet
9788130918877 Rs. 165

The Iliad
9788130907895 Rs. 145

Invisible Man
9788130906485 In Print

Heart of Darkness
9788130918815 Rs. 165

Jane Eyre
9788130918860 Rs. 195

Julius Caesar
9788130906492 Rs. 125

King Lear
9788130918853 Rs. 165

VIVA Modern Critical Interpretations

Available Titles in the Series

Viva

Long Day's Journey into Night

9788130904634 Rs. 99

Lord of the Flies

9788130904603 Rs. 145

The Lord of the Rings

9788130907956 Rs. 145

The Man without Qualities

9788130907499 Rs. 145

The Merchand of Venice

9788130906522 In Print

Macbeth

9788130906515 Rs. 125

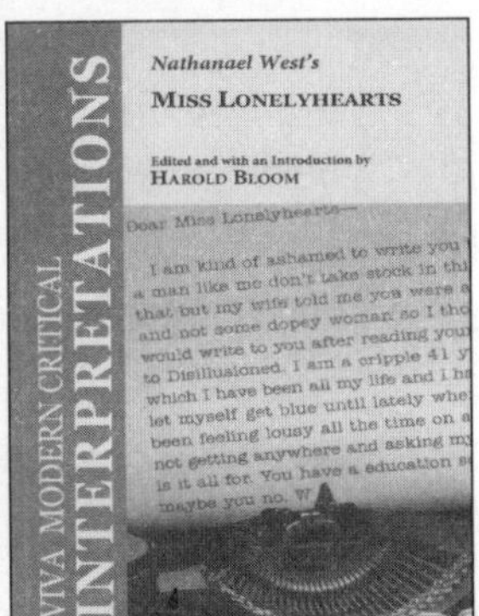

Miss Lonelyhearts

9788130907437 Rs. 125

A Midsummer Night's Dream

9788130918914 Rs. 165

The Metamorphosis

9788130904573 Rs. 99

VIVA Modern Critical Interpretations

Available Titles in the Series

Moby-Dick

9788130906546 Rs. 165

Oedipus

9788130906768 Rs. 165

One Flew Over the Cuckoo's Nest

9788130907444 Rs. 125

One Hundred Years of Solitude

9788130907451 In Print

The Old Man and the Sea

9788130906553 Rs. 125

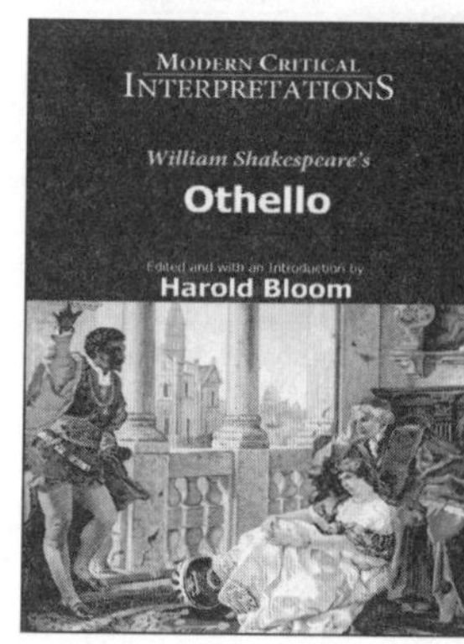

Othello

9788130918891 Rs. 165

Paradise Lost

9788130906560 In Print

The Pardoner's Tale

9788130904665 Rs. 125

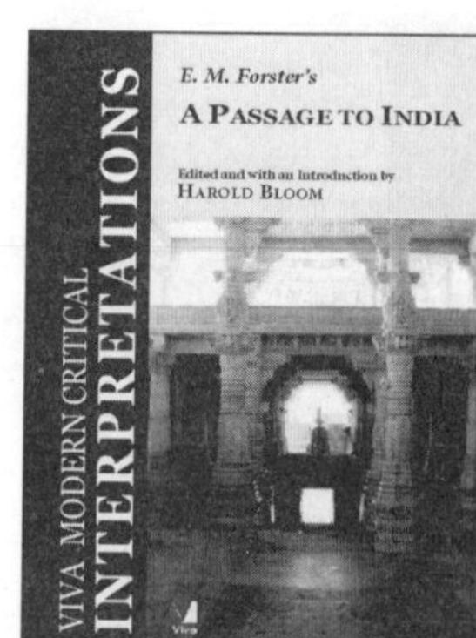

A Passage to India

9788130906584 Rs. 145

VIVA Modern Critical Interpretations

Available Titles in the Series

Viva

Persuasion

9788130906591 Rs. 175

Pride and Prejudice

9788130906607 Rs. 195

The Red Badge of Courage

9788130906614 Rs. 145

Romeo and Juliet

9788130906621 In Print

The Rubaiyat of Omar Khayyam

9788130904641 Rs. 145

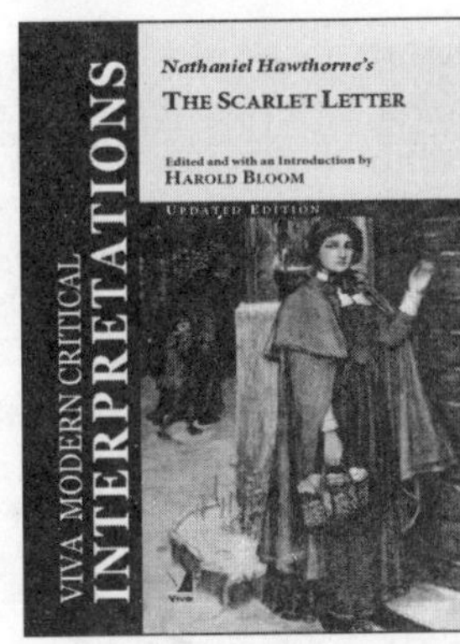

The Scarlet Letter

9788130907505 Rs. 175

Silas Marner

9788130906638 Rs. 125

Song of Solomon

9788130906645 Rs. 145

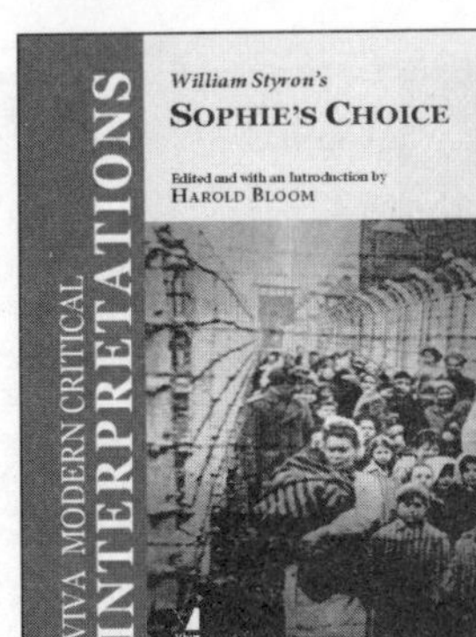

Sophie's Choice

9788130906652 Rs. 175

VIVA Modern Critical Interpretations

Available Titles in the Series

Viva

The Sound and The Fury

9788130906676 Rs. 195

A Streetcar Named Desire

9788130918716 Rs. 145

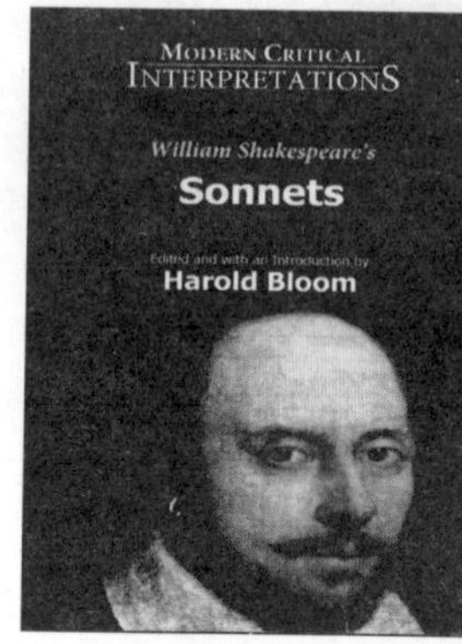

Sonnets

9788130918907 Rs. 165

A Tale of Two Cities

9788130906683 Rs. 145

The Tempest

9788130918822 Rs. 175

To Kill a Mockingbird

9788130906775 Rs. 125

Waiting for Godot

9788130906706 Rs. 99

Ulysses

9788130906690 Rs. 145

The Waste Land

9788130904689 Rs. 175

Wuthering Heights

9788130906713 Rs. 175

Young Goodman Brown

9788130906720 Rs. 125